Register This New Book

Benefits of Registering*

- ✓ FREE **replacements** of lost or damaged books

- ✓ FREE **audiobook** – *Pilgrim's Progress,* audiobook edition

- ✓ FREE information about new titles and other **freebies**

www.anekopress.com/new-book-registration

*See our website for requirements and limitations.

Knowing God the Father

Colombia para Cristo video introduction

Watch the *La Montaña* trailer, a film based on a true Stendal event

Knowing God the Father

A Commentary on the Gospel
and Epistles of John

Russell M. Stendal

ANEKO
PRESS

We love hearing from our readers. Please contact us
at www.anekopress.com/questions-comments with
any questions, comments, or suggestions.

Visit Russell M. Stendal website: www.cpcsociety.ca
Knowing God the Father – Russell M. Stendal
Copyright © 2018
First edition published 2018

Cover Design: J. Martin

Cover Painting: Matt Philleo

eBook Icon: Icons Vector/Shutterstock

Editors: Bronwen Jorel and Michelle Rayburn

Printed in the United States of America

Aneko Press

www.anekopress.com

Aneko Press, Life Sentence Publishing, and our logos are trademarks of

Life Sentence Publishing, Inc.
203 E. Birch Street
P.O. Box 652
Abbotsford, WI 54405

RELIGION / Biblical Commentary / New Testament

Paperback ISBN: 978-1-62245-535-5

eBook ISBN: 978-1-62245-536-2

10 9 8 7 6 5 4 3 2 1

Available where books are sold

Contents

Preface

The writings of the apostle John are unique in their tone and perspective. Some might call them utopian. However, just as Peter was the lead apostle to "the circumcision" (the Jews) and Paul was the lead apostle to "the uncircumcision" (the Gentiles),[1] John is the apostle linked to the future kingdom of God on earth, and we can hardly call a man's writings utopian when his work includes the book of Revelation. Although the kingdom he describes is of the future, it begins within us and is valid here and now, just as it has been over the past two millennia, even though its fullness is linked to the second coming of Jesus Christ.

As we enter the prophesied day of the Lord, the writings of John become clearer and even more pertinent. Jesus will return for a bride (a church) without spot or wrinkle or any such thing, but such a bride will be possible only if we love Him and one another.

You may wonder how a perfect bride can be formed from imperfect humanity, but make no mistake: prior to Jesus' return, the tares (to borrow a metaphor from one of his parables) will be removed from among the wheat. That is, the weeds that

---

1   See Galatians 2:7-8.

the devil has planted among the good crop will be removed from the midst of those who are truly born of God. The body of Christ will come to maturity (same word in the original as perfection), and prophecies – that until now many people have found unfathomable – will be fulfilled.

In fact, as you read this treatise you will see that the gospel of John is extremely prophetic and filled with living parables that offer great benefit, insight, and encouragement to every believer as the time for Jesus' triumphant return draws closer and closer.

When we study John's epistles in the light of his gospel, his words make more sense, because the tone, terminology, and sequence line up and harmonize perfectly with the rest of the Scriptures. It is of paramount importance, therefore, that each key word be properly defined according to the meaning God originally intended it to have.

The writings of John have a very special focus on God the Father. Many people who know Jesus, or claim to know him, have a limited or nonexistent personal knowledge of God the Father. It is, of course, essential for us to know Jesus, but his fervent desire is that we may also know the Father so intimately that we can ask him for whatsoever we will in Jesus' name and our prayers may be granted. By the Holy Spirit, we can have such deep and intimate communion with Jesus and the Father, that seeing our love for one another, *by this shall everyone know that ye are my disciples* (John 13:35).

Russell M. Stendal

August 27, 2018

Part I

The Gospel of John[2]

---

2   "John" means "the Lord has favored " (or "the Lord has extended his grace").

Introduction to Part I

The gospel accounts of Matthew, Mark, and Luke overlap quite a bit. Due to their many similarities, they are sometimes called the Synoptic Gospels – which basically means they are similar reports by different eye-witnesses. But the gospel of John is different – much of its content is not included in any of the other three accounts. For instance, John is the only one to mention Nicodemus, whom Jesus told, *Ye must be born again from above.* John is the only one to include the Samaritan woman at Jacob's well, and the resurrection of Lazarus. Yet despite these extra elements in his narrative, almost half of John's gospel is devoted to the last few days of Jesus' time here on earth.

While the Synoptic Gospels contain many parables that Jesus related in the second or third person, in the gospel of John he is depicted as speaking in the first person, and the entire narrative of what he actually did and said while traveling with his disciples is presented as a stream of living parables, each of which has profound spiritual and prophetic implications for us today.

The other gospels give us a more or less detailed account of Jesus' Olivet Discourse, that is, his extended teaching that took place on the Mount of Olives the week before his death. They record his answer to the disciples' question about when the destruction of the temple and the end of the age would take place. John, on the other hand, records Jesus' last-minute words of encouragement to his disciples after Judas's departure (John 14-17), focusing on the importance of knowing God the Father, on the coming of the Holy Spirit (the comforter), and on Jesus' new commandment that we love one another.

Matthew 5-7 (known as the Sermon on the Mount) has also been called the Little Gospel, or the Magna Carta of the Kingdom of Heaven. However, unless we (individually and corporately) implement Jesus' commandments and advice to us as recorded in John 14-16, the high ideals of the Sermon on the Mount will remain elusive. This is why Jesus, as our new high priest, prayed to his Father on behalf of his disciples (including us) in John 17. That prayer has not yet been completely answered or fulfilled, but soon it will be.

Chapter 1

Come and See

The gospel of John is written from a heavenly perspective and goes all the way back to *the beginning*.

The beginning of what?

In the beginning God created the heavens and the earth (Genesis 1:1).

John 1

1:1 *In the beginning was the Word, and the Word was with the God, and the Word was God.*

1:2 *The same was in the beginning with the God.*

1:3 *All things were made by him, and without him was not any thing made that was made.*

The Lord Jesus Christ is the living Word of God. The Jubilee Bible correctly translates this passage with the definite article (*the* God). This brings out the clear distinction between *the Word* and *the God* (that is, the distinction between the Father and the Son) that is evident in the original language. It's also clear that *the Word was God.*

Note the parallels between those verses and these:

> *For by him were all things created, that are in the heavens, and that are in earth, visible and invisible, whether they are thrones or dominions or principalities or powers: all things were created by him and in him; And he is before all things, and by him all things consist. And he is the head of the body, the congregation, who is the beginning, the firstborn from the dead, that in all things he might have the preeminence. For it pleased the Father that in him should all fullness dwell.* (Colossians 1:16-19)

Remember that in the creation account, God said, *Let **us** make man in **our** image, after **our** likeness* (Genesis 1:26a, emphasis added). This is speaking of the image and likeness of the Father and the Son.

> 1:4 *In him was life, and the life was the light of men.*

> 1:5 *And the light shines in the darkness, and the darkness apprehended it not.*

God says it is impossible for the darkness to apprehend (or extinguish) the light that is an intrinsic element of the life of the living Word of God. If we desire the light, we must seek the life of the Son.

> 1:6 *There was a man sent from God, whose name was John.*

> 1:7 *The same came for a witness, to bear witness of the Light, that all men through him might believe.*

> 1:8 *He was not the Light, but was sent to bear witness of the Light.*

1:9 *That Word was the true Light, which lightens*
every man that comes into this world.

Under Jewish law, in criminal cases involving a potential death
sentence, no decision could be rendered without hearing evidence from at least two or three witnesses (Numbers 35:30;
Deuteronomy 17:6).[3] John the Baptist was sent to bear witness
of Jesus Christ, and the decision we are called upon to make
as a result is indeed a matter of life or death for everyone who
comes into this world. Each of us has a conscience that enables
us to discern and acknowledge the truth. Everyone who genuinely seeks truth and light is really seeking him, for there is
no other source.

1:10 *He was in the world, and the world was made*
by him, and the world knew him not.

1:11 *He came unto his own, and his own received*
him not.

The world was made by him, but it was overtaken by corruption
when Adam rebelled against God and Satan usurped power
as the "prince" of this world. People were then beguiled into
thinking they were following the light, when in fact their own
self-righteous religious and humanistic ideas were leading them
into the darkness of bondage to Satan.

1:12 *But as many as received him, to them gave the*
power to become sons of God, even to them that
believe on his name,

1:13 *who are not born of blood, nor of the will of*
flesh, nor of the will of man, but of God.

When we receive Jesus and believe on his name (which is
linked to his nature), he gives us the *power to become the sons*

---

3   See also Deuteronomy 19:5.

of God. Our new birth has to do with faith and the Holy Spirit and the will of God.

> 1:14 *And the Word was made flesh and dwelt among us (and we beheld his glory, the glory as of the only begotten of the Father), full of grace and truth.*

The disciples were also witnesses of the glory of the *only begotten of the Father.* Jesus Christ is unique; he is one of a kind. The only way we can be born again is in and through his life. Our salvation is in him, and he is *full of grace and truth.*[4] We tend to think of grace as unmerited favor, but it is also power – the power of God to conform us to the truth so we may become his sons according to his nature. Without God's grace, it is impossible for us to successfully repent of our own way, no matter how fervently we want to do so (Romans 7:14-25).

> 1:15 *John bore witness of him and cried, saying, This is he of whom I spoke, He that comes after me is preferred before me, for he was before me.*

The natural birth of John the Baptist (Jesus' cousin) took place about six months before Jesus was born in Bethlehem, so in an earthly sense, Jesus came after John. However, in a spiritual sense, he came *before* John, being the incarnation of the Word of God that has existed from the beginning. He is the *only begotten Son* of the Father from before the creation of the heavens and the earth. This is the Messiah that John the Baptist came to announce.

> 1:16 *And of his fullness we have all received, and grace for grace.*

How did the disciples receive *of his fullness?*

It happened on the day of Pentecost, when God began to fulfill the prophecy of Joel by pouring out signs and wonders

---

4   God imparts his grace and truth to us by means of the Holy Spirit (the Comforter).

on those who had gathered together. Peter, standing with the disciples, reminded the amazed onlookers of Joel's words: *And it shall come to pass in the last days, saith God, I will pour out of my Spirit upon all flesh* (Acts 2:17a).

What is *grace for grace*?

It is what happens when, even though we don't deserve it, God graciously intervenes in our hearts and minds, working in and through us with his mighty power, changing us and transforming us according to his grace.

> 1:17 *For the law was given through Moses, but the grace and the truth of God came through Jesus, the Christ.*

> 1:18 *No man has seen God at any time; the only begotten Son, which is in the bosom of the Father, he has declared him.*

God gave the law of Moses to a people in the wilderness who refused to hear his voice (Exodus 20:19; Deuteronomy 5:23-33). Jesus, on the other hand, came as a man to declare the grace and the truth of God in word and deed. This is the very nature of God.

Before the coming of the Lord Jesus, no one had seen God the Father at any time. Even God's name was considered too sacred to pronounce, and his glory was hidden from sight in the realm of the holy of holies, because seeing it would be more than sufficient to kill any mortal. Everyone knew that if by any circumstance or error they came into the presence of God, they would certainly die.

Throughout the Old Testament, if anyone so much as saw the angel of the Lord, their response would not be to exult, "Glory to God! I just saw an angel!" but rather to wring their hands and rend their garments, crying, "Woe is me! I just saw the angel of the Lord, and now I'm going to die!"

But the advent of Jesus was entirely different. Although he was wholly God, he was also wholly man, and his earthly family was an obscure one. Since the Messiah was expected to be a warrior prince and not a humble carpenter, initially, almost no one seemed to recognize him. Accordingly, God sent John the Baptist as a witness to clearly identify Jesus as the Lamb of God.

> 1:19 *And this is the testimony of John, when the Jews sent priests and Levites from Jerusalem to ask him, Who art thou?*

> 1:20 *And he confessed and denied not, but confessed, I am not the Christ.*

Although John was the son of a respected priest, at this time he was living in the wilderness, wearing a leather girdle and a camel hair mantle after the fashion of Elijah, eating locusts and honey, and baptizing the people in the Jordan River (symbol of death).

> 1:21 *And they asked him, What then? Art thou Elijah? And he said, I am not. Art thou the prophet? And he answered, No.*[5]

> 1:22 *Then said they unto him, Who art thou? that we may give an answer to those that sent us. What sayest thou of thyself?*

> 1:23 *He said, I am the voice of one crying in the wilderness, Make straight the way of the Lord, as said the prophet Isaiah.*

> 1:24 *And those who were sent were of the Pharisees.*[6]

---

5   This is undoubtedly referring to Deuteronomy 18:15.

6   Interestingly, even though Jesus faced opposition from the Pharisees and had serious arguments with them, in the book of Acts, a number of them came to faith, and some of them even defended the apostle Paul after he was arrested in Jerusalem (Acts 5:34, 15:5, 23:9). It was the Sadducees who proved to be the worst enemies of the gospel.

John's response in verse 23 is a quote from Isaiah 40:3, and the Pharisees would have readily identified the entire passage with the Messiah.

> 1:25 *And they asked him and said unto him, Why dost thou baptize then if thou art not the Christ, nor Elijah, nor the prophet?*

According to tradition, when the Messiah came, he would find the people unclean; therefore, they would all need to be ceremonially washed, or baptized.

> 1:26 *John answered them, saying, I baptize with water, but there stands one among you, whom ye know not;*

> 1:27 *he it is, who coming after me is preferred before me, whose shoe's latchet I am not worthy to unloose.*

The phrase *preferred before me* would have undoubtedly been interpreted as messianic, as would the reference to the *shoe's latchet*. The shoe or sandal was symbolic of the preparation necessary to traverse the wilderness or to fight a war. Both Moses and Joshua had been required to remove their footgear in order to continue with what God had planned for them to do (Exodus 3:5; Joshua 5:15). In Jesus' case, however, the preparation for his mission to earth had taken place in heaven, and no one on earth was worthy to loosen or unfasten even so much as the latchet of his shoe.

> 1:28 *These things were done in Bethabara beyond Jordan, where John was baptizing.*

"Bethabara" means "house of passage." Since those who received John and were baptized by him were on their way to receiving Jesus, John's ministry was like a house of passage.

> 1:29 *The next day John saw Jesus coming unto him*

> and said, Behold the Lamb of God, who takes away
> the sin of the world.

On top of the messianic links, to hear John refer to Jesus as *the Lamb of God, who takes away the sin of the world* (which would include Gentiles as well as Jews) must have been mindboggling to the Jews. (And in many cases, it still is.)

> 1:30 *This is he of whom I said, After me comes a man who is preferred before me,*[7] *for he was before me.*

> 1:31 *And I knew him not; but that he should be made manifest to Israel, therefore am I come baptizing with water.*

> 1:32 *And John gave testimony, saying, I saw the Spirit descending from heaven like a dove, and it abode upon him.*

The fullness of the Spirit descended from heaven like a dove[8] upon Jesus *and it abode upon him.*

> 1:33 *And I knew him not; but he that sent me to baptize with water, the same said unto me, Upon whom thou shalt see the Spirit descending and abiding on him, the same is he who baptizes with the Holy Spirit.*

Who sent John to baptize with water?

The same God who sent him as a witness to identify Jesus as the Lamb of God. John's earthly mission had been prophesied by his father, the priest Zacharias: *And he shall go before him* [the Messiah] *in the spirit and power of Elijah* (Luke 1:17a). We find an echo of these words in Malachi 4:5-6 (the last verses

---

7 This is John's second use of the phrase *preferred before me*, referring to Jesus.

8 The dove is a symbol of the Spirit.

of the Old Testament). "Elijah" is a bit of a play on words in Hebrew and can mean "the LORD is God" or "God himself."

John was telling the truth when he declared to the Levites and priests of the Pharisees that he was not Elijah. However, it is clear that he went before Jesus in the spirit and power of Elijah (that is, of God himself). We see from this, therefore, that it was the Spirit of God who instructed John the Baptist on what to do and how to identify the Lamb of God as the one who not only takes away the sin of the world but also baptizes with the Holy Spirit.

John went further with his revelation by declaring:

> 1:34 *And I have seen and have given testimony that this is the Son of God.*

He announced Jesus' true identity at every opportunity.

> 1:35 *And again the next day John stood, and two of his disciples,*

> 1:36 *and looking upon Jesus as he walked, he said, Behold the Lamb of God!*[9]

> 1:37 *And the two disciples heard him speak and followed Jesus.*

Recognizing the truth of John's words, these two disciples started following Jesus instead of remaining with John.

> 1:38 *Then Jesus turned and saw them following and said unto them, What seek ye? They said unto him, Rabbi (which is to say, being interpreted, Master), where dwellest thou?*

> 1:39 *He said unto them, Come and see. They came*

---

9   This is the second time John calls Jesus *the Lamb of God*.

*and saw where he dwelt and abode with him that
day, for it was about the tenth hour.*[10]

Just as Jesus invited these first two disciples to come and stay
with him, so today he still desires us to follow him, to come and
see what he does, and to abide with him. Yet there are many
who would turn his invitation around and expect Jesus to follow *them* and come and see what *they* do. Instead of abiding
with him on his terms, they want him to abide with them while
they continue their old way of life.

1:40 *One of the two who heard John speak and followed him was Andrew, brother of Simon Peter.*

1:41 *He first found his own brother Simon and said
unto him, We have found the Messias, which is,
being interpreted, the Christ.*

"Messiah" or "Christ" means "anointed." In the Old Testament,
prophets, priests, and kings were anointed with a special oil that
had been prepared through meticulous adherence to a specific
formula (Exodus 30:22-25). There is, however, no evidence in
Scripture that Jesus Christ was ever anointed with this oil.
Rather, he was anointed when John *saw the Spirit descending
from heaven like a dove, and it abode on him.*

It was this testimony from John the Baptist that convinced
Andrew, who promptly went and found his brother, Simon,
and told him the news.

1:42 *And he brought him to Jesus. And when Jesus
beheld him, he said, Thou art Simon the son of
Jonah: thou shalt be called Cephas, which is by
interpretation, A stone.*

"Simon" means "to hearken" (to hear and obey) and "Jonah"
means "a dove" (symbol of the Holy Spirit). As soon as Jesus

---

10   The tenth hour was about four o'clock in the afternoon.

saw Simon, he put these two meanings together and told him that (future tense) he would be called "Cephas" (a stone pillar or monument). In other words, hearkening to the Holy Spirit would put Simon on such a rock-solid foundation that his very name (nature) would be changed.

> 1:43 *The day following Jesus desired to go forth into Galilee and found Philip and said unto him, Follow me.*

"Galilee" means "circle" or "circuit."[11] Jesus and most of the disciples were from that region. "Philip" means "lover of horses."[12] According to the law, the kings of Israel were not to multiply horses unto themselves (Deuteronomy 17:16), nor were they to attempt to return to "Egypt" (signifying the dead, legalistic ways of the natural man) in search of horses. Therefore, Jesus told Philip to follow him into Galilee (symbol of perfection). Following Jesus is the only way any of us may walk in perfection.

> 1:44 *Now Philip was of Bethsaida, the city of Andrew and Peter.*

"Bethsaida" means "house of fishing" or "house of nets," and Jesus would teach the disciples to be fishers of men. "Andrew" means "manly" (in the sense of free born or noble born). Jesus opened the way for all of us to be born again out of slavery to the flesh and sin, and into the glorious liberty of the sons of God (Romans 8:21). "Peter" means "small stone," but as noted above, Jesus took one look at Simon Peter and prophesied that in the future, he would be called "Cephas" (a stone pillar or monument).

> 1:45 *Philip found Nathanael and said unto him, We*

---

11 The ancients used the concept of a circle (a never-ending line) to describe perfection.

12 Horses are a symbol of man's natural strength.

have found him of whom Moses in the law and the
prophets wrote: Jesus of Nazareth, the son of Joseph.

"Nathanael" means "gift of God." "Nazareth" means "a branch" or "a shoot," and thus Jesus of Nazareth lines up with the prophecy of Isaiah 11:1. "Joseph" means "he shall add" or "let God add."

1:46 *And Nathanael said unto him, Can any good*
thing come out of Nazareth? Philip said unto him,
Come and see.

Philip lived in the same town as Andrew and Peter. Now he proclaimed to Nathanael (a native of Cana), "*We* have found him" (referring to Jesus) and responded to Nathanael's skeptical question by repeating Jesus' words to Andrew, "Come and see." This definitely got Nathanael's undivided attention.

1:47 *Jesus saw Nathanael coming to him and said of*
him, Behold a true Israelite, in whom is no guile!

1:48 *Nathanael said unto him, From where dost*
thou know me? Jesus answered and said unto him,
Before Philip called thee, when thou wast under the
fig tree, I saw thee.

Jesus called Philip, and Philip called Nathanael – who had literally been under a fig tree before being called. The fig tree, however, is also a symbol of the people of God under law. Evidently, Andrew, Peter, Philip, and Nathanael had been carefully studying the words of Moses and the prophets regarding the coming of the Messiah. It is likely they were following the prophecy of the seventy weeks of Daniel and knew they were at the beginning of the seventieth "week" of years.[13] This, together with the testimony of John the Baptist, would have had them all very excited, and now they had the wonderful opportunity to *come and see* Jesus in person. When Jesus told Nathanael he

---

13   Daniel 9:24-27.

had seen him under the fig tree, this was a third sign to them that he was indeed the Messiah.

> 1:49 *Nathanael answered and said unto him, Rabbi, thou art the Son of God; thou art the King of Israel.*

Nathanael linked being the Messiah, King of Israel, with being the Son of God, just as John the Baptist did.

> 1:50 *Jesus answered and said unto him, Because I said unto thee, I saw thee under the fig tree, believest thou? thou shalt see greater things than these.*

> 1:51 *And he said unto him, Verily, verily, I say unto you, Hereafter ye shall see the heaven open and the angels of God ascending and descending upon the Son of man.*[14]

Jesus didn't just tell Nathanael about his past; he also told him about his future. An open heaven is the realm of answered prayer; it is a revelation of the fullness of the kingdom of God behind the veil in the realm of the holy of holies where the Father dwells.

Let us pray

Lord, we ask that we may receive understanding and find the knowledge of the truth. But more than this, we ask that your truth and your grace and your light and your life may be found in us, so that if, on any occasion upon the paths of life, we encounter someone who has been desperately seeking your grace and your truth, we may be able to answer, "Come and see," as we lead them to you. Amen.

---

14 *Son of man* confirms Jesus' humanity. It also links to many additional Old Testament prophecies (particularly in the book of Ezekiel).

Chapter 2

The Third Day

John 2

2:1 And the third day there was a marriage in Cana of Galilee, and the mother of Jesus was there,

Apparently from the day when John identified Jesus as the Lamb of God, which was the same day Andrew and another disciple (whose name is not given) followed Jesus home. The third day,[15] however, is also a prophetic marker that is linked with Jesus' resurrection on the third temporal day after his death, as well as with the first resurrection (Revelation 20:4-5), which occurs on the third prophetic day[16] involving the body of Christ.

"Cana" means "favor" or "grace." The phrase "Cana of Galilee" suggests grace to the point of perfection; in this case, such perfect grace is to take place in the context of a "marriage," symbolizing Jesus Christ's relationship with his church. The

---

15   The *third day* is found in forty-nine Scriptures and occurs fifty-one times (two verses have it twice). This is the thirteenth reference to the *third day* in the New Testament and the forty-sixth such reference overall.

16   For the Lord, a (prophetic) day can be a thousand years (Psalm 90:4, 2 Peter 3:8).

mother of Jesus represents true people of God. Jesus said, *For whosoever doeth the will of God, the same is my brother and my sister and my mother* (Mark 3:35).

> 2:2 *and Jesus and his disciples were also called to the marriage.*

To be called to such an event is virtually the same as being invited. Jesus and all his disciples were invited to that wedding supper, just as they will also attend the great wedding supper that is soon to take place as our present age of grace ends.

> 2:3 *And being short of wine, the mother of Jesus said unto him, They have no wine.*

Wine is a symbol of life. There are, however, two very distinct types of life (or wine). There is the life of Adam, the old man, and there is the life of Jesus, the new man in Christ. The old man likes to get "inebriated" by excitedly centering on his own life. Nevertheless, the life of the old man will eventually come to an end.

> 2:4 *Jesus said unto her, Woman, what have I to do with thee? My hour is not yet come.*

Mary, though she was the mother of Jesus, had to learn that she no longer had authority over Jesus; and Jesus had to be very bold and tell his mother that he in no way could be under her authority anymore.

> 2:5 *His mother said unto the servants, Whatsoever he saith unto you, do it.*

Mary, the mother of Jesus, submitted to the authority of the Son of God. She earned the right to be symbolic of those who do the will of God. Even though Jesus did not deem the time to be ripe, Mary took a step of faith with her wise advice to the servants. If the clock is ticking (as it is right now at the end of this age) and if we realize that we are *short of wine* (time is running out for us, and the people of God are unable to produce *a bride without spot or wrinkle or any such thing* in the life of Adam, even with powerful gifts and ministries from God), it would behoove all of us to pay attention and follow Mary's advice: *Whatsoever he saith unto you, do it.*

> 2:6 *And there were set there six waterpots of stone, after the manner of the purifying of the Jews, containing two or three firkins*[17] *apiece.*

Six is the number that relates to man. Waterpots of stone symbolize the word of God that up until then had gone forth as law (the Jews received the Ten Commandments on tablets of stone). Under the law, there were many ways God's people could become unclean, and whenever that happened, they had to wash with water *after the manner of the purifying of the Jews.* Even the baptism of John was along these lines. It was extremely important that the waterpots be clean vessels, which is why God raised up the ministry of John in the wilderness, rather than communicating through the unclean priests at the contaminated temple.

> 2:7 *Jesus said unto them, Fill the waterpots with water. And they filled them up to the brim.*

The law brought the people into awareness of sin (Romans 7), and Jesus – the living Word – came to bring them life. Therefore, anyone who receives Jesus and his Word will be filled with the new wine of his life. This joyous opportunity was open to those who had been baptized into repentance by John.

> 2:8 *And he said unto them, Draw out now and bear unto the butler. And they bore it.*

Those who were cleansed and obedient to Jesus would soon be filled with the living Word of Life and would be able to minister

---

17   Various sources have defined a firkin as eight, nine, ten, or even eleven gallons (approximately one quarter-barrel).

life to others. This is symbolic of how God would later use Jesus' disciples and apostles in the kind of service described in the book of Acts, when they *turned the world upside down* (Acts 17:6b).

> 2:9 *When the butler had tasted the water that was made wine and knew not where it was from (but the servants who drew the water knew), the butler called the bridegroom*

> 2:10 *and said unto him, Every man at the beginning sets forth the good wine, and when they are well sat- isfied, then that which is worse; but thou hast kept the good wine until now.*

Who is the butler?

There are some clues in the Old Testament (OT), such as these verses in Genesis:

> *And it came to pass **the third day**, which was Pharaoh's birthday, that he made a banquet unto all his slaves, and he lifted up the head of the chief but- ler and of the chief baker among his slaves. And he restored the chief butler unto his butlership again, and he gave the cup into Pharaoh's hand. But he hanged the chief baker; as Joseph had interpreted to them. Yet the chief butler did not remember Joseph but forgot him.* (Genesis 40:20-23, emphasis added)

In this example, the chief baker was cut off and the chief butler was restored. This is symbolic of the cutting off of those who offered "bread" that was "leavened" by people such as Herod and the Pharisees, and the restoration of the ministry of the "butler" who served the cup of wine. Pharaoh's butler did not at first remember Joseph, who represents Jesus Christ, just as the butler at the wedding at Cana did not at first know from where the new wine came.[18]

In these examples, the butler represents those who have been serving the old wine, which is the old, lifeless religion; now God will use some of them to help serve the new wine, or new way of life through Jesus. Saul of Tarsus (later the apostle Paul) was one such "butler" who was dramatically converted when he came into direct contact with the overwhelming, unquenchable life of the Lord Jesus Christ.

John continues his narrative:

> 2:11 *This beginning of the signs Jesus did in Cana of Galilee and manifested forth his glory, and his disciples believed on him.*

Jesus' first recorded miracle of turning the water into wine at Cana of Galilee really happened, but it is also described as *this beginning of the signs.* The fullness of what this sign represents will be soon be revealed as this age closes, and the fullness of Jesus' glory (which is grace and truth) will be poured out to bring his bride to perfection.

The early believers, according to the descriptions in the book of Acts, relied on the Holy Spirit. Over the centuries, however, the leaven of man crept back in as the New Testament was distilled into principles and values that humanists could apply (or attempt to apply) on their own, without God. This quenched the Holy Spirit and gave rise to the bleak centuries known to secular and religious historians as the Dark Ages. Even today, many church leaders who are proud that they would never touch so much as a drop of alcohol are really serving the old wine of the humanistic life of Adam, thus allowing their people to remain in bondage to sin and the flesh.

---

18   Some parallels can also be drawn with the story of Nehemiah (meaning "the LORD comforts"), who was likewise the butler of a king, in relation to the restoration of the wall and the temple (Nehemiah 2:1).

Now, once again, Jesus is raising up servants and butlers who will serve the fullness of the new wine of the unadulterated life of Christ. This is the path to victory.

> 2:12 *After this he went down to Capernaum, he and his mother and his brethren and his disciples, and they continued there not many days.*

"Capernaum" means "village (or city) of Nahum (consolation)."

> 2:13 *And passover of the Jews was at hand, and Jesus went up to Jerusalem*

> 2:14 *and found in the temple those that sold oxen and sheep and doves, and the money changers seated;*

> 2:15 *and when he had made a scourge of small cords, he drove them all out of the temple, and the sheep and the oxen, and poured out the changers' money and overthrew the tables*

> 2:16 *and said unto those that sold the doves, Take these things away from here; do not make my Father's house a house of merchandise.*

When Jesus arrived at the temple, he didn't dillydally but immediately took action against those who were buying and selling for personal gain in his Father's house. If Jesus, in person, were to walk into our religious institutions today, what would be his reaction? In fact, *we* are now the temple of God, and when Jesus arrives into our life by the Spirit, rest assured that the very first thing he will do is clean house – and it will be awesome!

> 2:17 *Then his disciples remembered that it was written, The zeal of thine house has consumed me.*[19]

Now, under the new covenant, *we* are the temple.

---

19   Psalm 69:9a. It seems that Jesus' disciples were well versed in the Scriptures.

2:18 *Then the Jews answered and said unto him,*
What sign showest thou unto us, seeing that thou
doest these things?

The water turned to wine at the wedding supper was the *beginning of the signs Jesus did in Cana of Galilee* where he *manifested forth his glory*, but apparently the Jews of Jerusalem hadn't been paying much attention to what went on outside of the city.

2:19 *Jesus answered and said unto them, Dissolve*
this temple, and in three days I will raise it up.

2:20 *Then said the Jews, This temple was forty-six*
years in building, and wilt thou raise it up in three
days?

2:21 *But he spoke of the temple of his body.*

Jesus rose from the dead on the third day. And now, two thousand years later (that is, after two prophetic days of a thousand years each), the body of Christ (of which Jesus is the head) will come forth in the first resurrection as we enter the third prophetic day (Revelation 20:4-6).

2:22 *Therefore when he was risen from the dead,*
his disciples remembered that he had said this unto
them; and they believed the scripture and the word
which Jesus had said.

2:23 *Now when he was in Jerusalem at the passover,*
in the feast day, many believed in his name, seeing
the signs which he did.

How many signs had he done, and what were they?

In addition to the signs in Cana of Galilee, Jesus' cleansing of the temple was, in and of itself, a sign that had been written in a messianic psalm by King David more than a thousand years before.[20]

>2:24 *But Jesus did not trust himself unto them because he knew all men*
>
>2:25 *and needed not that any man should give testimony,*[21] *for he knew what was in man.*

Even though many believed in his name, *Jesus did not trust himself unto them.*

Why not?

They wanted a king who would free them from earthly bondage, but Jesus came to proclaim a kingdom that is not of this world. It is not enough to believe in his name; our hearts must be circumcised[22] and we must be filled with the Holy Spirit, for only then can our wrong desires and ambitions be neutralized.

Jesus *knew all men.* He knew that the heart of man is *deceitful above all things and desperately wicked* (Jeremiah 17:9). Therefore, he *needed not that any man should give him testimony.* Jesus, the creator of the universe, did not subscribe to the naïve humanistic philosophy that man is basically good. He *knew what was in man.*

Let us pray

Lord, we receive the water of your Word and ask that it be turned into new wine, new life. May we be cleansed by your Word, and may your life deliver us from corruption. May our hearts and minds be purified, and may we desire to do your will. Amen.

---

20   Joseph Benson, in his commentary of 1873, dates Psalm 69 at 1021 B.C.

21   The important testimony about Jesus Christ is described in detail in 1 John 5:6-9. There are three that bear witness in heaven (the Father, the Word, and the Holy Spirit) and three that bear witness on earth (the Spirit, the water, and the blood).

22   The circumcision of the heart is when the Word of God cuts the control of the flesh so our heart may become pure and clean and sensitive to the leading of the Holy Spirit.

Chapter 3

Ye Must Be Born Again
From Above

John 3

*3:1 There was a man of the Pharisees, named
Nicodemus, a prince of the Jews;*

Nicodemus" means "conquered his people." That he was
a prince of the Jews meant that he was on the council
or Sanhedrin. It is likely he was a priest.

*3:2 the same came to Jesus by night and said unto
him, Rabbi, we know that thou art a teacher come
from God, for no one can do these signs that thou
doest unless God is with him.*

Why would Nicodemus feel it was necessary to come to Jesus
by night?

Maybe he was afraid his control over the people would be
diminished if he were perceived as giving credence to Jesus or
being on amicable terms with him. Perhaps he was worried
about what other Pharisees would say if they knew he had

called on Jesus. He did, however, identify with some of the other Pharisees when he said, *Rabbi,* **we** *know that thou art a teacher come from God.* This deduction by at least some of the Pharisees was based on *these signs* that Jesus was doing.

Nicodemus acknowledged that Jesus really was performing the signs, but his response to this state of affairs seems to have been less than enthusiastic. For example, he came to Jesus by night instead of by day, and to some extent this may have made it harder for him to grasp what Jesus sought to teach him: God prefers to work in the light. Indeed, Scripture encourages us to allow God to do his work in us and through us during the day, because *the night comes, when no one can work* (John 9:4b).

> 3:3 *Jesus answered and said unto him, Verily, verily, I say unto thee, Except a person be born again from above, he cannot see the kingdom of God.*

Jesus told Nicodemus that spiritually he was like a fetus in the darkness of the womb (where hearing is possible to some extent, but seeing is totally impossible), and therefore if he was ever to see the kingdom of God, he must be birthed out of the womb and into the light. Even though his rightful king (the Messiah) was standing there in front of him, all that Nicodemus (and the other Pharisees who were aware of the signs Jesus had performed) could see was a rabbi, a teacher.

> 3:4 *Nicodemus said unto him, How can a man be born when he is old? Can he enter the second time into his mother's womb and be born?*

Confronted by Jesus about his spiritual blindness, Nicodemus, who considered himself a prince of the Jews, began to beat around the bush.

> 3:5 *Jesus answered, Verily, verily, I say unto thee, Unless a man is born of water and of the Spirit, he cannot enter into the kingdom of God.*

*3:6 That which is born of the flesh is flesh, and that
which is born of the Spirit is spirit.*

We are born into this fallen world in the flesh according to the
life of Adam, but only God can birth us in the Spirit according
to the life of Christ.

*3:7 Marvel not that I said unto thee, Ye must be
born again from above.*

*3:8 The wind blows where it desires, and thou hear-
est the sound of it, but canst not tell from where it
comes or where it goes; so is every one that is born of
the Spirit.*

The word translated as *wind* is essentially the same Greek word
translated as *Spirit* at the end of the verse.[23] Unless Nicodemus
(or anyone else for that matter) is born again from above, he
will never be able to perceive the things of the Spirit or understand how God moves his sons (and daughters) by the Spirit.

*3:9 Nicodemus answered and said unto him, How
can this be done?*

*3:10 Jesus answered and said unto him, Art thou a
teacher of Israel and knowest not this?*

When Nicodemus addressed Jesus in verse 2, he used the
Hebrew term "rabbi" (or "my master") and then acknowledged
that Jesus is a teacher or instructor[24] sent from God. When
Jesus, in response, referred to Nicodemus as a teacher, he used
the Greek word for "instructor" but did not call him "rabbi."

*3:11 Verily, verily, I say unto thee that we speak
what we know and testify that which we have seen,
and ye do not receive our witness.*

---

23   Greek *pneuma*.
24   Greek *didaskalos*.

Jesus made it very clear that Nicodemus had not received the witness of either John or himself. In order to receive John's witness, Nicodemus would have had to declare himself unclean and be baptized in water unto repentance in the light of day. This he had not even attempted to do. As a result, he was confused, seeking answers in the middle of the night and unable to perceive the kingdom of God, even though he was looking at the king of that realm.

> 3:12 *If I have told you earthly things and ye do not believe, how shall ye believe if I tell you of heavenly things?*
>
> 3:13 *And no one has ascended up to the heaven but he that came down from the heaven, even the Son of man, who is in the heaven.*[25]

Jesus came down from heaven and walked upon this earth as a man, yet even so, his real citizenship *is in the heaven*. Heaven can be defined as the place where God dwells, and God the Father lived inside of his Son while Jesus walked upon the earth as a man. This is why Jesus referred to himself as *this temple* in John 2:19.

Now Jesus wants to dwell in us by the Spirit so *we* will be *his* temple (1 Corinthians 3:16; 6:19; Ephesians 2:19-22). Jesus wants to give us a new heart to put his spirit within us.

> 3:14 *And as Moses lifted up the serpent in the wilderness, even so must the Son of man be lifted up,*

---

25   Scripture refers many times to the heavens (plural), while the earth is always singular. Paul referred to an experience he had in the "third heaven." The first heaven is the atmosphere, stars, and universe that we perceive with our natural eyes. The second heaven is the spiritual realm, where angels and even demons can interact (although the time will come when Satan and his angels are cast down). The third heaven, or in this case *the heaven* (with the definite article), is the dwelling place of the Father. Note that *the heaven* is mentioned three times in verse 13.

> *3:15 that whosoever believes in him should not perish but have eternal life.*

Moses lifted up the serpent in the wilderness to symbolize that Jesus would die on the cross for the sins of the world. In order to be saved from death by snake bite, the people had to lift up their eyes and gaze upon the serpent of brass (Numbers 21:4-9). This action could only take place in the daytime, when it was light enough to see the brass serpent, and it could only be performed in the public place where the serpent had been raised up. So, too, when we confess Jesus as our Lord and savior, we should not be ashamed to do so in daylight and in public.

> *3:16 For God so loved the world that he gave his only begotten Son, that whosoever believes in him should not perish but have eternal life.*

> *3:17 For God did not send his Son into the world to condemn the world, but that the world through him might be saved.*

The primary purpose of Jesus being sent into the world was to save the lost. His ministry was a ministry of reconciliation, not of condemnation. God's charity (or love) is manifest to the world in the form of his son Jesus Christ, but as we'll see in the following verses, there is no charity or mercy to be found outside of Jesus Christ.

> *3:18 He that believes on him is not condemned, but he that does not believe is condemned already because he has not believed in the name of the only begotten Son of God.*

To believe in Jesus is to trust and depend completely on him. This isn't simply a question of acknowledging the historical fact of his life; it is a question of recognizing that the only way our hearts and minds can be transformed is by the grace and power of God.

> 3:19 *And this is the condemnation, that the light is come into the world, and men loved darkness more than the light because their deeds were evil.*

> 3:20 *For every one that does evil hates the light, and does not come to the light, lest his deeds should be reproved.*

> 3:21 *But he that does truth comes to the light, that his deeds may be made manifest, that they are wrought in God.*

We can do evil and hate the light, or we can come to the light and do truth. This has been the choice offered to man since the beginning of time. Cain went one way, and his brother Abel went the other (Genesis 4:3-8). Whether they know it or not, anyone who loves and seeks the truth really loves and seeks Jesus.

Jesus desires to dwell in us. He longs to cleanse us by the Spirit so we may also come to know the Father. Jesus Christ is the beginning of the new creation, and he wants us to be first-fruits unto God as part of that creation, but this is only possible if we are members of the body of Christ. In the new creation, heaven and earth are no longer separated. What is more, in the Holy City, there will be no night (Revelation 21:25). Jesus could not get past the first step of explaining this to Nicodemus, however, because Nicodemus came him by night instead of by day. This "prince of the Jews" balked at the idea of undergoing a new birth into the light, just as he and many others like him balked at the idea of being publicly baptized by John. *And all the people that heard him [Jesus] and the publicans justified God, being baptized with the baptism of John. But the Pharisees and lawyers rejected the counsel of God against themselves, being not baptized of him* (Luke 7:29-30).

Regarding themselves as the elite, the Pharisees and lawyers attempted to cloak themselves in self-righteousness and, unlike the common people who had likewise heard Jesus' words, they refused to justify God. They *rejected the counsel of God against themselves* and chose to continue operating in the dark.

> 3:22 *After these things Jesus and his disciples came into the land of Judaea, and he tarried there with them and baptized.*

"Judea" means "the land of Judah" ("Judah" means "praise"). The Jews expected the coming Messiah to baptize people. It was culturally ingrained into them that the Messiah would find them unclean and they would all need to repent and be cleansed.[26]

> 3:23 *And John also was baptizing in Aenon near to Salim because there was much water there, and they came and were baptized.*

"Aenon" means "springs," and "Salim" means "(perfect) peace."

> 3:24 *For John was not yet cast into prison.*

> 3:25 *Then there arose a question between the disciples of John and the Jews about purifying.*

Many of the legalistic Jews undoubtedly argued that it was impossible for John, wearing an unclean mantle of camel's hair and eating locusts, to properly conduct baptisms unto purification.

> 3:26 *And they came unto John and said unto him, Rabbi, he that was with thee beyond Jordan of whom thou gave witness, behold, the same baptizes, and all men come to him.*

So they attempted to stir up some rivalry between John and Jesus.

---

26 The next chapter of the book of John clarifies that Jesus did not actually conduct the baptisms; he delegated this to his disciples (John 4:2).

*3:27 John answered and said, A man can receive
nothing except it is given him from the heaven.*

*3:28 Ye yourselves are my witnesses that I said, I am
not the Christ, but that I am sent before him.*

*3:29 He that has the bride is the bridegroom, but
the friend of the bridegroom, who stands and hears
him, rejoices greatly because of the bridegroom's
voice; this my joy therefore is fulfilled.*

John refused to be tempted by the politics of popularity. In fact,
he was delighted that Jesus was becoming the center of attention.

*3:30 It is expedient unto him to increase, but unto
me, to decrease.*

This is expedient for all of us. John continued to preach the
truth until Herod literally had the preacher's head chopped off.
Likewise, it is expedient for all of us to follow the truth, come
out from under our own headship, and place ourselves under
the government (headship) of the Lord Jesus Christ.

*3:31 He that comes from above is above all; he that
is of the earth is earthly and speaks earthly things:
he that comes from heaven is above all.*

Jesus is to be our government. He is to be our only head – our
only Lord – and we must recognize this in public. Only thus
can we become citizens of the kingdom of heaven and rise
above that which is earthly.

*3:32 And what he has seen and heard, that he testi-
fies; and no one receives his testimony.*

*3:33 He that has received his testimony has set to his
seal that God is true.*

No one in their natural state can receive Christ's witness or testimony. Unless God is working in our lives by the Spirit, it is impossible for us to witness to the truth. He is the only source of light, and without his light we have no possibility of proper discernment.

In Jesus' time, every official document, contract, or testament was authenticated with a seal. If we are to enter into a covenant with God, we must receive the testimony of Jesus, and we set our seal on that covenant when we demonstrate – not only in word, but also in deed – that God is true. Since Jesus finished his work of redemption by his death and resurrection, he has been able to place his seal, which is the Holy Spirit, on every believer.

> 3:34 *For he whom God has sent speaks the words of God; for God does not give the Spirit by measure unto him.*

Elijah had a powerful portion of the Spirit (or anointing). Elisha asked for and received a double portion. Jesus, who was sent from heaven by the Father, did not receive a partial anointing. God placed the Spirit without measure upon him, and his anointing was and is unlimited. We may participate in this unlimited anointing as part of the body of Christ, if and when God truly commissions us to do his will.

> 3:35 *The Father loves the Son and has given all things into his hand.*

Jesus, even now, is seated at the right hand of the Father with all power and authority, mediating the new covenant.

> 3:36 *He that believes in the Son has eternal life, and he that does not obey the Son shall not see life, but the wrath of God abides on him.*

Belief in Jesus is linked to obedience, and the first step is to admit in public that we are not clean and that we need to repent.

Repentance isn't just insincere tears; it's a one-hundred-and-eighty-degree change of course. Instead of favoring and feeding our own life, we must leave it behind and embrace Jesus so that his life and love may flow in us and through us. It is not possible for us to obey the Son and see life, unless by the grace of God we are born again and filled with the Holy Spirit. This is why he promised to pour out his Spirit on all flesh (Joel 2:28-29; Acts 2:17-18).

John 4

4:1 *When therefore the Lord knew how the Pharisees had heard that Jesus made and baptized more disciples than John*

4:2 *(though Jesus himself baptized not, but his disciples),*

4:3 *he left Judaea and departed again into Galilee.*

When the Pharisees tried to stir up rivalry between John and Jesus, John responded with a wonderful attitude and a clear revelation, announcing, *It is expedient unto him to increase, but unto me, to decrease.*

When Jesus heard what the Pharisees were up to, he demonstrated temperance and refused to play their little game; instead, he simply left Judaea and departed into Galilee. Both John and Jesus demonstrated a clean witness and example for all of us.

Let us pray

Lord, may we have the courage to follow you in the light of day and carry your banner in public; not the banner of the religion of men, but the banner of your truth. Amen.

Chapter 4

The Samaritan Woman

John 4

4:1 *When therefore the Lord knew how the Pharisees had heard that Jesus made and baptized more disciples than John*

4:2 *(though Jesus himself baptized not, but his disciples),*

4:3 *he left Judaea and departed again into Galilee.*

4:4 *And it was necessary that he go through Samaria.*[27]

Jesus (with his disciples) was on a journey from Judea (identified with the Jews) to Galilee (identified with perfection), and Samaria was on his route.

4:5 *Then he came to a city of Samaria, which is called Sychar, near to the parcel of ground that Jacob gave to his son Joseph.*

---

27 "Samaria" means "guard" or "watch" (i.e., outpost).

The Samaritans who lived there in Jesus' day were a residue of the ten tribes of the northern kingdom. Their ancestors had been carried away captive more than six hundred years previously and had subsequently intermarried with the pagans, thus losing their identity as tribes of Israel. The kings of Israel had gradually degenerated into a state of serious apostasy, setting up their own religious feast days and places of worship because they were afraid to let their people worship at Jerusalem at the prescribed times (Leviticus 23), lest they lose control. Even so, the Samaritans still identified with their ancestor Jacob. Some of them still lived on or near the parcel of ground that Jacob had given to his favorite son, Joseph.

4:6 *Now Jacob's well was there....*

Jacob's well is not directly mentioned in the Old Testament, although some historians think he must have dug this well on the plot of land that he bought at Shechem (which means "back" or "shoulder," symbolic of government). Remember it was Jacob who, almost five hundred years prior to the law of Moses (which formally instituted tithing as part of the law), offered God a tithe of all his income and increase as an incentive for God to bless him, after he had a dream and revelation from God on his journey to seek a wife from among his kin. *And Jacob vowed a vow, saying, If God will be with me and will keep me in this way that I go and will give me bread to eat and clothing to put on so that I come again to my father's house in peace, then shall the LORD be my God; and this stone, which I have set for a pillar, shall be God's house; and of all that thou shalt give me I will surely give the tenth part unto thee* (Genesis 28:20-22).

Jacob's well is thus symbolic of his commitment to tithe.

4:6 *... Jesus, therefore, being wearied with his*

journey, sat thus on the well; and it was about the
sixth hour.

Jesus, in his human condition, was tired from his journey. The sixth hour was noon, and the sun was undoubtedly hot. Six is a number associated with man (and with man's choices).[28]

4:7 *There came a woman of Samaria to draw water;*
Jesus said unto her, Give me to drink.

4:8 *(For his disciples were gone away unto the city to*
buy food.)

4:9 *Then said the Samaritan woman unto him, How*
is it that thou, being a Jew, askest drink of me, who
am a woman of Samaria? for the Jews have no deal-
ings with the Samaritans.

In Scripture, a woman can represent an entire congregation or group. Therefore, whom does this Samaritan woman represent?

Obviously, she is not a Jew. However, it is evident in the book of Acts that God planned to reach out not only to Samaria but to the uttermost parts of the earth (Acts 1:8; 8:25). The spiritual path that God would take from the age of the law (the time of the Jews) to the perfection of the kingdom would go through Samaria, in that he would pour out his grace on the Gentiles, many of whom throughout history would identify with Jacob and his well. The OT tithe would become one of the foundational doctrines of the NT church as their source of blessing. It would provide much of the financing for the institutional church, and the individuals who tithed would be promised that God would slake their thirst with his blessing.

Sadly, over time, many church leaders became obsessed with promoting a ten percent commitment to the church's coffers rather than stressing a total surrender to the Lord. You

---

28   Man was created on the sixth day (Genesis 1:26-31). Psalm 6 demonstrates the consequences of man's choices, and so on.

will recall that Jacob's well was located at or near the city of Shechem, meaning "shoulder," symbolic of government. That city's name was subsequently changed to "Sychar," which means "drunken," and it is true to say that much of the church became inebriated over the concept of ten percent for God and ninety percent to do whatever they pleased.

In this true example or living parable, Jesus comes walking by, tired from his journey, and then sits on the edge of the well and asks the woman for some of the water. What would happen today if he (or someone he sent) were to enter one of our modern churches that depends on the concept of tithing, sit down on the edge of "Jacob's well," and ask the woman (the congregation) to give him some of the "water" to drink? After all, to whom does the water really belong?

> 4:10 *Jesus answered and said unto her, If thou knewest the gift of God and who it is that saith to thee, Give me to drink, thou wouldest have asked of him, and he would have given thee living water.*

In this gospel account, it has already been established (in John 3:16) that God gave his only begotten son. Therefore, Jesus is the gift of God. Jesus now makes it clear that Jacob's well does not contain living water. No amount of tithing to a congregation, minister, or church can produce this water. Only Jesus can supply us with living water, and we must recognize who he really is and personally ask him to provide it.

> 4:11 *The woman said unto him, Sir, thou hast nothing to draw with, and the well is deep; from where then hast thou that living water?*

> 4:12 *Art thou greater than our father Jacob, who gave us the well and drank thereof himself, and his sons and his cattle?*

Apparently, the original well was cut out of stone and was quite deep. In fact, when Jacob made the commitment to tithe, he set up a stone pillar and said that from that time forward, this would be called *God's house*. Does any of this sound familiar?[29] Later on, the children of Israel would receive the commandments of God on tablets of stone instead of having them engraved on the tablets of their hearts.

The woman at the well, even though she is a Samaritan rather than a Jew, refers to *our father Jacob*. "Jacob" means "heel catcher" or "supplanter," and he was so named because he was born grasping his twin brother's heel. Jacob spent much of his early life strategizing how to get the best deal for himself, even if this meant tripping up his brother Esau and having to flee the country as a result. Years later, Jacob set off to return to his homeland, and while en route, he learned that Esau was coming to meet him with four hundred men. Not surprisingly, given his history with his brother, Jacob feared his entire family would be slaughtered. He spent that night wrestling with the angel of the Lord, and when he refused to let go until the Lord blessed him, God touched him in the sinew of his thigh, blessed him, and changed his name to Israel, meaning "God prevails" (or "he who prevails with God"). This change of name symbolized a change of nature (i.e. conversion).

Jacob gave the well to those who are like the Samaritan woman (and like many church congregations). Verse 12 tells us that he drank from the well himself (he instituted the tithe for himself), and his sons and cattle also drank thereof (he also instituted it for his descendants). Sons and cattle are symbols of those who are converted (having a new name or nature) and those who are unconverted respectively, but since the tithe became part

---

29   Have you ever attended a worship service where they welcomed you (and your tithe if you were so disposed) to the house of God?

of the law, it may be applied to those who are unconverted just as easily as to the genuine sons.

Jesus, however, would soon prove to the woman that he was, indeed, much greater than *our father Jacob.*

> 4:13 *Jesus answered and said unto her, Whosoever drinks of this water shall thirst again,*

> 4:14 *but whosoever drinks of the water that I shall give him shall never thirst, but the water that I shall give him shall be in him a fountain of water springing up into eternal life.*

For the ancients, living water was water that flowed (and was cleansed by the force of the flow). A static pool of water at the bottom of a deep well was not considered to be living water. Jesus desires us to voluntarily place all our time, money, and resources under his control so he may flow in and through us by the Holy Spirit. The static giving of a tithe by a law set in stone can never compare with the living *fountain of water springing up into eternal life* as we make every decision (financial and otherwise) by the Spirit, based on the witness and prompting of Jesus.[30]

> 4:15 *The woman said unto him, Lord, give me this water, that I not thirst, neither come here to draw.*

The woman was bantering with Jesus, trying to decide whether or not he meant what he said.

> 4:16 *Jesus said unto her, Go, call thy husband and come here.*

Under the old covenant (and the entire concept of Jacob's well is OT), a covenant could only be made between males (females could be included in the covenant's provisions because they were

---

30   See *The Truth About Tithing,* Russell Stendal, Life Sentence Publishing, Abbotsford, WI.

married to a husband or were the daughter of a father, etc.). The sign of the old covenant is the circumcision of the flesh (and in this sense, it is impossible to circumcise a woman). Under the new covenant, however, in Christ there is *neither male nor female* (Galatians 3:28), and the covenant's sign is circumcision of the heart (as discussed in chapter 2).

> 4:17 *The woman answered and said, I have no husband. Jesus said unto her, Thou hast well said, I have no husband;*
>
> 4:18 *for thou hast had five husbands, and he whom thou now hast is not thy husband; this hast thou said with truth.*

This woman had a problem with fidelity to her husbands, and a substantial segment of the church that she represents has the same problem with regard to Jesus, the church's bridegroom.

Just as the woman had five husbands, so there are five ministries mentioned in Scripture: apostles, prophets, evangelists, pastors, and teachers (Ephesians 4:11). Five is also a number that is linked to mercy and grace. On the fifth day of creation, God created the fish and other living creatures of the sea and every winged fowl that could fly above the earth (Genesis 1:20-23), and it's his plan to fish us out of the sea of lost humanity, change our nature (our name), and give us (as citizens of heaven) wings like eagles to soar high above the problems and obstacles on earth. God accomplishes this by his mercy and grace, and he uses the five ministries *for the perfecting of the saints in the work of the ministry, unto the edifying of the body of the Christ until we all come forth in the unity of the faith and of the knowledge of the Son of God unto a perfect man* (Ephesians 4:12-13a).

Different sectors of the church at different times have attempted to "marry" the ministry (or vice versa), and in doing so they have displaced Jesus Christ from his position as its bridegroom (even to the point of returning to laws set in stone, such as the tithing represented by Jacob's well). The attitude of John the Baptist was quite the opposite. He called himself *the friend of the bridegroom* and declared himself overjoyed to see Jesus increase, even if this meant that John's own position as an important prophet must decrease.

Some in the church have considered themselves married to doctrines and or to ministries emphasizing God's mercy and grace (symbolized by the number five[31]) and have completely disregarded many warnings and admonitions throughout the Scriptures. The Samaritan woman, like many today, had been with five husbands and the one she was presently with was not her husband. When confronted directly by Jesus, she had to admit the truth.[32]

> 4:19 *The woman said unto him, Lord, I perceive that thou art a prophet.*

The woman thought she was being confronted by a prophet, and indeed she was, but her position was much more serious than this, since the man confronting her was not only a prophet, but the Son of God. Nevertheless, Jesus continued to extend mercy and grace to her.

Even in the midst of all of the promiscuous things that have been done and are currently being done in his name, he continues to extend mercy and grace, hoping there will be a harvest of those who will voluntarily place everything on the altar and commit to him one hundred percent.

> 4:20 *Our fathers worshipped in this mountain, and ye say that in Jerusalem is the place where it is necessary to worship.*

---

31   I am presently writing a commentary on the Psalms that will help clarify the meanings of the numbers according to their use by God in Scripture.

32   *For thy Maker shall be thine husband; the LORD of the hosts is his name; and thy Redeemer the Holy One of Israel; The God of the whole earth shall he be called* (Isaiah 54:5).

Jacob instituted the ten percent commitment (and called the stone memorializing it *God's house*) almost a thousand years before David captured the citadel of Zion at Jerusalem and received plans from God for the temple that his son, Solomon, would build. Now, about a thousand years after Solomon, Jesus had found the temple to be filled with dishonest people who had made his Father's house a house of merchandise. Among the Jews, Jesus had so far cloaked his true identity in secrecy, but now he was about to give this woman – who was a total stranger to his absent disciples – a startling revelation of not only his identity but his plans for the next two thousand years. This was a very important sign (as in signs and wonders), and the events of the two days following this revelation would be breathtaking for the disciples.

> *4:21 Jesus said unto her, Woman, believe me, the hour comes when neither in this mountain nor in Jerusalem shall ye worship the Father.*
>
> *4:22 Ye worship what ye know not; we worship what we know, for saving health is of the Jews.*
>
> *4:23 But the hour comes, and now is, when the true worshippers shall worship the Father in spirit and in truth, for the Father seeks such to worship him.*
>
> *4:24 God is a Spirit and those that worship him must worship him in spirit and in truth.*

Jesus revealed to the Samaritan woman – and to us – that the hour comes, and now is, when the city of Bethel, stone monuments such as Jacob's well, the temple at Jerusalem, medieval cathedrals, modern houses of worship, and all the religious structure of obligatory tithing sustaining an intermediary priest or clergy class will be displaced, because *God is a Spirit and those that worship him must worship him in spirit and in truth.*

We ourselves are to be the temple! Jesus is the only mediator of the new covenant (1 Timothy 2:5; Hebrews 8:6; 9:15; 12:24), and he will settle for nothing less.

And now this woman with a somewhat shabby and sordid past, who had been faithfully drawing water from the depths of Jacob's well to quench Jesus' thirst, received the truth that he spoke directly into her life, and a great revelation began to dawn on her. Thoughts of the promised Messiah filled her mind as a wonderful hope welled up in her heart.

> *4:25 The woman said unto him, I know that the Messiah is to come, who is called the Christ; when he is come, he will declare unto us all things.*

> *4:26 Jesus said unto her, I AM that speak unto thee.*

I AM is the sacred name of God (Exodus 3:14). The Israelites thought this name too sacred to pronounce, on pain of blasphemy (a crime that carried the death penalty they eventually carried out on Jesus), and yet this Samaritan woman was transformed by a direct revelation and word from the Lord Jesus.

> *4:27 And upon this came his disciples and marvelled that he talked with that woman; yet no one said, What askest thou? or, What talkest thou with her?*

Jesus' conversation with "that woman" included an important revelation that he had not yet shared openly with the Jewish general public or even with his disciples. In fact, the disciples would not be privy to some aspects of that revelation until after being filled with the Holy Spirit on the day of Pentecost, several years in the future.

> *4:28 The woman then left her waterpot and went into the city and said to those men,*

> *4:29 Come, see a man who told me all that I have done; is perchance this the Christ?*

The woman knew that when the Messiah was come, *he will declare unto us all things.* Incredibly, this was what had just happened to her. Now she left her waterpot and went into the city with an important declaration for "those men."

What city? Who were those men?

She went into the city that received their water from Jacob's well. Here she encountered those men (the five men, or ministries, that she had been under, none of which turned out to have been the real husband) who had built fortresses of religion with tithe money that had been laboriously extracted from the depths of Jacob's well with the waterpot that belonged to the woman. And in her excitement about her encounter with Jesus, she exclaimed to the men, *Come, see a man who told me all that I have done; is perchance this the Christ?*

She certainly got their attention, especially when they saw that she had left her waterpot and was no longer inclined to use it. The water from Jacob's well would never really satisfy. Now she had a fountain of water springing up into eternal life inside her being, and she could worship the Father in Spirit and in truth anywhere.

4:30 *Then they went out of the city and came unto him.*

In order to come to Christ, the men had to go out of the city.

The proper purpose of ministry isn't to attract people and make them dependent on the ministry or on church institutions; it's to connect the people directly to Jesus. Then the true universal body of Christ is edified.

4:31 *In the meanwhile his disciples entreated him, saying, Rabbi, eat.*

While Jesus was having his little discussion with the woman regarding Jacob's well, the disciples had gone away into the city to buy food (verse 8). While the woman (representing major elements of the church) has been obsessed with Jacob's well and with those who are not her real husband, any true disciple has been hard pressed to find good (spiritual) food that does not require payment of some kind of price. In fact, it seems that Jesus refused to eat the food the disciples bought in that city.

> 4:32 *But he said unto them, I have a food to eat that ye know not of.*

> 4:33 *Therefore said the disciples one to another, Has anyone brought him anything to eat?*

> 4:34 *Jesus said unto them, My food is to do the will of him that sent me and to finish his work.*

Jesus' purpose in engaging with the Samaritan woman at the well wasn't just to kill some time while the disciples were in town buying food. No, he was doing the will of his Father, which was much more important to Jesus than any physical food. The provision from Jacob's well could never *finish his* (the Father's) *work*; that task requires living water from Jesus, *a fountain of water springing up* (from inside us) *into eternal life.*

> 4:35 *Do ye not say, There are yet four months and then comes harvest? Behold, I say unto you, Lift up your eyes and look on the fields, for they are white already to harvest.*

Jesus and the disciples had just come from celebrating the Passover at Jerusalem, and it would literally be four more months until harvest time, yet he wanted them to be able to see that they were in the season for a great spiritual harvest (even among the Samaritans, whom the Jews regarded as their apostate enemies).

> 4:36 *And he that reaps receives wages and gathers fruit unto eternal life, that both he that sows and he that reaps may rejoice together.*

> *4:37 And herein is that saying true, One sows and another reaps.*

> *4:38 I have sent you to reap that upon which ye bestowed no labour; others laboured, and ye have entered into their labours.*

This was the case for Jesus' disciples at the end of the age of the Jews, and so it is for us now at the end of the church age.

> *4:39 And many of the Samaritans of that city believed in him by the word of the woman, who testified, He told me all that I have done.*

> *4:40 So when the Samaritans were come unto him, they asked him to abide with them; and he abode there two days.*

Two prophetic days represent two thousand years. On the spiritual journey from Judea ("of the Jews") toward Galilee ("perfection"), Jesus ended up spending two days with the Samaritans. This is symbolic of the two-thousand-year age of grace, which falls between the age of the law and the coming day of the Lord.

> *4:41 And many more believed by his own word*

> *4:42 and said unto the woman, Now we believe, not because of thy speech; for we have heard him ourselves and know that this is indeed the Christ, the Saviour of the world.*

When Jesus has a woman, or congregation, filled with a fountain of living water springing up into eternal life, we will find plenty of action. Many will believe her testimony, and many more will be brought near enough to hear the voice of the Lord for themselves and believe.

> 4:43 *Now after two days he departed from that place and went into Galilee.*

> 4:44 *For Jesus himself testified that a prophet has no honour in his own country.*

After the two prophetic days of the age of grace unto the Gentiles, Jesus will once again focus on Galilee ("maturity" or "perfection").[33] There will be an end-time restoration of Israel (that is, the people of God, including both Jews and Gentiles) linked to the second coming of Jesus Christ and to the events leading up to his return. Up until now, Jesus has had *no honour in his own country*, but this is about to change.

> 4:45 *Then when he was come into Galilee, the Galilaeans received him, having seen all the things that he had done in Jerusalem at the feast, for they had also gone to the feast.* [34]

The feast in question is Passover, and Jesus is the Lamb of God that takes away the sins of the world. The Galilaeans (those who are on the way to "perfection") who had gone to the feast received him. As we know, Jesus will soon return for a bride without spot or wrinkle or any such thing. This "bride" will consist of those who have *gone to the feast*, that is, believers who are on their way to maturity in Christ having celebrated Passover (being saved by the blood of the Lamb of God who gave his life for us) and Pentecost (the infilling of the Holy Spirit) on our way to the Feast of Tabernacles (where we will dwell or tabernacle with God for all eternity).[35]

---

33 Maturity and perfection are the same word in both Greek and Hebrew.

34 Remember that the Jews were required to go to three feasts a year in Jerusalem: Passover, Pentecost, and Tabernacles (Leviticus 23) and that these three feasts are symbolic of our path to maturity or perfection in Christ.

35 Leviticus chapter 23 spells out the three annual feasts of the Lord. Attendance was mandatory for all males in Israel. All three feasts are fulfilled in Christ and are symbolic of our spiritual journey. The Feast of Pentecost is also known as the Feast of Weeks (it was seven weeks after the Passover on the fiftieth day) and the Feast of Tabernacles is also known as the Feast of Harvest.

> 4:46 *So Jesus came again into Cana of Galilee,*
> *where he had made the water wine. And there*
> *was a certain nobleman whose son was sick at*
> *Capernaum.*

A nobleman is someone who was born free. The only way to truly be born free, however, is to be born again from above. The son of this nobleman was sick at Capernaum, the city of Nahum (or "comforter"). The real comforter, of course, is the Holy Spirit.

Why was the nobleman's son sick?

It has been said that God has sons but not grandsons, because the faith of the fathers is not sufficient for the salvation of their children. This situation is tragic, and it is playing out in many congregations today. It is also true that the sins (or the iniquity) of the fathers affect their descendants, even unto the third or fourth generation of those that hate God (Exodus 20:5). This particular nobleman was of the court of Herod Antipas, a ruler whose family hated even the idea of the coming of the Messiah. Herod's father, known as Herod the Great, had ordered the murder of all the babies in Bethlehem in an effort to eliminate the infant Jesus.

> 4:47 *When he heard that Jesus was come out of*
> *Judaea into Galilee, he went unto him and besought*
> *him that he would come down and heal his son, for*
> *he was at the point of death.*

> 4:48 *Then Jesus said unto him, Except ye see signs*
> *and wonders, ye will not believe.*

This seems to have been true of Herod, who even then was rejecting John the Baptist.

> 4:49 *The nobleman said unto him, Sir, come down*
> *before my child dies.*

This particular nobleman knew that the only hope for his dying son lay in Jesus.

> 4:50 *Jesus said unto him, Go; thy son lives. And the man believed the word that Jesus spoke unto him, and he went.*

Compare the nobleman's attitude with that of the disciple Thomas, whom Jesus would later chide for his lack of belief in his resurrection: *Thomas, because thou hast seen me, thou hast believed; blessed are those that have not seen and yet have believed* (John 20:29). This nobleman represents those who have not seen and yet have believed. There have been a number of them over the centuries.

> 4:51 *And as he was now going down, his slaves met him and told him, saying, Thy son lives.*

> 4:52 *Then he enquired of them the hour when he began to get better. And they said unto him, Yesterday at the seventh hour the fever left him.*

> 4:53 *So the father knew that it was at the same hour in which Jesus said unto him, Thy son lives; and he believed, and his whole house.*

The mature faith of this father helped trigger the salvation of *his whole house.*

> 4:54 *This again is the second sign that Jesus did when he was come out of Judaea into Galilee.*

If this is the second sign Jesus did on his trip from Judaea into Galilee, what was the first?

The woman at the well.[36]

The first sign began to take place at the sixth hour at Jacob's well. Six is the number of man and of man's ability to choose.

---

36   This is counting the signs on Jesus' trip from Judea to Galilee (not from the beginning of his ministry).

The second sign took place at the seventh hour at Galilee. Seven is the number of God and of his rest (Genesis 2:1-3). The first sign means that Jesus will have a people who have chosen him above and beyond anyone or anything else, because of who he is. The second sign means that one by one, these individuals will believe and enter into God's rest without having to see the results of Jesus' promises up front. All of this will trigger a significant end-time harvest among Gentiles and Jews.

Let us pray

Lord, we ask that there may be opportunity for your Word to reach all the people and groups that for any reason have been too far away, or seemingly forgotten, or passed over until now. May they receive a clean word through your clean and worthy messengers. Amen.

Chapter 5

The Pool of Bethesda

John 5

5:1 After these things there was a feast of the Jews, and Jesus went up to Jerusalem.

After what things?

After the two signs described in the previous chapter, with the Samaritan woman at Jacob's well and with the nobleman whose son was dying in Capernaum. Since Jesus had traveled to Galilee via Samaria after celebrating the Passover in Jerusalem, the feast mentioned here is probably the feast of Pentecost.

5:2 Now in Jerusalem there is a pool by the sheep gate,[37] which in Hebrew is called, Bethesda, having five porches.

The pool of Bethesda (meaning "house of mercy") was by the sheep gate or sheep market, and it had five porches. Five is the number linked to grace and mercy (as well as to ministry).

---

37   At the time of the return from the Babylonian captivity, the sheep gate was restored by the high priest, Eliashib ("whom God restores"), and his brethren, the priests (Nehemiah 3:1).

> 5:3 *In these lay a great multitude of those who were sick, blind, halt, withered, waiting for the moving of the water.*

When God took the children of Israel out of Egypt and into the wilderness, he promised them, *If thou wilt diligently hearken to the voice of the LORD thy God and wilt do that which is right in his sight and wilt give ear to his commandments and keep all his statutes, I will put none of these diseases upon thee, which I have brought upon the Egyptians; for I am the LORD thy Healer* (Exodus 15:26). And while it is true they had not undergone the plagues that had been visited on Egypt, they were certainly experiencing a wide variety of physical problems.

> 5:4 *For an angel went down at a certain time into the pool and troubled the water; whosoever then first after the troubling of the water stepped in was made whole of whatever disease he had.*

There was *a great multitude of those who were sick, blind, halt, withered, waiting …*

The water of the pool of Bethesda wasn't much more curative than the static water at the bottom of Jacob's well. Every so often an angel went down and troubled (stirred) the water, but the effect only lasted long enough for one person to be healed.

> 5:5 *And a certain man was there who had an infirmity thirty-eight years.*

The number thirty-eight[38] is connected with remembering how far the people of God have fallen from grace, yet how he can deal with their iniquity and remove it (iniquity is known sin that the person or group, or even the entire nation, is trying to hide).

---

38   Thirty-eight is nineteen doubled. Compare Psalm 19 (the wisdom and glory of God) to Psalm 38 (the actual state of many of the people of God then and now). Some people may not feel that chapter and verse numbers in Scripture are really inspired. However, I am confident that the Psalms are in the original order and therefore the number of each Psalm is significant.

> 5:6 *When Jesus saw him lying there and knew that he had been now a long time in that case, he said unto him, Dost thou desire to be made whole?*

> 5:7 *The impotent man answered him, Sir, I have no man when the water is troubled to put me into the pool, but while I am coming, another steps down before me.*

> 5:8 *Jesus said unto him, Rise, take up thy bed, and walk.*

Jesus earnestly desires to make us whole. Without him, we are "impotent," no matter how long we "lie at the pool of Bethesda in front of the sheep gate."

> 5:9 *And immediately the man was made whole and took up his bed and walked, and on that day was the sabbath.*

This unnamed man was healed by the grace of God. He didn't even know who Jesus was, and there is no indication here that he expressed either repentance or faith. He had been in this dire predicament for a long time until Jesus came by, noticed him, and asked him if he wanted to be healed. Then, with a direct order, Jesus cut right through his doleful explanation of how, for so many years, he had been unable to find healing at what was supposed to be the "house of mercy" with its five porches. At a word from Jesus, he was made whole.

> 5:10 *The Jews therefore said unto him that was cured, It is the sabbath day; it is not lawful for thee to carry thy bed.*

The Sabbath, being the seventh day of the week, is the day on which man was commanded to rest (Exodus 20:8-11). After finishing creation, God also rested on the seventh day (Genesis

2:2). However, *one day before the Lord is as a thousand years, and a thousand years are as one day* (2 Peter 3:8; Psalm 90:4). We are now entering into the seventh prophetic day, when God will finish his **new** creation.

> 5:11 *He answered them, He that made me whole, the same said unto me, Take up thy bed and walk.*

> 5:12 *Then they asked him, Who is the man that said unto thee, Take up thy bed and walk?*

> 5:13 *And he that was healed did not know who it was; for Jesus had conveyed himself away, a multitude being in that place.*

> 5:14 *Afterward Jesus found him in the temple and said unto him, Behold, thou art made whole; sin no more, lest a worse thing come unto thee.*

In this case, the number thirty-eight also has to do with being saved from the consequences of sin. Having *found him in the temple*, Jesus gave this man a direct word to *sin no more, lest a worse thing come unto thee*. When Jesus saves us by grace, he does not want us to go on sinning. If we hear his voice, we will receive the grace and power to do what he says and overcome the lure of our previous sin.

> 5:15 *The man departed and told the Jews that it was Jesus who had made him whole.*

> 5:16 *And for this reason the Jews persecuted Jesus and sought to kill him: because he had done these things on a sabbath.*

For untold centuries, God's people had sickened and died, yet when the Lord himself came on the scene and began to heal people, all of a sudden the Jews revealed themselves as his mortal enemies because God was choosing not to operate within their narrow rules.

> 5:17 *But Jesus answered them, My Father works until now, and I work.*

Jesus told them in no uncertain terms that since his Father worked on the Sabbath day, he did likewise. What he did not explicitly tell them at that time was that God can not only use the Sabbath or any other day to raise up those who are paralyzed and impotent, he can also give resurrection life through his Son on any day of the week.

> 5:18 *Therefore the Jews sought the more to kill him, because he not only had broken the sabbath but also called God his own Father, making himself equal with God.*

If we are truly born again from above, what does that make us?

It makes us part of the family of God, part of the body of Christ under the headship (or government) of Jesus.

> 5:19 *Then Jesus answered and said unto them, Verily, verily, I say unto you, The Son can do nothing of himself but what he sees the Father do; for all that he does, this also the Son does together with him.*

> 5:20 *For the Father loves the Son and shows him all the things that he does, and he will show him greater works than these that ye may marvel.*

This is a theme that is developed more and more throughout the course of John's gospel account.

> 5:21 *For as the Father raises up the dead and gives them life; even so the Son gives life unto whom he will.*

> *5:22 For the Father judges no man but has commit-*
> *ted all judgment unto the Son*

> *5:23 that everyone should honour the Son, even as*
> *they honour the Father. He that does not honour the*
> *Son does not honour the Father who has sent him.*

Jesus is a perfect representation of the Father.

> *5:24 Verily, verily, I say unto you, He that hears my*
> *word and believes him that sent me has eternal life*
> *and shall not come into judgment but has passed*
> *from death unto life.*

> *5:25 Verily, verily, I say unto you, The hour shall*
> *come, and now is, when the dead shall hear the*
> *voice of the Son of God, and they that hear shall live.*

The impotent man lacked the power to do anything to save himself (he couldn't even get into the pool of Bethesda in time, when the angel troubled the water). He could, however, still hear, and when he heard Jesus tell him, *Rise, take up thy bed, and walk,* to his utter astonishment, he found that he was able to do so.

How many "impotent" people have heard the voice of the truth (and Jesus is the truth) in the depths of their conscience and have suddenly found it possible to take steps or even giant leaps of faith?

> *5:26 For as the Father has life in himself, so has he*
> *given to the Son to have life in himself*

> *5:27 and has also given him power and authority to*
> *execute judgment because he is the Son of man.*

Religious people like the scribes and Pharisees do not execute true judgment. Only Jesus, *the Son of man*, can do so. What's more, the life of the flesh is not, and never will be, eternal. If we are to have eternal life, we must believe upon the Lord Jesus Christ and depend on him alone.

> 5:28 *Marvel not at this, for an hour shall come when all that are in the graves shall hear his voice,*

> 5:29 *and those that have done good shall come forth unto the resurrection of life; but those that have done evil, unto the resurrection of judgment.*[39]

We see that there are two very different kinds of resurrection.

> 5:30 *I can of my own self do nothing; as I hear, I judge, and my judgment is just because I seek not my own will, but the will of the Father who has sent me.*

Jesus chose to have mercy on the impotent man, and this was the will of the Father.

> 5:31 *If I bear witness of myself, my witness is not true.*

> 5:32 *There is another that bears witness of me, and I know that the witness which he witnesses of me is true.*

> 5:33 *Ye sent unto John, and he bore witness unto the truth.*

Jesus is the truth.

> 5:34 *But I receive not testimony from man, but I say these things that ye might be saved.*

> 5:35 *He was a burning and a shining light, and ye were willing to rejoice for one hour in his light.*

John the Baptist evidenced the presence and comfort of the

---

39 In the original Greek, both the word "good" and the word "evil" are plural. This seems to convey the idea that a person will continually be engaged in some form of one or the other.

Spirit of God from very early on (Luke 1:41,80). He was a burning, shining light because the Spirit operated in him and through him.

> 5:36 *But I have greater testimony than that of John; for the works which the Father has given me to finish, the same works that I do, bear witness of me that the Father has sent me.*

> 5:37 *And the Father himself, who has sent me, has borne witness of me. Ye have neither heard his voice at any time nor seen his appearance.*

The Father spoke from heaven when John baptized Jesus, and many who were present heard his voice, yet the unbelieving Jews did not (Matthew 3:16, 17).

> 5:38 *And ye do not have his word abiding in you; for whom he has sent, him ye do not believe.*

> 5:39 *Search the scriptures, for in them ye think ye have eternal life; and they are those who testify of me.*

Those who testify of Jesus include John the Baptist (by the Spirit of God), the Father (by the mighty works done through Jesus), and the Scriptures (with inspired prophecy written hundreds or even thousands of years in advance).

> 5:40 *And ye will not come to me, that ye might have life.*

Eternal life is only available through Jesus. The Scriptures (the written Word) are inspired, but they testify of Jesus (the living Word), and we must receive him in order to have life.

> 5:41 *I do not receive glory from men.*

Glory relates to light, and Jesus' illumination and clarity came from his Father, not from men.

> *5:42 But I know you that ye have not the love of God in you.*

Jesus knew that the unbelieving Jews did not have the love of God within them, not only because he knew their hearts, but also because they demonstrated their lack of such love by their words and their actions. Not satisfied with rejecting all the signs and witnesses of Jesus' identity, they expressed an intense desire to kill him and ultimately succeeded in having him crucified.

> *5:43 I have come in my Father's name, and ye receive me not; if another shall come in his own name, him ye will receive.*

> *5:44 How can ye believe, who take glory one from another, and seek not the glory that comes only from God?*

Religious men receive those who come in their own name (nature), yet Jesus came in his Father's name (nature) and was not received. Rather than seeking true glory (light or illumination), which comes only from God, those who come in their own name settle for taking a false glory from one another, but this so-called glory is really darkness. Therefore *men loved darkness more than the light, because their deeds were evil* (John 3:19).

God's glory cleanses and transforms because it is linked to his very presence. If we desire to partake of the glory of God, we must accept Jesus' authority and presence in our lives, so that he will cleanse us from all unrighteousness. This, however, is what the self-righteous Jews fervently sought to avoid.

> *5:45 Do not think that I will accuse you to the Father; there is one that accuses you, even Moses, in whom ye trust.*

> *5:46 For had ye believed Moses, ye would have believed me, for he wrote of me.*

*5:47 But if ye do not believe his writings, how shall
ye believe my words?*

Let us pray

*Lord, we thank you for your Word, and we seek your glory and
your righteousness instead of our own. May the brightness of
your presence illuminate us. Amen.*

Chapter 6

Communion with Jesus and the Father

John 6

6:1 After these things Jesus went over the sea of Galilee, which is the sea of Tiberias.

The Sea of Galilee is described by four different names in Scripture. Here it is also called the Sea of Tiberias, named for the Roman Emperor at the time of Jesus. Tiberias means "son of Tiber" or simply "of Tiber" (the Tiber is the river that flows through Rome). This sea is now symbolic of the sea of lost Gentiles that Jesus came to save (John 3:16). Note that Jesus went *over the sea* and began to minister on the other side (there were Jews on one side and Gentiles on the other).

6:2 And a great multitude followed him because they saw his signs which he did on the sick.

6:3 And Jesus went up into a mountain, and he sat there with his disciples.

6:4 And the passover, the feast of the Jews, was near.

This is the second Passover explicitly mentioned in this gospel account. Here it is also called *the feast of the Jews.*

> 6:5 *Then Jesus lifted up his eyes and saw a great company come unto him; he said unto Philip, From where shall we buy bread that these may eat?*

> 6:6 *But he said this to prove him, for he knew what he would do.*

> 6:7 *Philip answered him, Two hundred denarius of bread is not sufficient for them, that each one of them may take a little.*

A denarius was a day's wages.

> 6:8 *One of his disciples, Andrew, Simon Peter's brother, said unto him,*

> 6:9 *There is a lad here, who has five barley loaves and two small fishes, but what are they among so many?*

> 6:10 *Then Jesus said, Make the men sit down. Now there was much grass in the place. So the men sat down, in number about five thousand.*[40]

As mentioned earlier, five is a number linked to grace, mercy, and ministry. Barley is linked to the Holy Spirit (the feast of Pentecost was at the time of the barley harvest). Jesus had told his disciples that if they followed him, he would make them fishers of men, and here two small fish speak of the small remnant of believers that Jesus planned to multiply.

> 6:11 *And Jesus took the loaves, and when he had given thanks, he distributed to the disciples and the disciples to those that were sitting down; and likewise of the fishes as much as they desired.*

40   See *The Gospel of Jesus Christ – A Study in Mark*, Russell Stendal, Aneko Press.

In this miracle, Jesus used the disciples to bring about the multiplication of the barley loaves and the fish.

> 6:12 *When they were filled, he said unto his disciples, Gather up the fragments that remain that nothing be lost.*

> 6:13 *Therefore they gathered them together and filled twelve baskets with the fragments of the five barley loaves which were left over from those that had eaten.*

The number twelve symbolizes divine order. It represents Jesus' desire to fill us with his mercy and grace as he multiplies his godly remnant (symbolized by the two fish) until he brings his people into divine order, that is, until they depend upon him and are under his government (Genesis 49:10). When that order prevails, the *five barley loaves* (representing the five ministries of grace and mercy) and the *two fishes* (representing the godly remnant) are intermingled. Under divine order there is no ruling class of chief brethren lording it over the people of God and the one who is the greatest is the servant of all.

> 6:14 *Then those men, as they had seen the sign that Jesus did, said, This is of a truth the prophet that was to come into the world.*

What prophet did they mean? The one described by Moses, who wrote:

> *The LORD thy God will raise up unto thee a Prophet from the midst of thee, of thy brethren, like unto me; unto him ye shall hearken, according to all that thou didst desire of the LORD thy God in Horeb in the day of the assembly, saying, Let me not hear again the voice of the LORD my God, neither let me see this great fire any more, lest I die.*

*And the LORD said unto me, They have well spoken
that which they have spoken. I will raise them up a
Prophet from among their brethren, like unto thee,
and will put my words in his mouth; and he shall
speak unto them all that I shall command him. And
it shall come to pass that whoever will not hearken
unto my words which he shall speak in my name, I
will require it of him.* (Deuteronomy 18:15-19)

The Pharisees had sent messengers to ask John the Baptist
whether he was the Christ, and if not, whether he was Elijah
or the prophet, that is, the prophet Moses mentioned (John
1:19-22). Does anyone wonder why they were much less eager
to ask Jesus the same questions?

Later, John recorded that *the testimony of Jesus is the spirit
of prophecy* (Revelation 19:10b).

6:15 *Jesus therefore knowing that they would
come and take him by force to make him king, he
departed again into a mountain himself alone.*

The feeding of the five thousand was a wonderful, prophetic,
living parable that went well beyond the reality of the actual
situation. Afterwards, Jesus *departed again into a mountain
himself alone* because he did not want the people to *take him
by force to make him king* at the wrong time and for the wrong
reasons.

6:16 *And when evening was come, his disciples went
down unto the sea*

6:17 *and entered into a ship and were crossing the
sea toward Capernaum. And it was now dark, and
Jesus had not come to them.*

The disciples were attempting to cross the sea toward Capernaum
without Jesus on board.

6:18 And the sea arose by reason of a great wind that blew.

6:19 So when they had rowed about twenty-five or thirty furlongs, they saw Jesus walking upon the sea and drawing nigh unto the ship, and they were afraid.

6:20 But he said unto them, I AM; be not afraid.

I AM is the sacred name of God (Exodus 3:14) that the Jews were not to pronounce, upon pain of death. In their dire situation, however, the disciples were reassured not only by the sound of Jesus' voice but by the words he used to signify his authority.

6:21 Then they willingly received him into the ship, and immediately the ship was at the land where they went.

The disciples were sailing toward Capernaum ("city of consolation"), but in reality, Jesus is all the consolation we need, no matter what problem or storm we may be facing, and we should welcome him aboard with gratitude and joy. Once they *received him into the ship*, immediately the ship was at their destination.

6:22 The day following when the multitude which was on the other side of the sea saw that there was no other boat there except the one in which his disciples had entered and that Jesus had not gone with his disciples into the boat, but that his disciples had gone away alone

6:23 (but other boats came from Tiberias near unto the place where they ate bread after the Lord had given thanks);

6:24 when the people therefore saw that Jesus was

not there, nor his disciples, they also entered into the
boats and came to Capernaum, seeking for Jesus.

There are many "boats" from "Tiberias," but true disciples need
only one boat, for Jesus promised that wherever two or three
are gathered together in his name, he will be in our midst, even
though those on the outside may not perceive him. There are
many groups, denominations, congregations, etc., but there is
only one body of Christ.

> 6:25 *And when they had found him on the other*
> *side of the sea, they said unto him, Rabbi, when*
> *didst thou come here?*[41]

> 6:26 *Jesus answered them and said, Verily, verily, I*
> *say unto you, Ye seek me, not because ye have seen*
> *the signs, but because ye ate of the loaves and were*
> *filled.*

There are many who seek and follow after Jesus for earthly
reasons, even in the midst of great revival. They are led by the
desires of their belly and are oblivious to *the signs* that point
to his spiritual authority, purity, and power.

> 6:27 *Labour not for the food which perishes, but for*
> *the food which abides unto eternal life, which the*
> *Son of man shall give unto you, for him has God the*
> *Father sealed.*

The seal of God is the Holy Spirit, and Jesus received the Spirit
without measure (John 3:34). God's seal also signifies that Jesus
is set apart from everyone else as the only way to eternal life.
We must hear and obey him by the grace of God.

> 6:28 *Then they said unto him, What shall we do*
> *that we might work the works of God?*

41　Job 9:8-11 is a parallel passage.

6:29 Jesus answered and said unto them, This is the work of God, that ye believe in him whom he has sent.

Grace is when God works in and through us, and when he does for us what we cannot do for ourselves. The Jews were accustomed to working their own self-righteousness under the law, but this had so far proved to be an unmitigated disaster.

6:30 They said therefore unto him, What sign showest thou then that we may see and believe thee? what dost thou work?

6:31 Our fathers ate manna in the desert, as it is written, He gave them of the bread from the heaven to eat.

6:32 Then Jesus said unto them, Verily, verily, I say unto you, Moses gave you not that bread from the heaven, but my Father gives you the true bread from the heaven.

This is what Moses wrote: *And he afflicted thee and caused thee to hunger and sustained thee with manna, food of which thou knewest not, neither did thy fathers know, that he might make thee know that man does not live by bread alone, but by every word that proceeds out of the mouth of the LORD shall man live* (Deuteronomy 8:3; also see Matthew 4:4; Luke 4:4).

6:33 For the bread of God is he who descended from heaven and gives life unto the world.

6:34 Then said they unto him, Lord, always give us this bread.

6:35 And Jesus said unto them, I AM the bread of life; he that comes to me shall never hunger, and he that believes in me shall never thirst.

6:36 But I said unto you, That even though ye have seen me, ye do not believe.

6:37 All that the Father gives me shall come to me, and he that comes to me I will in no wise cast out.

6:38 For I came down from the heaven, not to do my own will, but the will of him that sent me.

6:39 And this is the Father's will who has sent me, that of all whom he has given me I should lose nothing but should raise it up again in the last day.

What is the last day?

In the highest sense, the last day is the seventh millennium, the seventh prophetic day, also known as the day of the Lord.[42] The first resurrection takes place at the beginning of the last prophetic thousand-year day (Revelation 20:4).

6:40 And this is the will of him that sent me, That every one who sees the Son and believes in him may have eternal life, and I will raise him up in the last day.

Even with Jesus standing right in front of them, it was difficult for many to see him as the Son of God. Here, the promise of eternal life is for *every one who sees the Son and believes in him.* Astonishingly, many people who saw Jesus perform signs and miracles still did not really believe in him (verse 36).

Some may wonder how they can see Jesus today if he died and rose from the dead and is ascended on high, seated at the right hand of the Father. Hopefully they will see him through the loving actions of those who make up the body of Christ in the world today.

6:41 The Jews then murmured of him because he

---

42   We must bear in mind, however, *that one day before the Lord is as a thousand years, and a thousand years are as one day* (2 Peter 3:8b).

said, I AM the bread which descended from the heaven.

The fact that Jesus pronounced that sacred name again is bound to have added to the controversy.

6:42 And they said, Is not this Jesus, the son of Joseph, whose father and mother we know? How is it then that he says, I descended from heaven?

6:43 Jesus therefore answered and said unto them, Murmur not among yourselves.

6:44 No one can come to me unless the Father who has sent me draws him, and I will raise him up in the last day.

6:45 It is written in the prophets, And they shall all be taught of God. Every man therefore that has heard from the Father and has learned comes unto me.

How do we hear directly from the Father and learn so that we can come to Jesus?

It all starts with listening to the voice of our conscience. God created all of us with a conscience to act as our moral compass, and it is through our conscience that he can speak to us if we choose to hear.

6:46 Not that anyone has seen the Father, except he who is of God, he has seen the Father.

6:47 Verily, verily, I say unto you, He that believes in me has eternal life.

6:48 I AM the bread of life.

6:49 Your fathers ate manna in the wilderness and are dead.

> 6:50 *This is the bread which comes down from heaven, that anyone may eat of it and not die.*

> 6:51 *I AM the living bread which came down from heaven; if anyone eats of this bread, they shall live for ever; and the bread that I will give is my flesh, which I will give for the life of the world.*

This speech greatly complicated the situation for the religious Jews listening to Jesus' discourse. Now, not only was he proclaiming himself to be the living bread that came down from heaven and that people must eat in order to live forever, and not only was he pronouncing the sacred name of God in conjunction with his own (five times in this chapter alone), but he was also linking these revolutionary concepts to his flesh.

> 6:52 *The Jews therefore contended among themselves, saying, How is he able to give us his flesh to eat?*

Instead of tempering his message, Jesus doubled down on it.

> 6:53 *Then Jesus said unto them, Verily, verily, I say unto you, Unless ye eat the flesh of the Son of man and drink his blood, ye shall have no life in you.*

> 6:54 *Whosoever eats my flesh and drinks my blood has eternal life, and I will raise him up at the last day.*

The last day is mentioned only ten times in all of Scripture, yet this is the fourth mention of resurrection *at the last day* in this discourse.

> 6:55 *For my flesh is food indeed, and my blood is drink indeed.*

> 6:56 *He that eats my flesh and drinks my blood abides in me, and I in him.*

This is really a lesson on communion (and not the ground rules for some cannibal sect). Jesus' "flesh" is his body, and his "blood" is his life. They are respectively symbolized by bread and wine, which early in Scripture are the elements of covenant (Genesis 14:18-20). Jesus is setting the stage to announce the new covenant that will require his own death in order for it to be valid.

> *6:57 As the living Father has sent me, and I live by the Father, so he that eats me, he shall also live by me.*
>
> *6:58 This is the bread which came down from heaven; not as your fathers ate manna and are dead; he that eats of this bread shall live eternally.*
>
> *6:59 He said these things in the synagogue as he taught in Capernaum.*

Just as Jesus lives by the Father, so the person who feeds on Jesus shall live by Jesus. This way, the death of our mortal body will not mean the death of our soul. As the apostle Paul wrote, *We are confident, I say, and willing rather to be absent from the body and to be present with the Lord* (2 Corinthians 5:8).

> *6:60 Many therefore of his disciples when they had heard this said, This is a hard word; who can hear it?*
>
> *6:61 But Jesus, knowing in himself that his disciples murmured at it, said unto them, Does this offend you?*
>
> *6:62 What if ye shall see the Son of man ascend up where he was before?*
>
> *6:63 The Spirit is he[43] that gives life; the flesh profits*

---

43   Note that the Spirit is linked to a personal pronoun here. The Spirit operates in people like us and joins us to one another and to Jesus and to the Father.

*nothing; the words that I have spoken unto you, they
are Spirit and they are life.*

By now, Jesus had pretty much made sure that anyone who did
not really believe in him would not continue to follow him. In
fact, this message was hard to digest (so to speak) even for true
believers. Having just told them they must eat his flesh and
drink his blood to have eternal life, he now says *the flesh profits
nothing*. And it's true: although our flesh profits nothing, the
living words of Jesus can give us life by the Spirit.

6:64 *But there are some of you that do not believe.
For Jesus knew from the beginning who they were
that did not believe and who should betray him.*

6:65 *And he said, Therefore I said unto you that no
one can come unto me unless it is given unto them
of my Father.*

We tend to think in terms of having to meet some minimum
conditions to come to Jesus, at which point he will want us
to meet his Father. This text, however, shows that everything
really originates with the Father. It is the Father who desires
us to submit to Jesus so that he may baptize us with the Holy
Spirit and fire to cleanse us, in order that we may then have an
intimate relationship with Jesus and the Father by the Spirit.

6:66 *After this, many of his disciples went back and
walked no more with him.*

6:67 *Then Jesus said unto the twelve, Will ye also go
away?*

6:68 *Then Simon Peter answered him, Lord, to
whom shall we go? thou hast the words of eternal
life.*

6:69 *And we believe and know that thou art the*
Christ, the Son of the living God.

Simon Peter was given this revelation by the Father (Matthew 16:15-17).

6:70 *Jesus answered them, Have not I chosen you*
twelve, and one of you is a devil?

This and similar comments undoubtedly caused many of the disciples to seriously consider their commitment to the Lord, and a number of them abandoned him at this point. The next verse was likely added in hindsight when John wrote this gospel, since it appears that Jesus left all the disciples in suspense regarding which of them was a devil. It was up to the Father to give them a sense of well-being and security in the depths of their conscience if this was warranted.

6:71 *He spoke of Judas Iscariot the son of Simon, for*
it was he that should betray him, being one of the
twelve.

Let us pray

Lord, we thank you for your Word and ask that by your Spirit
we may understand. Please cleanse our hearts until we are able
to clearly see things from your perspective. Amen.

Chapter 7

Jesus Appears in the Temple

John 7

7:1 After these things Jesus walked in Galilee, for he would not walk in Judea because the Jews sought to kill him.

Jesus walked in Galilee (symbol of perfection). He would not walk in Judea (or among the Jews) because even though the Jews had been waiting for their Messiah for fifteen hundred years, now that he had come at last, they sought to kill him.

7:2 Now the feast of the Jews, of the tabernacles, was at hand.

This is the third time John uses the phrase *feast of the Jews*. The OT refers to feast(s) of (or unto) the LORD. It appears that a subtle change had taken place, however, as the Jews had apparently displaced the LORD as the focal point of the feast (Isaiah 1:14).

7:3 His brethren therefore said unto him, Depart

*from this place and go into Judea that thy disciples
also may see the works that thou doest.*

*7:4 For no one who seeks to be clearly known does
anything in secret. If thou doest these things, show
thyself to the world.*

7:5 For not even his brethren believed in him.

It's startling to see how little respect Jesus' kinfolk had for him
at this point, even taunting him, *If thou doest these things.*
Evidently they could not conceive of having such power and
not making a public display of it. Yet Jesus had no desire to
grandstand or to draw attention to himself. He came to bear
witness to his Father. The reason Jesus did signs and miracles
was not simply because he had the power. He only did the will
of his Father.

*7:6 Then Jesus said unto them, My time is not yet
come, but your time is always ready.*

*7:7 The world cannot hate you, but it hates me
because I testify of it that its works are evil.*

If we are faithful to Jesus and to the Father, the world will hate
us as it hated him (Matthew 5:10-12).

*7:8 Go ye up unto this feast; I go not up yet unto this
feast, for my time is not yet fulfilled.*

*7:9 And having said these things unto them, he
abode still in Galilee.*

So far, according to history, the first two feasts have been fulfilled
(Passover, with Jesus as the Lamb of God that takes away the
sin of the world, and Pentecost, with the coming of the Holy
Spirit upon the early Christians). The third feast, Tabernacles,
has yet to be fulfilled. This is the feast at the end of the harvest

(Leviticus 23:34-44), and prophetically, it has to do with Jesus' second coming.

> 7:10 *But when his brethren were gone up, then he also went up unto the feast, not openly, but as it were in secret.*

> 7:11 *Then the Jews sought him at the feast and said, Where is he?*

> 7:12 *And there was much murmuring among the people concerning him, for some said, He is a good man; others said, No, but he deceives the people.*

> 7:13 *But no one spoke openly of him for fear of the Jews.*

> 7:14 *Now about the midst of the feast Jesus went up into the temple and taught.*

Under the new covenant, we believers are the temple (1 Corinthians 3:16; 2 Corinthians 6:16). At the time of harvest, Jesus will return to fulfill the Feast of Tabernacles in and among his people. At a later date, John wrote, *Beloved, now we are the sons of God, and it is not yet made manifest what we shall be; but we know that if he shall appear, we shall be like him; for we shall see him as he is* (1 John 3:2).

> 7:15 *And the Jews marvelled, saying, How does this man know letters, having never learned?*

> 7:16 *Jesus answered them and said, My doctrine is not mine, but his that sent me.*

> 7:17 *If anyone desires to do his will, he shall know of the doctrine, whether it is of God or whether I speak of myself.*

Anyone who genuinely desires to do the will of God will receive discernment regarding doctrine.

> 7:18 *He that speaks of himself seeks his own glory,*
> *but he that seeks the glory of him that sent him, the*
> *same is true, and no unrighteousness is in him.*

Those who would promote a given school of human thought are different from those who are truly sent by God.

> 7:19 *Did not Moses give you the law, and yet none of*
> *you keeps the law? Why do ye go about to kill me?*

> 7:20 *The people answered and said, Thou hast a*
> *demon; who goes about to kill thee?*

> 7:21 *Jesus answered and said unto them, I have*
> *done one work, and ye all marvel.*

> 7:22 *Moses therefore gave unto you circumcision*
> *(not because it is of Moses, but of the fathers), and ye*
> *on the sabbath day circumcise a man.*

> 7:23 *If a man on the sabbath day receives circumci-*
> *sion without the law of Moses being broken, are ye*
> *angry at me because I have made a man entirely*
> *whole on the sabbath day?*

> 7:24 *Judge not according to the appearance, but*
> *judge with righteous judgment.*

More than a year had passed since Jesus had healed the impotent man on the Sabbath, but the Jews were still attempting to kill him over it.

> 7:25 *Then one of those of Jerusalem said, Is not this*
> *he whom they seek to kill?*

> 7:26 *But, behold, he speaks boldly, and they say*

nothing unto him. Have the rulers truly understood that this is indeed the Christ?

7:27 But we know where this man is from; but when the Christ comes, no one shall know where he is from.

The Enemy had been hard at work spreading lies about the coming of the Christ (or Messiah), and apparently, he had convinced many people that when the Christ came, no one would know where he was from. (Rest assured that the same Enemy will also be spreading lies about the second coming.)

7:28 Then Jesus cried out in the temple as he taught, saying, Ye know me, and ye know from where I come, but I have not come of myself, but he that sent me is true, whom ye know not.

7:29 But I know him, for I am from him, and he has sent me.

7:30 Then they sought to take him, but no one laid hands on him because his hour was not yet come.

7:31 And many of the people believed in him and said, When the Christ comes, will he do more signs than these which this man has done?

7:32 The Pharisees heard the people that murmured such things concerning him, and the princes of the priests and the Pharisees sent officers to take him.

The princes of the priests and the Pharisees feared they would lose control of the people.

7:33 Then Jesus said unto them, Yet a little while I shall be with you, and then I shall go unto him that sent me.

7:34 Ye shall seek me and shall not find me, and where I shall be, ye shall not be able to come.

7:35 Then the Jews said among themselves, Where will he go that we shall not find him? Will he go unto the dispersed among the Greeks and teach the Greeks?

7:36 What manner of saying is this that he said, Ye shall seek me and shall not find me, and where I shall be ye shall not be able to come?

Jesus was referring to the coming events of his death, resurrection, and ascension to the right hand of his Father.

7:37 In the last day, that great day of the feast, Jesus stood and cried out, saying, If any man thirsts, let him come unto me and drink.

7:38 He that believes in me, as the scripture has said, out of his belly shall flow rivers of living water.[44]

7:39 (But this he spoke concerning the Spirit, which those that believe on him should receive, for the Holy Spirit was not yet given because Jesus was not yet glorified.)

7:40 Then many of the people, when they heard this word, said, Truly this is the Prophet.

---

44 The Scripture that Jesus is referring to is difficult to locate. There are only a handful of Scriptures that mention "living water." The only one that I can find that could possibly relate is: *And it shall be in that day that living waters shall go out from Jerusalem: half of them toward the eastern sea and half of them toward the western sea; in summer and in winter it shall be* (Zechariah 14:8). In the context of what Jesus said above, this Scripture would therefore depict the coming of the fullness of the Spirit on the day of the Lord. (The outpouring on the day of Pentecost was the earnest or down payment of the Spirit [2 Corinthians 1:22; Ephesians 1:13, 14].)

7:41 *Others said, This is the Christ. But some said, Shall the Christ come out of Galilee?*

7:42 *Has not the scripture said, That the Christ comes of the seed of David and out of the town of Bethlehem where David was?*

It never occurred to most of them that the prophet described by Moses could be the Christ, nor did Jesus attempt to clear up any of this controversy. He could have called upon his mother, other members of his family, or even his neighbors to testify that he had really been born in Bethlehem and that he was of the line of David. In and through it all, however, Jesus limited himself to conforming to his Father's will.

7:43 *So there was a division among the people because of him.*

7:44 *And some of them would have taken him, but no one laid hands on him.*

7:45 *Then the officers to the chief priests and Pharisees came, and they said unto them, Why have ye not brought him?*

7:46 *The officers answered, Never has anyone spoken like this man.*

There was division and even confusion among the people because of Jesus, mostly related to the question of his identity. However, the officers of the chief priests and Pharisees who had been sent to arrest him were so struck with admiration – and even awe – at Jesus' way of speaking that they found themselves unwilling or unable to comply with their orders.

Jesus' attitude had not been that of a man attempting to defend himself as if before an earthly court. Even the servants of the priests and Pharisees could see he was manifesting the presence and glory of God.

> 7:47 *Then the Pharisees answered them, Are ye also deceived?*

> 7:48 *Have any of the princes or of the Pharisees believed on him?*

> 7:49 *But this people who do not know the law are cursed.*

The Pharisees obviously felt they had not only a superior intellect but a superior knowledge of the law, and they looked down on those who did not share their knowledge, calling them cursed. Actually, it was the other way around. The Pharisees should have known that to fail at keeping even one point of the law would bring the curse of the entire law upon the infractor(s).

> 7:50 *Nicodemus said unto them (he that came to Jesus by night, being one of them),*

> 7:51 *Does our law judge any man before it hears him and knows what he does?*

> 7:52 *They answered and said unto him, Art thou also of Galilee? Search and see, for a prophet has never arisen out of Galilee.*

> 7:53 *And each one went unto his own house.*

The officers refused to arrest Jesus, Nicodemus went on public record with a statement that favored Jesus, and the princes of the priests and the Pharisees each went home from the feast to his own house, more determined than ever to rid themselves of this upstart.

John 8

8:1 *Jesus went unto the mount of Olives.*[45]

Let us pray

Lord, may we be willing to seek your kingdom and your righteousness instead of our own. May you write your laws upon our hearts and in our souls. Amen.

---

45 This is the thirteenth and final mention of the Mount of Olives in Scripture. The number thirteen symbolizes the kingdom of God. Remember that when Jesus walked around with his twelve disciples preaching the kingdom of God they numbered thirteen.

Chapter 8

Confrontation at the Temple

John 8

8:1 *Jesus went unto the mount of Olives.*

8:2 *And early in the morning he came again into the temple, and all the people came unto him; and he sat down and taught them.*

J esus did not spend the night in the city of Jerusalem. He preferred the more peaceful atmosphere of the Mount of Olives.

8:3 *Then the scribes and Pharisees brought unto him a woman taken in adultery, and when they had set her in the midst,*

8:4 *they said unto him, Master, this woman was taken in adultery in the very act.*

8:5 *Now Moses in the law commanded us that such should be stoned, but what sayest thou?*

On an earlier occasion, Jesus had said: *Think not that I am come to undo the law or the prophets; I am not come to undo, but to fulfil. For verily I say unto you, Until heaven and earth pass away, not one jot or one tittle shall pass from the law until all is fulfilled* (Matthew 5:17-18). What would he say now?

> 8:6 *This they said, tempting him, that they might be able to accuse him. But Jesus stooped down and with his finger wrote on the ground.*

There has been quite a bit of speculation over the centuries as to exactly what Jesus may have written with his finger on the ground. Here is at least part of what I think he could have written: *And when a man lies carnally with a woman that is a bondmaid, betrothed to a husband and has not been completely ransomed nor been given her freedom, both shall be scourged; they shall not be put to death because she is not free* (Leviticus 19:20).

Remember that a woman can symbolically represent an entire congregation. At this point, all Israel was a "bondmaid" under the law because Jesus had not yet completed his work of redemption. Those who are under the law have not yet been fully ransomed, nor have they been given their freedom, and thus Jesus came to save them (and us). In our natural state, all of us are slaves to the flesh and to sin, which is why we must be redeemed (Leviticus 25:55).

> 8:7 *So when they continued asking him, he lifted himself up and said unto them, He that is without sin among you, let him be the first to cast a stone at her.*
>
> 8:8 *And again he stooped down and wrote on the ground.*

I believe Jesus continued to make the legal case that this woman (and the entire nation, including each of her accusers) was in bondage to sin and that under the law, slaves are treated differently from those who are free. Jesus' written words also may have questioned why her accusers had only brought the woman involved in the adultery. Where was the man? Jesus may even have been writing down the names of her accusers and the specific sins they had committed.

> 8:9 *And those who heard it, being convicted by their own conscience, went out one by one, beginning at the eldest even unto the last; and Jesus was left alone and the woman that had been in the midst.*

> 8:10 *Jesus, lifting himself up and seeing no one but the woman, said unto her, Woman, where are thine accusers? Has no one condemned thee?*

Remember that in order for an accused person to be convicted in matters of life or death, two or three witnesses were required, and these witnesses were supposed to cast the first stones (Deuteronomy 17:6-7; 19:15). Before Jesus could even finish what he was writing on the ground, the woman's accusers had all left, one by one, beginning with the eldest. The fact that they left one by one may indicate that Jesus was bearing down on each one of them individually. Soon no witnesses remained on the scene.

> 8:11 *And she said, No one, Lord. Then Jesus said unto her, Neither do I condemn thee; go and sin no more.*

The children of Israel received the law on two tablets of stone because they refused to continue to hear the voice of the Lord. They only wanted to hear from God through an intermediary, and this distanced them from God's necessary grace. Without that grace, it was legally appropriate and even necessary to have the death penalty available. However, with the advent of Jesus Christ, everything changed. If the woman were to embrace the personal word that Jesus gave her, she would be given sufficient grace to comply with his directive. Under the circumstances, the need for the death penalty could be abolished under the new covenant, and the law of God could be written in her heart and in her soul.

> 8:12 *Then Jesus spoke again unto them, saying, I AM the light of the world; he that follows me shall not walk in darkness but shall have the light of life.*

Once again Jesus pronounced the sacred name of God (I AM) and linked it to himself as the light of the world. The Father has eternal existence, and so does Jesus.

> 8:13 *Then the Pharisees said unto him, Thou dost bear witness of thyself; thy witness is not true.*

The legalistic Pharisees were disgruntled over the spectacular collapse of their case against the woman they had taken such care to catch in the very act of adultery. They were also embarrassed by the failure of their plot, and they decided to recoup their loss of face by challenging Jesus' authority to bear witness to his own identity.

> 8:14 *Jesus answered and said unto them, Though I bear witness of myself, my witness is true, for I know from where I came and where I go; but ye do not know where I came from and where I go.*

> 8:15 *Ye judge after the flesh, but I judge no one.*

> 8:16 *And yet if I judge, my judgment is true, for I am not alone, but I and the Father that sent me.*

> 8:17 *It is also written in your law that the testimony of two men is true.*

> 8:18 *I AM one that bears witness of myself, and the*
> *Father that sent me bears witness of me.*

In his response, Jesus doubles down on the name (nature) of God. Jesus does not judge anyone after the flesh. However, the judgments that he pronounces as God are an entirely different matter. As God, Jesus was fully capable of forgiving sins, even before his death and resurrection. This is another very important point in the case of the woman caught in adultery.

> 8:19 *Then they said unto him, Where is thy Father?*
> *Jesus answered, Ye neither know me, nor my Father;*
> *if ye had known me, ye should have known my*
> *Father also.*

When Jesus says *if ye had known me*, he means "if you had recognized me for who I really am."

> 8:20 *Jesus spoke these words in the treasury as he*
> *taught in the temple, and no one laid hands on him,*
> *for his hour was not yet come.*

His enemies undoubtedly wanted to lay hands on Jesus and kill him for what they regarded as blasphemy.

> 8:21 *Then Jesus said again unto them, I am going*
> *away, and ye shall seek me, but ye shall die in your*
> *sins; where I go, ye shall not be able to come.*

Those who die in their sins will not go to be with Jesus.

> 8:22 *Then the Jews said, Will he kill himself?*
> *because he says, Where I go, ye shall not be able to*
> *come.*

After his death and resurrection, Jesus would ascend *up far above all the heavens* (Ephesians 4:10).

> 8:23 *And he said unto them, Ye are from below, I*

am from above; ye are of this world, I am not of this world.

8:24 Therefore I said unto you that ye shall die in your sins, for if ye do not believe that I AM, ye shall die in your sins.

It is not enough to believe in a historical Jesus who died on a cross. We must believe (and depend entirely) upon him as the living Son of God.

8:25 And said they unto him, Who art thou? Then Jesus said unto them, He that I said unto you also from the beginning.

8:26 I have many things to say and to judge regarding you, but he that sent me is true; and those things which I have heard of him, I speak in the world.

8:27 But they did not understand that he spoke to them of the Father.

8:28 Then Jesus said unto them, When ye have lifted up the Son of man, then ye shall know that I AM and that I do nothing of myself, but as my Father has taught me, I speak these things.

8:29 And he that sent me is with me: the Father has not left me alone, for I always do those things that please him.

Jesus described himself as his Father's temple (Matthew 12:6; John 2:19-21) because the Father dwelt in him by the fullness of the Spirit.

8:30 As he spoke these words, many believed in him.

Many rejected Jesus (who is the personification of the truth), but many believed in him. Few were able to remain indifferent. This is still the case today.

> 8:31 *Then Jesus said to those Jews who had believed him, If ye abide in my word, ye shall be my disciples indeed;*
>
> 8:32 *and ye shall know the truth, and the truth shall set you free.*

Even now, many people seem to think it is not necessary to abide in Jesus' word. However, the more we know about the truth (and Jesus *is* the truth), the more we will realize our own inadequacy and our inescapable need to remain in fellowship with him.

> 8:33 *They answered him, We are Abraham's seed, and we have never served anyone; how sayest thou, Ye shall be set free?*
>
> 8:34 *Jesus answered them, Verily, verily, I say unto you, Whosoever commits sin is the slave of sin.*

When we are slaves to sin, we are not free to do the will of God. This was the case with the woman caught in adultery. Jesus set her free to *go and sin no more*.

> 8:35 *And the slave does not abide in the house for ever, but the Son abides for ever.*
>
> 8:36 *If the Son therefore shall set you free, ye shall be free indeed.*

We can only *abide in the house for ever* if we are born again from above by the Spirit and become part of the body of Christ.

> 8:37 *I know that ye are Abraham's seed, but ye seek to kill me because my word has no place in you.*

When Jesus says, *but ye*[46] *seek to kill me*, he is referring to the corporate Jewish nation.

> 8:38 *I speak that which I have seen with my Father,*
> *and ye do that which ye have seen with your father.*

> 8:39 *They answered and said unto him, Abraham*
> *is our father. Jesus said unto them, If ye were*
> *Abraham's sons, ye would do the works of Abraham.*

What are the works of Abraham?

For one thing, *Abraham believed God, and it was counted unto him for righteousness* (Romans 4:3). For another, he followed God by faith, for *the just in his faith shall live* (Habakkuk 2:4b).

> 8:40 *But now ye seek to kill me, a man that has told*
> *you the truth, which I have heard of God; Abraham*
> *did not do this.*

> 8:41 *Ye do the deeds of your father. Then they said*
> *to him, We are not born of fornication; we have one*
> *Father, even God.*

> 8:42 *Jesus said unto them, If God were your Father,*
> *ye would surely love me, for I proceeded forth and*
> *came from God; neither did I come of myself, but he*
> *sent me.*

Those who are sons of God by faith love Jesus. They also love everyone else who loves Jesus, due to the shared bond with God by the Spirit.

> 8:43 *Why do ye not understand my speech? even*
> *because ye cannot hear my word.*

> 8:44 *Ye are of your father the devil, and the desires*
> *of your father ye desire to do. He was a murderer*
> *from the beginning and abode not in the truth*

---

46   Remember that the pronouns, ye, and, you, are always plural in old English.

*because there is no truth in him. When he speaks
a lie, he speaks of his own, for he is a liar and the
father of it.*

8:45 *And because I tell you the truth, ye do not
believe me.*

Those who embrace the truth (that is, those who truly believe
in Jesus, who is the very essence of truth) become sons of God.
Those who embrace the lies of the Enemy, on the other hand,
become sons of the devil. Lies and murder are linked and are
directly opposed to the truth. It's one thing to be a slave to the
flesh and to sin, but it's quite another to willfully choose the lie
over the truth. This is the difference between the woman caught
in adultery and the enemies of Jesus. The woman trusted Jesus,
and he set her free to *go and sin no more.* Those who refuse to
believe him – and who thus reject the truth – cannot understand
his message because the truth he speaks does not comport with
the lies they have accepted from the Father of Lies.

8:46 *Which of you reproves me of sin? And if I say
the truth, why do ye not believe me?*

8:47 *He that is of God hears God's words; ye therefore hear them not because ye are not of God.*

8:48 *Then the Jews answered, and said unto him, Do
we not say well that thou art a Samaritan and hast
a demon?*

Unable to face the fact that Jesus spoke the truth, the Jews
claimed he was a demon-possessed Samaritan. They not only
failed to believe, their discernment was a hundred and eighty
degrees off.

8:49 *Jesus answered, I do not have a demon; but I
honour my Father, and ye do dishonour me.*

> 8:50 *And I seek not my own glory; there is one that*
> *seeks it and judges.*

It is the Father who seeks Jesus' glory; it is the Father who judges. In fact, the day will come when the entire body of Christ will be glorified (Romans 8:30).

> 8:51 *Verily, verily, I say unto you, If anyone keeps*
> *my word, he shall not see death forever.*

> 8:52 *Then the Jews said unto him, Now we know*
> *that thou hast a demon. Abraham died and the*
> *prophets; and thou sayest, If a man keeps my word,*
> *he shall not taste death forever?*

> 8:53 *Art thou greater than our father Abraham who*
> *died? and the prophets died; whom makest thou*
> *thyself?*

> 8:54 *Jesus answered, If I glorify myself, my glory is*
> *nothing; it is my Father that glorifies me, of whom*
> *ye say that he is your God;*

> 8:55 *yet ye have not known him, but I know him;*
> *and if I should say, I do not know him, I shall be*
> *a liar like unto you; but I know him and keep his*
> *word.*

> 8:56 *Your father Abraham rejoiced to see my day,*
> *and he saw it and was glad.*

Scripture clearly states that no one has ever seen the Father at any time. Therefore when the LORD appeared unto Abraham in the form of a man (Genesis 18), we can infer that this was a direct encounter with the Lord Jesus Christ.[47]

---

47   *No man has seen God at any time; the only begotten Son, which is in the bosom*
     of the Father, he has declared him (John 1:18).

> 8:57 *Then the Jews said unto him, Thou art not yet fifty years old, and hast thou seen Abraham?*

> 8:58 *Jesus said unto them, Verily, verily, I say unto you, Before Abraham was, I AM.*[48]

The prophets were allowed to pronounce the sacred name if they were directly under the anointing of the Spirit of God. However, when Jesus persisted in applying this name to himself, it caused profound consternation among the Jews, many of whom thought he should immediately be stoned to death for what they viewed as blasphemy.

> 8:59 *Then they took up stones to cast at him, but Jesus concealed himself and went out of the temple, and going through the midst of them, went away.*

Jesus' enemies were also his Father's enemies. They were unable to understand his speech because they could not hear his word (verse 43); instead, they blocked their ears with lies. Now, enraged, they sought to attack him with stones, not understanding that if Jesus chose to conceal himself, he could simply depart *through the midst of them.*

Let us pray

Lord, may we have ears to hear and eyes to see. May we willingly embrace the truth and be set free no matter what the cost. Amen.

---

48 The sacred name of God is I AM (Exodus 3:14). The Jews believed it would be blasphemy to say this name aloud, so they wrote it with four consonants (YHWH) and read it as *Adonai* (Lord) in the sacred writings of the Scriptures. In many English Bible translations, including the Jubilee Bible, this sacred name is rendered as LORD (all in uppercase) close to 7,000 times. When this name is used in the NT, the Jubilee Bible renders it as I AM (again all in uppercase).

Chapter 9

Special Provision for
Those Who Are Blind

The previous scene of confrontation with the religious leaders at the temple had just ended with Jesus concealing himself and exiting through their midst in order to avoid being stoned.

John 9

9:1 *And as Jesus passed by, he saw a man who was blind from his birth.*

All of us are born into this world spiritually blind. Unless we are born again from above by the Spirit of God, it is impossible for any of us to perceive the spiritual realm.

9:2 *And his disciples asked him, saying, Rabbi, who sinned, this man or his parents, that he was born blind?*

9:3 *Jesus answered, Neither has this man sinned nor his parents, but that the works of God should be made manifest in him.*

If we are all born spiritually blind, then it follows that our blindness did not stem from our sin or the sins of our immediate parents (Romans 5:14). This does not, of course, mean that we can excuse or ignore the behavior of Adam and Eve and the lie of the serpent that led to the curse and to death, yet even so, Jesus continues to desire that the works of God be manifest in each of us. For God is *not willing that any should perish, but that all should come to repentance* (2 Peter 3:9; also see Matthew 18:14).

When God created the heavens and the earth and man, he pronounced everything to be *very good*. However, he was well aware that by giving man free will, he was opening the door to the possibility of Adam's rebellion. When this rebellion arose, God had a plan of redemption that had been determined from the very beginning, which is why Jesus is described as *the Lamb of God* (John 1:29, 36) who was *already ordained from before the foundation of the world* (1 Peter 1:19-20).

In this now fallen world, the birth of children is accompanied by pains that did not previously exist (Genesis 3:16), and man must work for his food by the sweat of his brow until he returns to the ground from which he was taken (Genesis 3:19). Men and women are subject to the law of sin and death and are born into spiritual darkness. Nevertheless, we have the opportunity to respond to the light, and it is possible for us to obtain righteousness, albeit in only one way, which is by faith in Jesus, so that *the law of the Spirit of life in Christ Jesus* may free us from the law of sin and death (Romans 8:2). God, in his infinite wisdom, has allowed this situation to continue for the past six thousand or so years. This great opportunity, however, will not be available indefinitely.

> 9:4 *It is expedient that I do the works of him that sent me while it is day; the night comes, when no one can work.*

There is a time when opportunity can be seized (day) and a time when opportunity has passed (night), and *every will under the heaven has its time determined* (Ecclesiastes 3:1b). When we are given the chance to choose, we will be held accountable for our choice (Hebrews 9:27).

> 9:5 *As long as I am in the world, I am the light of the world.*

Jesus told his disciples, *Ye are the light of the world* (Matthew 5:14). This presages the many-membered body of Christ.

> 9:6 *When he had thus spoken, he spat on the ground and made clay of the spittle, and he anointed the eyes of the blind man with the clay*

Under Jewish law, spitting on someone made that person ceremonially unclean (Numbers 12:14). In addition, if a Jew became extremely upset about something, they could throw dust into the air in an attempt to make everyone around them unclean (Acts 22:23). Thus Jesus would have been seen as rendering the man unclean as a preliminary to healing him. Why would he do this? Because he also intended to show all of us that our natural way of viewing or perceiving things is unclean.

> 9:7 *and said unto him, Go, wash in the pool of Siloam (which is by interpretation, Sent). Then he went and washed and came back seeing.*

We will not be able to see properly into the spiritual realm unless and until we are sanctified and cleansed *in the washing of water by the word* (Ephesians 5:25-27). It is not until we hear the word of Jesus, and begin to obey when he sends us to do something, that our spiritual vision will start to function.

> 9:8 *The neighbours, therefore, and those who before had seen him that he was blind said, Is not this he that sat and begged?*

In that society at that time, because this man was blind, he had little choice but to be a beggar. When we are spiritually blind, we tend to behave in a similar way, continually begging for guidance from others or depending on them for insight and advice. But after Jesus opens our eyes, we are able to follow him with confidence, and we no longer feel compelled to depend on therapists or spiritual directors. When Jesus opens our eyes, one of the first things we see is that we are not the center of the universe. This may induce a "poor me" complex at first, but such a response soon dissipates in the splendor of the light of Jesus as he lines us up with the truth (in the terminology of God according to its use in the Scriptures, this is called "reconciliation").

> 9:9 *Some said, This is he; others said, He is like him; but he said, I am he.*

I am he?

I AM is the name (or nature) of God. God wants to place his name upon us so we can be confident of our eternal existence in the new life we have found in Jesus Christ.

> 9:10 *Then they said unto him, How were thine eyes opened?*

In spite of all the lies we have been told by entities ranging from the serpent in the garden of Eden to those who consider themselves moral authorities today, there is only one way our spiritual eyes can be opened, only one way out of our spiritual blindness, and that is for us to meet Jesus, accept him as Lord, and go wherever he sends us.

> 9:11 *He answered and said, A man that is called Jesus made clay and anointed my eyes and said unto me, Go to the pool of Siloam, and wash; and I went and washed, and I received sight.*

9:12 *Then said they unto him, Where is he? He said,
I know not.*

Jesus didn't heal this man as a means of calling attention to himself. He had no interest in parading the formerly blind man around town to impress a crowd. By the time the man washed the clay from his eyes at the pool of Siloam and found that his sight had been restored, Jesus had disappeared, and the man he had healed didn't even know where he was.

9:13 *They brought to the Pharisees him that before-hand had been blind.*

9:14 *And it was the sabbath day when Jesus had made the clay and had opened his eyes.*

Virtually every detail of the astounding account of the man who had been blind from birth was politically incorrect from the perspective of a religious Jew. To top it off, it was the Sabbath day[49] when Jesus *had made the clay and had opened his eyes.*

9:15 *Then again the Pharisees also asked him how he had received his sight. He said unto them, He put clay upon my eyes, and I washed and do see.*

9:16 *Therefore some of the Pharisees said, This man is not of God because he does not keep the sabbath day. Others said, How can a man that is a sinner do such signs? And there was a division among them.*

The Pharisees knew from their extensive study of the Scriptures that only God can open the eyes of the blind. They were aware that this was one of the specific miracles that would take place at the coming of the Messiah (Psalm 146:8 and Isaiah 29:18; 35:5; 42:7).

---

49 Jesus kept performing powerful signs and miracles on the Sabbath day according to the will of his Father – a fact that may very well have prophetic significance for us as we enter the seventh prophetic day (the seventh millennium) on the eve of his second coming.

> 9:17 *They said unto the blind man again, What say-*
> *est thou of him, that has opened thine eyes? He said,*
> *He is a prophet.*

A prophet is someone who is sent from God and who speaks God's words instead of his own.

> 9:18 *But the Jews did not believe concerning him*
> *that he had been blind and received his sight until*
> *they called the parents of him that had received his*
> *sight.*

> 9:19 *And they asked them, saying, Is this your son,*
> *who ye say was born blind? how then does he now*
> *see?*

The Jews and the Pharisees seemed to be primarily concerned with finding out exactly how the blind man received his sight, but this attitude was strictly a smokescreen. They didn't want to deal with the implications of what had happened and who had done it, nor could they bring themselves to face the fact that the restoration of this man's sight was undoubtedly a major prophetic sign.

> 9:20 *His parents answered them and said, We know*
> *that this is our son and that he was born blind;*

> 9:21 *but by what means he now sees, we know not;*
> *or who has opened his eyes, we know not; he is of*
> *age, ask him; he shall speak for himself.*

> 9:22 *These words spoke his parents because they*
> *feared the Jews, for the Jews had agreed already*
> *that if anyone did confess that he was the Christ, he*
> *should be put out of the synagogue.*

> 9:23 *Therefore his parents said, He is of age, ask*
> *him.*

9:24 Then they called again the man that had been blind and said unto him, Give glory to God; we know that this man is a sinner.

9:25 He answered and said, Whether he is a sinner or not, I do not know; one thing I know, that having been blind, now I see.

The personal testimony of the man who had been blind sent a powerful message that blew away the religious smokescreen behind which the Jews had been hiding.

9:26 Then said they to him again, What did he do to thee? How did he open thine eyes?

9:27 He answered them, I have told you already, and ye have heard; what more would ye hear? Do ye also desire to be his disciples?

After the Lord has opened someone's eyes and they see clearly; after their spiritual discernment is functioning perfectly; after they are able to read the Bible and its depths are revealed unto them by the Spirit; after the Lord opens their understanding regarding the whole of creation and begins to reveal his plan and purpose for everything; after they find themselves meditating night and day while the Lord speaks directly into their conscience, their heart, and their soul; then they will no longer be fooled by false piety, self-righteousness, and religious humanism whose proponents attempt to snow them with doctrines, theological thought, and the politics of human control. This person is now able to joyfully proclaim *that having been blind, now I see.*

9:28 Then they reviled him and said, Be thou his disciple, but we are disciples of Moses.

9:29 We know that God spoke unto Moses; as for this fellow, we do not know where he is from.

God continues to raise up witnesses and send them forth to testify to those who are enveloped in religious franchises. Those who are devoid of spiritual discernment always want to know:

Where are you from?

Who is your covering (that is, your "shepherd" or spiritual guide and counselor)?

Where did you undertake your theological studies?

What is your eschatology?

Where do you congregate?

How did you do this? How did you do that? And so on, and so on, and so on.

These questions were, of course, irrelevant in the case of men like Moses, Elijah, Jesus, or the NT apostles. God himself backed them up with powerful signs and wonders, and it didn't matter that they had no earthly credentials. They were able to simply state, "I come from the presence of God."

> 9:30 *The man answered and said unto them, Indeed this is a marvellous thing that ye do not know where he is from, and yet he has opened my eyes.*
>
> 9:31 *Now we know that God does not hear sinners, but if anyone should fear God and do his will, him he will hear.*
>
> 9:32 *Since the world began it has not been heard of that anyone opened the eyes of one that was born blind.*
>
> 9:33 *If this man were not of God, he could do nothing.*

For the man whose vision had been restored, it was a no-brainer. The fact of his healing gave him the courage to confront the intellectual religious wizards with the short and simple truth.

9:34 *They answered and said unto him, Thou wast altogether born in sins, and dost thou teach us? And they cast him out.*

The Jews and Pharisees didn't mind having a blind man in their congregation, but they strongly objected when Jesus intervened. Jesus had opened his eyes spiritually as well as physically, and these men now perceived him as a threat to their usurped authority over the people of God.

9:35 *Jesus heard that they had cast him out; and finding him, he said unto him, Dost thou believe in the Son of God?*

As soon as this unnamed man realized his vision had been restored, he knew it was Jesus who had healed him, but he couldn't find him to thank him (verse 12). Now that he had taken a stand for the truth, even in the face of hardened religious leaders who cast him out of their synagogue for this attitude, he didn't have to search for Jesus because Jesus came looking for him. And having found him, Jesus went straight to the point, immediately asking him if he believed in the Son of God.

9:36 *He answered and said, Who is he, Lord, that I might believe in him?*

9:37 *And Jesus said unto him, Thou hast seen him, and it is he that talks with thee.*

9:38 *And he said, Lord, I believe. And he worshipped him.*

The Lord loves to cultivate our hearts and then plant seeds of faith. Jesus opened the eyes of the blind man so the man might see him. He asked the man if he believed *in the Son of God*, and he answered the man's question about the Son of God's identity. *Thou hast seen him, and it is he that talks with thee.*

Jesus is the same yesterday, today, and forever. He continues to reveal himself and to pour out his grace upon people, even unlikely people like us, so that we may have a strong foundation for our faith.

> 9:39 *And Jesus said, For judgment I have come into this world, that those who do not see might see and that those who see might be blinded.*

After the formerly blind man believed and worshipped Jesus, the next sentence Jesus spoke to him was ripe with revelation about judgment.

> 9:40 *And some of the Pharisees who were with him heard these words and said unto him, Are we blind also?*

Some of the Pharisees now wondered if there might be some truth in Jesus' words after all. Others may have asked this question satirically.

> 9:41 *Jesus said unto them, If ye were blind, ye should have no sin; but now because ye say, We see, therefore your sin abides.*

Under the law, there is special provision for those who are blind (Leviticus 19:14; Deuteronomy 27:18). A blind person is not responsible for their inability to see. However, those who declare themselves to be religious experts are responsible not only for their own sin but also, to some extent, for the sins of those whom they have misled.

Let us pray

Lord, we ask that although we may enjoy an apparent position of prosperity in this world, you will open our eyes that we may see from the perspective of your reality. That we may see people (including ourselves) as you see us. That we may trust you completely instead of leaning upon our own understanding. Amen.

Chapter 10

The Good Shepherd

The parables found in John 10 are ones Jesus told in the context of an intense debate with the Jews and Pharisees regarding his healing of a man who had been blind since birth. Wanting to give his listeners every chance to understand who he was and why he had come, he continued to address the issues that had been under discussion.

John 10

> 10:1 *Verily, verily, I say unto you, He that enters not by the door into the sheepfold, but climbs up some other way, the same is a thief and a robber.*

Those who do not enter by the "door" are not real shepherds. They are thieves and robbers. The legitimate shepherd of the sheep uses the door.

How many thieves and robbers continue to wreak havoc among the sheep of God today?

> 10:2 *But he that enters in by the door is the shepherd of the sheep.*

10:3 *To him the porter opens, and the sheep hear his voice, and he calls his own sheep by name and leads them out.*

10:4 *And when he puts forth his own sheep, he goes before them; and the sheep follow him, for they know his voice.*

Those who hear his voice and recognize that it is the voice of the shepherd will follow him. As we hear his voice and follow Jesus' instructions, our hearts will be cleansed and our vision will be clarified, for *the pure in heart ... shall see God* (Matthew 5:8).

10:5 *And they will not follow a stranger, but will flee from him, for they do not know the voice of strangers.*

10:6 *Jesus spoke this parable unto them, but they did not understand what it was that he spoke unto them.*

Those who didn't understand the parable Jesus told them were unable to follow him, their hearts were never cleansed, and they were never able to perceive him for who he was and is.

The religious authorities were jealous of Jesus because so many people were following him, and every sign and miracle Jesus performed drew more people to him. The leaders of the temple and the synagogues used fear to keep the people in line, exaggerating the tenets of the law so greatly and applying the rules so strictly that it was almost impossible for the average person not to be continually loaded up with the guilt of serial infractions, but this is not the way of the Good Shepherd.

10:7 *Then said Jesus unto them again, Verily, verily, I say unto you, I AM the door of the sheep.*

10:8 *All that ever came before me are thieves and robbers, but the sheep did not hear them.*

> 10:9 *I AM the door; whosoever enters in by me shall*
> *be saved and shall go in and out and find pasture.*

Jesus is the door. Any religious leaders who are not directly commissioned by him aren't shepherds at all but thieves and robbers, and the true sheep of God will not hear them. Jesus continues to use the sacred name of God (I AM), linking himself to the name of God throughout the OT. He and the Father have worked together from the beginning of creation.

Whosoever enters in by Jesus *shall be saved and shall go in and out.* We shall go *in* and have fellowship with Jesus and with those who are his, and we shall also be able to go *out* and overcome the world.

> 10:10 *The thief comes not but for to steal and to kill*
> *and to destroy the sheep; I am come that they might*
> *have life and that they might have it in abundance.*

Those like the devil who would steal, kill, and destroy Jesus' sheep have no ability to heal or to defend them. Only Jesus can provide his charges with saving health and protection.

> 10:11 *I AM the good shepherd; the good shepherd*
> *gives his life for the sheep.*

This works both ways, for those who belong to the good shepherd will also be willing to lay down their lives for Jesus and for the brethren (1 John 3:16).

> 10:12 *But the hireling, who is not a shepherd, whose*
> *own the sheep are not, sees the wolf coming and*
> *leaves the sheep and flees; and the wolf catches them*
> *and scatters the sheep.*

> 10:13 *The hireling flees because he is a hireling, and*
> *the sheep do not belong to him.*

> 10:14 *I AM the good shepherd, and know my sheep*
> *and am known of mine.*

Jesus knows all about sheep because he is one. He is not only the Lion of the tribe of Judah, he is also the Lamb of God.

> 10:15 *As the Father knows me, even so I know the Father, and I lay down my soul for the sheep.*

> 10:16 *And I have other sheep which are not of this fold; it is expedient that I bring them also, and they shall hear my voice, and there shall be one fold and one shepherd.*[50]

In Christ there is neither Jew nor Gentile but one new man (Galatians 3:28-29; Ephesians 2:11-22), nor should we imagine that there shall always be many shepherds and many folds. Even though there are many congregations of believers, there is only one body of Christ (Ephesians 4:4), and Jesus is the *great shepherd of the sheep through the blood of the eternal testament* (Hebrews 13:20).

> 10:17 *Therefore does my Father love me, because I lay down my soul that I might take it again.*

> 10:18 *No man takes it from me, but I lay it down of myself. I have power to lay it down, and I have power to take it again. This commandment I have received of my Father.*

Even though Jesus was making these striking declarations right in front of the Jews, most of them remained – or found it expedient to appear to be – oblivious to his meaning.

> 10:19 *There was a division therefore again among the Jews for these words.*

> 10:20 *And many of them said, He has a demon and is beside himself; why do ye hear him?*

---

50   Greek *poimen*. "Shepherd" and "pastor" are the same Greek word.

> 10:21 *Others said, These are not the words of him that has a demon. Can a demon open the eyes of the blind?*

Demons cannot open the eyes of the blind (it is the other way around). Hirelings (verses 12-13) would likely be willing to try, but they too lack that kind of power. Only Jesus can open the eyes of the blind, and he desires to work in and through those he chooses.

> 10:22 *And they celebrated the dedication in Jerusalem, and it was winter.*

> 10:23 *And Jesus walked in the temple in Solomon's porch.*

> 10:24 *Then the Jews came round about him and said unto him, Until when wilt thou hold our soul in suspense? If thou art the Christ, tell us plainly.*

> 10:25 *Jesus answered them, I have told you, and ye do not believe; the works that I do in my Father's name, they bear witness of me.*

> 10:26 *But ye believe not because ye are not of my sheep, as I said unto you.*

> 10:27 *My sheep hear my voice, and I know them, and they follow me;*

For the third time in this chapter, Jesus defines his sheep as those who hear or know his voice.

> 10:28 *and I give unto them eternal life; and they shall never perish, neither shall anyone pluck them out of my hand.*

> 10:29 *My Father, who gave them to me, is greater*

*than all; and no one is able to pluck them out of my
Father's hand.*

10:30 *I and my Father are one.*

His Father, who is greater than all, gives Jesus' sheep to him, and
Jesus gives his sheep eternal life. No one can pluck Jesus' sheep
out of his hand, nor can anyone pluck them out of the hand
of the Father. To be in Jesus' hand is to also be in his Father's
hand. God's desire is for us to be one with Jesus as Jesus is one
with his Father (John 17). Jesus has chosen to do the will of his
Father so that he and the Father are one.

10:31 *Then the Jews took up stones again to stone
him.*

10:32 *Jesus answered them, Many good works have
I showed you from my Father; for which of those
works do ye stone me?*

10:33 *The Jews answered him, saying, For a good
work we do not stone thee, but for blasphemy; and
because thou, being a man, makest thyself God.*

Jesus was not simply a man, nor was he a man who made himself God. Rather, he *is* God, and yet he came to earth as a man.

10:34 *Jesus answered them, Is it not written in your
law, I said, Ye are gods?*[51]

This is written in the law (in the Psalms), and it is true in the
sense that God has created all of us in his image and has given
us free will (for which we are responsible).[52]

---

51 The quoted verse is: *I have said, Ye are gods; and all of you are sons of the most
High* (Psalm 82:6). Interestingly, the word for God in Hebrew, *Elohim*, is plural,
even though it is almost always translated as singular. (In Hebrew, the plural
can be used for emphasis.) The Scripture clearly states: *Hear, O Israel: The
LORD our God is one LORD* (Deuteronomy 6:4). Devout Jews therefore found
it almost impossible to accept that God could have an *only begotten Son* who
was capable of representing him as he is.

52 *God stands in the congregation of the mighty; he judges among the gods* (Psalm 82:1).

10:35 If he called them gods unto whom the word of God came (and the scripture cannot be broken),

10:36 do ye say of him whom the Father has sanctified and sent into the world, Thou blasphemest, because I said, I am the Son of God?

The person *whom the Father has sanctified* is set apart exclusively to serve the Father and to carry out his will (and works).

10:37 If I do not do the works of my Father, do not believe me.

10:38 But if I do, though ye do not believe me, believe the works that ye may know and believe that the Father is in me and I in him.

10:39 Therefore they sought again to take him, but he escaped out of their hand

10:40 and went away again beyond Jordan into the place where John at first baptized, and there he abode.

10:41 And many came unto him and said, John certainly did no sign, but all the things that John spoke of this man were true.

10:42 And many believed in him there.

Let us pray

Lord, we ask that we may understand and assimilate your Word. May your Word penetrate our heart and cleanse us from the corruption that is inherent in all of us, so we may become your worthy representatives. Amen.

Chapter 11

The Resurrection of Lazarus

John 11

11:1 Now a certain man was sick, named Lazarus, of Bethany, the town of Mary and her sister Martha.

Lazarus" means "without help." He lived in the town of Bethany, meaning "house of dates." The date comes from a type of palm tree, which is a symbol of righteousness (the date is thus the fruit of righteousness). "Mary" means "bitter" (in the sense of myrrh, which is symbolic of the way of the cross), and "Martha" means "lady" (in the sense of someone born free).

Lazarus could represent any of us who are members of the body of Christ. We live to produce the fruit of righteousness (we live in "Bethany"). Mary and Martha are our "sisters," and they represent the congregations of believers who know about the way of the cross and who are born again into freedom in Christ.

11:2 (It was that Mary who anointed the Lord with ointment and wiped his feet with her hair whose brother Lazarus was sick.)

After the crucifixion, several other women who were also named

Mary made a concerted effort to anoint Jesus (a venture that failed because when they arrived at the tomb, it was already empty). Mary of Bethany was the only woman who, in effect, anointed his body for burial, having poured her costly ointment on his feet while he was still alive (John 12:3,7). She represents those who, using their God-given gifts and abilities, anoint the "feet" of Jesus (the members of the body of Christ who walk here upon this earth).

> *11:3 Therefore his sisters sent unto him, saying,*
> *Lord, behold, he whom thou lovest is sick.*

All of us who are individual members of the body of Christ (and loved by the Lord) are sick in the sense that our physical bodies are subject to sickness and death.

> *11:4 When Jesus heard that, he said, This sickness*
> *is not unto death, but for the glory of God, that the*
> *Son of God might be glorified thereby.*

God does not perceive death from our natural perspective. In his view, our sickness is not unto death but rather for the glory of God. Its purpose is that through it, the Son of God might be glorified (and there is a mystery here, because if we are part of the body of Christ, eventually we will be raised up and included in Jesus' glory).

> *11:5 Now Jesus loved Martha and her sister and*
> *Lazarus.*

Jesus loves the entire family of those who dwell in Bethany (the house of the fruit of righteousness). He considers those who bear good fruit to be his very own brothers and sisters. Jesus has made us members of his family.

> *11:6 When he had heard therefore that he was sick,*
> *he abode two days still in the same place where he*
> *was.*

When Jesus lived here among us, he "heard" about all of our sickness. However, that was about two thousand years ago (two prophetic days, in which one day before the Lord is as a thousand years). For these past two "days," Jesus has remained *in the same place where he was*, that is, at the right hand of the Father in the heavens.

> 11:7 *Then after that he said to his disciples, Let us go into Judea again.*

Jesus will soon return to "Judea." "Judah" means "praise," and Judea is the land of the people of Judah (of those who praise God). When Jesus returns, he will come with all of his saints, or disciples (Jude v. 14).

> 11:8 *His disciples said unto him, Rabbi, the Jews of late sought to stone thee, and goest thou there again?*

Jesus was not well received by many of the Jews at his first coming. What will happen at his second coming?

> 11:9 *Jesus answered, Are there not twelve hours in the day? If anyone walks in the day, he does not stumble because he sees the light of this world.*

> 11:10 *But he who walks in the night stumbles because there is no light in him.*

Twelve is a number that is symbolic of divine order. The natural day, on average, is twelve hours long. Jesus wants us to walk by day in his light (in divine order), instead of stumbling around in spiritual night as do those who are in bondage to the flesh and to sin. Jesus is the light of the world, and he desires to shine his light in and through us (Matthew 5:14).

> 11:11 *Having said that he said unto them, Our friend Lazarus sleeps, but I go that I may awake him out of sleep.*

11:12 Then his disciples said, Lord, if he sleeps, he shall be saved.

There are several Scriptures in the Old Testament, such as Psalm 13:3 and Daniel 12:2, that equate sleep with death (at least under certain circumstances). Similarly, in the New Testament, when Jairus' daughter died, Jesus said that she was asleep (Luke 8:52), and when Stephen was martyred, Luke described his death as falling asleep in the Lord (Acts 7:60).

11:13 But Jesus had spoken of his death, and they thought that he had spoken of taking of rest in sleep.

11:14 Then Jesus said unto them plainly, Lazarus has died.

Over the past two thousand years, many people have fallen asleep in the Lord (1 Corinthians 15:6; 1 Thessalonians 4:13-15).

11:15 And I am glad for your sakes that I was not there, in order that ye may believe; nevertheless let us go unto him.

11:16 Then Thomas said, who is called Didymus, unto his fellowdisciples, Let us go also, that we may die with him.

Why was Jesus glad he wasn't there prior to Lazarus's death? Because he wanted the disciples to see the sequence of events that he knew would take place after the burial, so they would understand he, Jesus, had the power of life and death. Even so, Thomas, who is on record here as being willing to die with Jesus, later had trouble believing Jesus had risen from the dead, even when others testified that this was indeed the case. Thomas (meaning "twin" in Hebrew) is also called Didymus (which is "twin" in Greek). Many of us are also "twins," in that one minute we yield to the Spirit of God and are ready to lay down our lives for Jesus, but the next minute we refuse to believe in his power unless we have witnessed it with our own eyes.

11:17 *Then when Jesus came, he found that he had lain in the grave four days already.*[53]

After learning the initial news about Lazarus, Jesus waited an additional two days (symbolic of the 2000-year church age that would take place) before announcing to the disciples that he had decided to go to the scene. Now, having arrived, he found that Lazarus *had lain in the grave for four days already.* God's plan for having a corporate people of God began four thousand years ago (four prophetic days ago) with Abraham.[54] If Lazarus represents any or all of the individual members of the corporate people of God, then our corporate problem with sickness and death has been going on for four days (four thousand years).

11:18 *Now Bethany was near unto Jerusalem, about fifteen furlongs off;*

Fifteen is a number that can symbolize the good fruit that is produced in our lives by God's grace and mercy (fifteen is three times five). Even though most of Jerusalem had become an apostate city of religion, fifteen furlongs away was Bethany, an enclave producing the fruit of righteousness. Similar situations abound today.

11:19 *and many of the Jews had come to Martha and Mary to comfort them concerning their brother.*

---

53 This verse may turn out to be prophetic on at least two levels: (1) The four days (of corruption) in which Lazarus had lain in the tomb may indicate that the corruption of mankind through the sin of Adam and Eve took place exactly four thousand years earlier. (2) The four days, if measured from the beginning of the corporate people of God starting with Abraham (two prophetic days before this situation with Lazarus, coupled with the two additional days that Jesus waited before going mentioned in v. 6) could mean that the second coming of Jesus will be two thousand years after this event. Time will tell.

54 It is also true that Adam and Eve entered into sin and death about four thousand years prior to the actual resurrection of Lazarus. Prior to God's friendship with Abraham, there are only three individuals whom Scripture describes in a favorable light: Abel, Enoch, and Noah.

Martha and Mary are members of the same family (representing the family of God), yet God would reveal different and important facets of truth through each of them. Many religious Jews had come to comfort them, yet the true comforter is the Holy Spirit (who, at the time of this living parable, had not yet been given). Jesus, however, was full of the Spirit of God, and he came to comfort Martha and Mary in a way that the Jews knew nothing about.

> 11:20 *Then Martha, as soon as she heard that Jesus was coming, went and met him; but Mary sat still in the house.*

Martha (her name means a freeborn, noble lady) was active. She dedicated her time and energy to personally serving Jesus and his disciples and friends, even though she could have had a life of ease. As soon as she heard Jesus was coming, she went out and met him. On the other hand, Mary (her name relates to myrrh and to the way of the cross), sat still in the house (in Bethany, the house of dates, the house of the fruit of righteousness). Mary was patient and at rest even in the midst of tribulation.

> 11:21 *Then Martha said unto Jesus, Lord, if thou hadst been here, my brother would not have died.*

> 11:22 *But I know that even now whatsoever thou wilt ask of God, God will give it unto thee.*

Martha believed that if Jesus had been there with the family, things would have been different. Even so, her faith was strong.

> 11:23 *Jesus said unto her, Thy brother shall rise again.*

Humanly speaking, Lazarus was dead. From Jesus' (God's) perspective, however, he was only asleep. This is true regarding all of those of faith who have died throughout the long history of the people of God. Earlier, Jesus had said: *The hour shall* come, and now is, when the dead shall hear the voice of the Son of God, and they that hear shall live (John 5:25). We are now rapidly approaching the fullness of this promise.

> 11:24 Martha said unto him, I know that he shall rise again in the resurrection in the last day.

Although many people have heard of the general resurrection that is to take place at the end of the last (prophetic) day (Revelation 20:11-15), only a few seem to know there is a first resurrection that will take place at the beginning of the last day (Revelation 20:4-5). This first resurrection is the hidden subject of the following two-verse parable.

> 11:25 Jesus said unto her, I AM the resurrection and the life; he that believes in me, though he is dead, yet shall he live;
>
> 11:26 and whosoever lives and believes in me shall never die. Believest thou this?

Martha may have found Jesus' words a little puzzling, but she did not question or contradict him.

> 11:27 She said unto him, Yes, Lord, I believe that thou art the Christ, the Son of God, who should come into the world.

Having reaffirmed her faith that he was the Christ, the Son of God, she became aware that he wanted to say something special to her sister, Mary.

> 11:28 And having said this, she went away and called Mary her sister secretly, saying, The Master is come, and calls for thee.
>
> 11:29 As soon as she heard that, she arose quickly and came unto him.

Mary didn't make a move until she knew Jesus was calling for her.

11:30 *(Now Jesus was not yet come into the town, but was in that place where Martha met him.)*

11:31 *Then the Jews who were with her in the house and comforted her, when they saw Mary, that she rose up hastily and went out, followed her, saying, She goes unto the grave to weep there.*

11:32 *Then when Mary was come where Jesus was and saw him, she fell down at his feet, saying unto him, Lord, if thou hadst been here, my brother would not have died.*

Mary's initial words to Jesus were exactly the same as Martha's.

11:33 *When Jesus therefore saw her weeping and the Jews also weeping who came with her, he became enraged in the Spirit and stirred himself up*

11:34 *and said, Where have ye laid him? They said unto him, Lord, come and see.*

11:35 *Jesus wept.*

11:36 *Then the Jews said, Behold how he loved him!*

The Jews completely misinterpreted Jesus' tears, as they had misinterpreted so many other things regarding his ministry and intention. Yes, Jesus loved Lazarus very much, but that was not why he wept.

11:37 *And some of them said, Could not this man, who opened the eyes of the blind, have also caused that this man should not have died?*

11:38 *Jesus therefore, becoming enraged again in himself, came to the grave. It was a cave, and a stone lay upon it.*

Jesus' emotions were in turmoil because he knew what was about to happen and was aware that, although the coming miracle was a sign or parable pointing to the first resurrection – and incidentally would bring great joy to Mary and Martha – the fullness of this sign would not be possible without his own suffering, death, and resurrection. Because he was fully God, he knew his suffering and death would be only transient, but because he was also fully human, their inevitability must have cost him some qualms, even in that age of violent death. On the other hand, he realized that by raising Lazarus, he was about to set in motion a train of events that would bring about the defeat of the Prince of This World and all his evil principalities. What a triumph that would be!

> 11:39 *Jesus said, Take ye away the stone. Martha,*
> *the sister of him that had died, said unto him, Lord,*
> *by this time he stinks, for he has been dead four*
> *days.*

Martha, always practical, brought up the fact that removing the stone would allow what she thought would be a most unpleasant smell to escape from her brother's grave.

> 11:40 *Jesus said unto her, Did I not say unto thee*
> *that if thou wouldest believe thou shalt see the glory*
> *of God?*

Martha (and, I suspect, most of those present) clearly thought removing the stone would release the stench of corruption of a body that had been dead for four days. Jesus, on the other hand, said removing it would reveal the glory of God, a glory that is more than capable of destroying every trace of bodily corruption.

Whom would the onlookers believe?

What does the stone represent? It represents every legalistic impediment to faith. The stone had to be removed before Jesus would speak life into the situation. Therefore Jesus ordered them collectively, *Take ye away the stone.*

> 11:41 *Then they took away the stone from the place where the dead was laid. And Jesus, lifting up his eyes, said, Father, I thank thee that thou hast heard me.*

> 11:42 *And I knew that thou hearest me always, but because of the people who stand by I said it, that they may believe that thou hast sent me.*

> 11:43 *And having said these things, he cried with a loud voice, Lazarus, come forth.*

Without help, all of us are like Lazarus. But no matter how dead we think we are, Jesus wants to give life to our dead bodies. Will we trust him and take away the "stone"?

> 11:44 *Then he that had been dead came forth, bound hand and foot with graveclothes, and his face was bound about with a napkin. Jesus said unto them, Loose him, and let him go.*

After Lazarus responded to Jesus' voice and came out of the tomb, he still had to be released from the graveclothes and napkin with which he had been bound in accordance with Jewish traditions of burial. Jesus came to set us free from religious tradition. All we have to do is hear his word and respond to it. Jesus came as the Lamb of God to fulfill the law by offering himself as the once-and-for-all sacrifice for each of us.

> 11:45 *Then many of the Jews who had come to Mary and had seen what Jesus did believed on him.*

Many who had previously found it difficult to trust Jesus did believe on him when they saw how he had raised a man from the dead.

11:46 *But some of them went unto the Pharisees and told them what Jesus had done.*

11:47 *Then the high priests and the Pharisees gathered a council and said, What shall we do? for this man does many signs.*

11:48 *If we let him thus alone, everyone will believe on him, and the Romans shall come and take away both our place and the nation.*

Once again, the religious leaders were motivated by fear of man instead of fear of God.

11:49 *And one of them, named Caiaphas, being the high priest that same year, said unto them, Ye know nothing at all*

11:50 *nor consider that it is expedient for us that one man should die for the people, and not that the whole nation be lost.*

"Caiaphas" means "dell" or "depression" (that is, a hollow in the earth). Caiaphas was most likely of the sect of the Sadducees who, unlike the Pharisees, did not believe in the possibility of *resurrection, neither angel nor spirit* (Acts 23:8; see also Matthew 22:23 and Acts 5:17). Modern Sadducees are still found today.

11:51 *And this he spoke not of himself; but being high priest that year, he prophesied that Jesus should die for the nation;*

11:52 *and not for that nation only, but that he should also gather together in one the sons of God that were scattered abroad.*

God is an expert at using our enemies to fulfill his own purpose.

11:53 *So that from that day forth they took counsel together to kill him.*

God used the corrupt, unbelieving, and cynical high priest Caiaphas and his religious cohorts to help bring about the single all-sufficient sacrifice of Jesus as the Lamb of God. Although Caiaphas prophesied that Jesus should *die for the nation*, he was unaware that the "nation" included all *the sons of God that were scattered abroad* and that Jesus' death and resurrection would *gather together in one* every true son of God – Gentile as well as Jew.

> 11:54 *Jesus therefore no longer walked openly among the Jews, but went from there unto a country near to the wilderness into a city called Ephraim and there continued with his disciples.*

"Ephraim" means "double ash heap" or, conversely, "double fruitfulness." It is worth noting that Joseph (after being sold into slavery in Egypt) named his second son Ephraim because, he said, God *has caused me to be fruitful in the land of my affliction* (Genesis 41:52).[55] This was also to be the case with Jesus, but on a much higher plane. Jesus would open the way (in fact, he *is* the way) for us to be born again from above by the Spirit of God, as part of God's plan to take us from a double ash heap through all manner of trials and tribulations and bring us into double fruitfulness for his kingdom.

Jesus, led by his Father, now went *unto a country near to the wilderness into a city called Ephraim and there continued with his disciples* because this would be the starting point for his last journey to Jerusalem, along what would be the way of the cross. Satan and his sons and his demonic principalities and powers knew nothing about the way of the cross (and they still do not seem to understand it), and so they overplayed their

---

55 Later, when Joseph's father, Israel, blessed Joseph's two sons he placed his right hand (of power and authority) on Ephraim, the second born and his left hand on Manasseh, the first born (Genesis 48:13-20). Joseph, thought his almost blind father was making a mistake but Israel did this on purpose. Israel (Jacob) was a second born son.

hand. Indeed, with their hatred and strong desire to kill Jesus, they not only failed to hinder God's plan, they actually helped accomplish it. In the two millennia since then, they do not seem to have learned much, if anything, from their mistakes, as they have continued to hate, defame, revile, persecute, and attempt to kill Jesus' followers (Matthew 5:11-12).

> 11:55 *And the passover of the Jews was now at hand, and many went out of the country up to Jerusalem before the passover to purify themselves;*

> 11:56 *and they sought for Jesus and spoke among themselves as they stood in the temple, What think ye, that he will not come to the feast?*

> 11:57 *Now both the high priests and the Pharisees had given a commandment, that if anyone knew where he was he should show it, that they might take him.*

The stage was now set. Some of the most important events that would ever take place in human history were about to be accomplished in accordance with the infinite wisdom and plan of God. The resurrection of Lazarus was a watershed. Many who had seen this or heard about it were now believers, but the high priests and the Pharisees doubled down on their wicked plot to kill Jesus right on the eve of the Passover. And the path from double ash heap to double fruitfulness (the way of the cross) continues all the way to the first resurrection, when those who have chosen to lay down their own lives so that Jesus' life may come forth in them will be resurrected. Then they *shall live and reign with Christ the thousand years* that Satan will be bound, prior to the general resurrection and judgment at the end of that time (Revelation 20:4-6).

Let us pray

Lord, May we truly understand the parable of Martha and Mary and Lazarus. May we embrace the way of the cross. May your Holy Spirit lead and guide us from the double ash heap into double fruitfulnesss, according to the will of the Father. May we come out from under our own headship so we may reign with you under your government. Amen.

Chapter 12

The Triumphal Entry and the Second Coming

John 12

12:1 Jesus, therefore, six days before the passover, came to Bethany, where Lazarus was who had been dead, whom he raised from the dead.

I f Lazarus is a representation of God's plan to have a first resurrection at the beginning of the last day, also known as the day of the Lord (prophetically the seventh millennium), let's look back at what happened almost six prophetic days ago (six days before the Passover). In the immediate aftermath of the fall of Adam and Eve that took place roughly six thousand years ago, God made an important promise and prophetic declaration unto the serpent: *and I will put enmity between thee and the woman and between thy seed and her seed; that seed shall bruise thy head, and thou shalt bruise his heel* (Genesis 3:15).

The seed of the woman that would bruise Satan's head is Jesus Christ (and remember that we may become part of the body of Christ under Jesus' headship). The enmity between the seed of the serpent and the seed of the woman is clearly evident throughout this book and has been raging for almost six thousand years.

> 12:2 *There they made him a supper; and Martha served, but Lazarus was one of those that sat at the table with him.*

> 12:3 *Then Mary took a pound of ointment of spike-nard, very costly, and anointed the feet of Jesus and wiped his feet with her hair; and the house was filled with the odour of the ointment.*

In a certain sense, this supper at Bethany (the house of the fruit of righteousness) served by Martha (symbolic of free women, she here represents the people Jesus has redeemed and set free), with Lazarus, *who had been dead*, seated at the table, is also a celebration of Jesus being designated and anointed by the Father as *the Lamb that was slain from the foundation of the world* (Revelation 13:8b). The full celebration is yet to come and is called the *marriage supper of the Lamb* (Revelation 19:7-9).

In the parable that John records, Mary represents the bride, and here she has taken a pound of ointment of spikenard and poured it on Jesus' feet. This very costly ointment or anointing is made from the lily and represents all the wonderful gifts, anointings, and ministries that Jesus has given us. The lily is linked to the pillars of the temple[56] and to the bridegroom (1 Kings 7:19; Song of Solomon 2:1, 16; 5:13). That Mary *wiped his feet with her hair* is also very significant. Her hair represents glory, and normally in that culture, a woman would cover her hair because *the woman is the glory of the man* (1 Corinthians

---

56 *And he stood up the pillars in the porch of the temple. And when he had set up the right pillar, he called the name of it Jachin* [Hebrew "The LORD establishes"]; *and in standing up the left pillar, he called its name Boaz* [Hebrew "Only in Him is there strength"]. *And upon the top of the pillars was lily work, and so the work of the pillars was finished* (1 Kings 7:21-22).

11:7b). Here, however, the glory of the bride is part of her gift to Jesus.

Jesus referred to Mary's act with some striking words: *Verily I say unto you, Wherever this gospel shall be preached throughout the whole world, this also that she has done shall be spoken of for a memorial of her* (Mark 14:9).[57] This statement gives us a hint that the gospel really is not complete without mentioning Mary and the bride she symbolizes. The Song of Solomon sheds more light on this subject.[58]

> 12:4 *Then said one of his disciples, Judas Iscariot, Simon's son, who should betray him,*
>
> 12:5 *Why was this ointment not sold for three hundred denarius[59] and given to the poor?*
>
> 12:6 *This he said, not that he cared for the poor, but because he was a thief and had the bag and would take from what was put therein.*

This is where the nature of Judas Iscariot, the traitor, begins to be revealed as a thief and robber who had come to kill and destroy. The devil thought he had cleverly infiltrated Jesus' inner circle with one of his own people. There are still many "tares" – that is, weeds disguised as wheat – that the devil has sown among the people of God and who steal that which belongs to Jesus when they think no one is looking. This situation, however, is about to end.

---

57 The account of this incident recorded by Mark states that ointment was poured on Jesus' head, and Jesus said that the woman (whom Mark does not name) had anticipated anointing his body for burial (Mark 14:3-8). Jesus, the head, would proceed almost immediately to the cross. Those who were of his body would follow, and obviously the anointing poured all the way down from his head to his feet. For greater detail on Mark's account, See *The Gospel of Jesus Christ – A Study in Mark*, Russell Stendal, Aneko Press, Abbotsford, WI.

58 See *Until the Day Breaks and the Shadows Flee Away* (previously *The Mystery of the Will of God*), Russell Stendal, Aneko Press, Abbotsford, WI.

59 Three hundred denarius was about a year's wages for an agricultural field worker.

12:7 *Therefore Jesus said, Let her alone; against the day of my burying she has kept this;*

12:8 *for the poor ye always have with you, but ye shall not always have me.*

12:9 *A great multitude of the Jews therefore knew that he was there; and they came not only for Jesus' sake, but that they might see Lazarus also, whom he had raised from the dead.*

In another parable of the marriage supper, described in the gospel of Matthew, many of the invited guests failed to show up, and the king ordered his servants to invite everyone they encountered on the public roads instead. Subsequently, someone who accepted the servants' invitation was found to not be wearing the proper attire at the feast; he should have been clad in a wedding garment, symbolic of submitting to the authority of Jesus Christ and doing what he desires (for we must be found clothed in Jesus' righteousness, and not in our own self-righteousness of the type Judas displays here). *Then the king said to the slaves, Bind him hand and foot and take him away and cast him into the darkness outside; there shall be weeping and gnashing of teeth. For many are called, but few are chosen* (Matthew 22:13-14).

12:10 *So the princes of the priests took counsel that they might also put Lazarus to death*

12:11 *because by reason of him many of the Jews went away and believed on Jesus.*

Judas's hypocritical remarks regarding his concern for the poor, and his putdown of Mary's humble act of adoration, marked the beginning of the end of his fellowship with Jesus and the other disciples. It would not be long before he would be in the employ of the princes of the priests, who not only refused to glorify God for restoring Lazarus to life but were now so blinded by jealousy and hatred that they planned to kill the resurrected man to eliminate his witness.

> 12:12 *On the next day[60] the multitude that were come to the feast, when they heard that Jesus was coming to Jerusalem,*

> 12:13 *took branches of palm trees and went forth to meet him and cried, Hosanna; Blessed is he that comes in the name of the Lord, the King of Israel.*

The palm tree is a symbol of righteousness, and the date is the fruit of the date palm. Bethany, the house of dates, is a symbol of the fruit of righteousness. Some (perhaps even all) of the palm branches used by the crowd applauding Jesus' triumphal entry likely came from date palms found in and around Bethany. The use of the palm branches welcomed Jesus as the King of Righteousness (Revelation 7:9). The word "Hosanna" – which means "Oh, save!" – links this passage to Revelation 7:10.

> 12:14 *And Jesus, when he had found a young ass, sat upon it, as it is written,*

> 12:15 *Fear not, daughter of Sion; behold, thy King comes, sitting on an ass's colt.[61]*

Man is born like a wild ass's colt (Job 11:12b). Jesus rode into

---

60 The previous day was six days before the Passover (verse 1), thus these events take place five days before the Passover. It's not likely that the supper prepared for Jesus on the previous day would have taken place on the Sabbath; therefore, it's not likely that his triumphant entry into Jerusalem took place on a Sunday. The dates for the Passover were set by a lunar calendar in which the Passover was the fourteenth day of the first month, and the month began with the new moon. This means there was only one chance in seven that the Passover would fall on any given day of the week. See: The *Gospel of Jesus Christ – a Study in Mark*, Russell Stendal, Aneko Press, Abbotsford, WI.

61 *Rejoice greatly, O daughter of Zion; shout with joy, O daughter of Jerusalem; behold, thy King shall come unto thee: just, and a saviour; humble, and riding upon an ass, even upon a colt the foal of an ass* (Zechariah 9:9).

Jerusalem on a young ass *upon which no man ever sat* (Mark 11:2b), demonstrating that only he can bring our wild flesh under perfect control.

> 12:16 *His disciples did not understand these things at first, but when Jesus was glorified, then they remembered that these things were written of him and that they had done these things unto him.*

> 12:17 *The multitude, therefore, that was with him when he called Lazarus out of his grave and raised him from the dead, bore witness.*

> 12:18 *For this cause the multitude also met him, for they had heard that he had done this sign.*

The sign Jesus had done *when he called Lazarus out of his grave and raised him from the dead* is symbolic of the first resurrection, which will take place at Jesus' return at the beginning of the last (prophetic) day. Lazarus and the multitude of people who bore witness to Lazarus's resurrection have counterparts among those described in Revelation 7:13-17.

When Jesus returns, he will be accompanied by a huge multitude who will bear witness. Those who are asleep in the Lord, of whom Lazarus is a symbol, are described by the apostle Paul this way: *And these all, approved by testimony of faith, received not the promise, God having provided some better thing for us, that they without us should not be made perfect* (Hebrews 11:39-40). Paul also states, *For this, we say unto you by the word of the Lord, that we who are alive and remain unto the coming of the Lord shall not precede those who are asleep* (1 Thessalonians 4:15).

Those of us who are *alive and remain* when Jesus comes back will witness what happens when he calls those who are his out of their graves and raises them from the dead. Paul paints the picture for us: *For the Lord himself shall descend from heaven with a shout, with the voice of the archangel, and with the trumpet of God; and the dead in Christ shall rise first; then we who are alive and remain shall be caught up together with them in the clouds, to meet the Lord in the air, and so shall we ever be with the Lord* (1 Thessalonians 4:16-17).

The triumphal entry into Jerusalem, and the joyous response of the multitude who had earlier witnessed the resurrection of Lazarus, is also a portrayal of Jesus' second coming. Needless to say, however, the Pharisees failed to share the joy felt by the crowd.

> 12:19 *The Pharisees therefore said among themselves, Perceive ye how ye prevail nothing? behold, the world is gone after him.*

Modern counterparts of the scribes and Pharisees and Sadducees continue to usurp control over large segments of the people of God. What will they say when Jesus returns and calls all of the heroes of the faith out of their graves and raises them from the dead?

Remember that *the Lord himself shall descend from heaven with a shout* (perhaps like the commanding tone he used when he told Lazarus to come forth). Remember that this will take place *with the voice of the archangel, and with the trumpet of God.* Remember that *the dead in Christ shall rise first.* Remember that after all of this, **then** *we who are alive and remain shall be caught up together with them in the clouds, to meet the Lord in the air.*

When we are *caught up together with them in the clouds, to meet the Lord in the air,* we will be witnesses to all of the prior events, just as the multitude who met Jesus outside the city and accompanied him into Jerusalem had earlier witnessed the resurrection of Lazarus. By this time, we will have heard the shout when the Lord himself descended from heaven, we will have heard the voice of the archangel, we will have heard the blast of the trumpet, and we will have witnessed the resurrection of the dead in Christ who shall rise first. Then we will be caught up together with the resurrected ones and will be changed from mortal to immortal (1 Corinthians 15:50-54), and all of us will accompany Jesus on the final segment of his glorious return to earth as we, like the multitudes described in John 12:13, cry out, *Hosanna; Blessed is he that comes in the name of the Lord, the King of Israel.*

> 12:20 *And there were certain Greeks among them that came up to worship at the feast;*

> 12:21 *the same came therefore to Philip, who was of Bethsaida of Galilee, and asked him, saying, Lord, we desire to see Jesus.*

> 12:22 *Philip came and told Andrew, and then Andrew and Philip told Jesus.*

These *certain Greeks* showed Philip a great deal of respect, addressing him as Lord. This happened on the day of Jesus' triumphal entry into Jerusalem. If we are among those who are chosen for the first resurrection at the beginning of the last day, and are thus selected to reign with Christ, and if we are among those who meet Jesus in the air and accompany him on the final segment of his triumphant return to earth, people from all over the world will view us with similar respect.

The Greek Gentiles seemed drawn to Philip, whose name means "lover of horses" (an animal that can symbolize the natural capability of the Gentiles). Philip listened to their request and told Andrew about it. Both Philip and Andrew were from Bethsaida, which means "house of fishing" or "house of nets" (and Jesus had told them from the beginning that if they followed him, he would make them fishers of men). Not wanting to introduce the wrong sort of people to Jesus, Philip did not go alone to him to pass on this request, but instead involved Andrew as a witness.

> 12:23 *And Jesus answered them, saying, The hour comes in which the Son of man shall be clarified.*

"Clarified" may seem an unusual word to use, especially given that many versions of the Bible use "glorified" instead, but it is the proper translation of the word used by Casiodoro de Reina in his Spanish Bible published in 1569, on which the Jubilee Bible is based. However, in this context, there is no conflict between the two words. Even the disciples were at this point seeing Jesus *as through a mirror, in darkness* (1 Corinthians 13:12); however, his dimly seen image would soon be sharpened and *clarified* by the events that were about to unfold. And when we see Christ clearly, our response is to *glorify* him through our praise and worship.

At this time, Jesus' listeners (which here included not only Philip and Andrew but also the Greeks who had asked to speak to him, as well as anyone else within earshot) did not understand that his death and resurrection would also serve to clarify many things to an extraordinary degree, proving to be a turning point in human history. Historians have noted a major difference between the time before Christ's birth (BC) and the time after it (AD, signifying *anno Domini*, or "in the year of our Lord"). Yet Jesus' second coming, which will make his nature still clearer to us, will make an even more profound difference and will mark the true division of time and history.

> 12:24 *Verily, verily, I say unto you, Except the grain of wheat falls into the ground and dies, it abides alone; but if it dies, it brings forth much fruit.*
>
> 12:25 *He that loves his life shall lose it, and he that*

*hates his life in this world shall keep it unto life
eternal.*

12:26 *If anyone serves me, let them follow me; and
where I am, there shall my servant be also; the one
that serves me, will my Father honour.*

This is Jesus' message to his disciples (represented by Philip and
Andrew) and to the world (represented by the distinguished
Greek visitors). His words are crystal clear in the light of his
death and resurrection. Jesus desires for all of us to follow him
along the way of the cross, the way of death and resurrection.

12:27 *Now is my soul troubled; and what shall I say?
Father, save me from this hour, but for this have I
come in this hour.*

Jesus called on his disciples (including us) to take up their cross
and follow him. He knew that the purpose of his coming was
to lead the way, but the very nature of the way of the cross is
troubling to the human soul.

12:28 *Father, clarify thy name. Then there came a
voice from the heaven, saying, I have clarified it and
will clarify it again.*

On a previous occasion the Father had spoken from heaven
and clarified that Jesus *is my beloved Son, in whom I am well
pleased* (Matthew 3:17). The name of the Father is linked to
his nature, so when Jesus now requests that his Father clarify
his name, he is asking that glory of the Father's true nature be
made clear to his people.

Since Jesus, the only begotten Son, still had the same heavenly nature as the Father (even though he had humbled himself
and had become incarnate as a mere man), when his Father's
name/nature was clarified, their profoundly shared nature would
also become clear to the world – or at least, to those who had

eyes to see it. It was because their nature was shared that Jesus could continue to pronounce the sacred name of God (I AM), linking himself to the Father, without committing blasphemy.

> 12:29 *The people, therefore, that were present and heard it, said that it thundered; others said, An angel spoke to him.*

Who were *the people that were present and heard it*?

It appears that they included Philip and Andrew and the Gentile visitors who had addressed Philip as Lord and politely expressed their desire to see Jesus. No matter who was there, however, it seems safe to say that they certainly did not expect to hear *a voice from the heaven* in the middle of Jesus' discourse. This astounding event caused them to dispense with protocol and discuss what had happened. Some identified the voice as thunder, while others believed they had heard an angel speaking to Jesus. Apparently none of them were able to identify the Father's voice.

> 12:30 *Jesus answered and said, This voice came not because of me, but for your sakes.*

The Father decided to back up Jesus' message and testimony with a second witness from heaven at the precise moment when *certain Greeks* were evaluating Jesus and his message. The visit of the Greeks was important to both Jesus and his Father, as it was one of the first signs that Gentiles were interested in Christ's message, even though many Jews rejected it, and Jesus now shared very sensitive information with them about the meaning of coming events (just as he had gently revealed subtle hidden truths to the Samaritan woman).

> 12:31 *Now is the judgment of this world; now shall the prince of this world be cast out.*

Satan has continued to operate with his demons in the spiritual realm called heaven, where he is known as the accuser of the brethren (Revelation 12:10), but his days there are numbered. As we enter the time of the end, we will soon see the following Scripture fulfilled: *And there was war in heaven: Michael and his angels fought against the dragon; and the dragon fought and his angels, and did not prevail; neither was their place found any more in heaven. And the great dragon was cast out, the serpent of old, who is called Devil and the Satan, who deceives the whole world; he was cast out into the earth, and his angels were cast out with him* (Revelation 12:7-9).

Jesus continued his discourse to his audience of Greeks and Jews:

> 12:32 *And I, if I be lifted up from the earth, will draw all men unto me.*
>
> 12:33 *This he said, signifying what death he should die.*
>
> 12:34 *The people answered him, We have heard out of the law that the Christ abides for ever; and how sayest thou, It is expedient that the Son of man be lifted up? Who is this Son of man?*

The term "son of man" is used extensively in the OT. The prophet Ezekiel, who is also a type and shadow of the Messiah, is referred to by God on numerous occasions as "son of man." The prophet Daniel saw the Messiah as a son of man (Daniel 7:13; 10:16). Son of Man depicts Jesus' humanity and Son of God his divinity. Jesus is one hundred percent man and one hundred percent God. He shares the same nature (name) as his Father, and he wants us to become members in particular of the body of Christ so we may have eternal existence in him. His death and resurrection make this possible (Romans 6:5; Philippians 3:10).

12:35 Then Jesus said unto them, Yet a little while is the Light with you. Walk while ye have the light, lest darkness come upon you; for he that walks in darkness does not know where he goes.

12:36 While ye have the Light, believe in the Light that ye may be the sons of light. Jesus spoke these things and departed and hid himself from them.

The temple, the city of Jerusalem, and even what the religious leaders perceived as the entire nation of Israel, all began living on borrowed time when those leaders rejected Jesus, the Light of the World. Even after they crucified him, they still had the chance to witness to the light of God that was present in his apostles and disciples, but most of them continued to fail miserably until the darkness they had chosen enveloped and destroyed them. The kingdom of darkness belongs to Satan and has no capacity to save or to heal.

12:37 But although he had done so many signs before them, yet they did not believe in him,

12:38 that the word of Isaiah the prophet might be fulfilled, which he spoke, Lord, who shall believe our report? and to whom has the arm of the Lord been revealed?[62]

12:39 Therefore they could not believe, because Isaiah said again,

12:40 He has blinded their eyes and hardened their heart, that they should not see with their eyes nor understand with their heart and be converted, and I should heal them.[63]

---

62   Isaiah 53:1.
63   Isaiah 6:10.

12:41 *Isaiah said these things when he saw his glory and spoke of him.*

The children of Israel made a fatal mistake at the foot of Mount Sinai when, even before the giving of the law, they refused to continue to hear the voice of the LORD, despite Moses's attempts to reason with them. Moses described it this way:

And ye said, Behold, the LORD our God has shown us his glory and his greatness, and we have heard his voice out of the midst of the fire; we have seen this day that God does talk with man, and he lives. Now, therefore, why should we die? For this great fire will consume us; if we hear the voice of the LORD our God any more, then we shall die. For what is all flesh that it should hear the voice of the living God that speaks out of the midst of the fire, as we heard, and live? Go thou near and hear all that the LORD our God shall say, and thou shalt tell us all that the LORD our God shall speak unto thee; and we will hear it, and do it. (Deuteronomy 5:24-27)

And so they settled for a secondhand revelation and commissioned Moses to act as their intermediary, not realizing that in order for God's grace and mercy to effectively transform and empower us to do his will, we must have personal contact with him. And it is impossible to hear the voice of the living God and continue to live our own life according to our own ways. Continuing to hear God's voice will kill something in us, but it will also bring us to a new birth in the life of God. None of this became clear, however, until the death and resurrection of Jesus Christ opened the way for the Holy Spirit to be poured out upon all flesh (Joel 2:28; Acts 2:17).

12:42 *Nevertheless, even among the princes many believed in him, but because of the Pharisees they*

*did not confess him, lest they should be put out of
the synagogue;*

12:43 *for they loved the glory of men more than the
glory of God.*

Even today, many love the glory of men more than the glory of
God. Such people continue to go along with things that, in the
depths of their own conscience, they know are not right, simply
because they are not willing to confront those who insist that
everyone must be religiously and politically correct.

12:44 *But Jesus cried and said, He that believes in
me, believes not in me, but in him that sent me,*

12:45 *and he that sees me sees him that sent me.*

12:46 *I am come as a light into the world that whosoever believes in me should not abide in darkness.*

Jesus did not come on his own. He came to represent his Father.
If Jesus is received, the Father is received. If Jesus is received,
we will walk in the light.

12:47 *And if anyone hears my words and believes
not, I judge him not, for I came not to judge the
world but to save the world.*

12:48 *He that rejects me and does not receive my
words has one that judges him: the word that I have
spoken, the same shall judge him in the last day.*

12:49 *For I have not spoken of myself; but the Father
who sent me, he gave me a commandment, what I
should say and what I should speak.*

12:50 *And I know that his commandment is eternal
life; whatsoever I speak therefore, even as the Father
said unto me, so I speak.*

Those who reject Jesus and do not receive his words are really rejecting the Father and the words of the Father. Jesus is the living Word of God, and his word flows according to the commandment of the Father, whose *commandment is eternal life.*

Let us pray

Lord, please open our understanding. May we embrace your Word, and may it penetrate deep inside our being and change us from the inside out, until our hearts are cleansed and we perceive things from your point of view. Amen.

Chapter 13

The Last Supper and a New Commandment

John 13

13:1 *Now before the feast of the passover, when Jesus knew that his hour was come that he should depart out of this world unto the Father, having loved his own who were in the world, he loved them unto the end.*

13:2 *And supper being ended, the devil having now put into the heart of Judas Iscariot, Simon's son, to betray him,*

This is now the day of preparation for the Passover at what has become known as the Last Supper (Mark 14:18). Jesus would be dead in less than twenty-four hours, and he knew it, but he loved his disciples to the end.

13:3 *Jesus knowing that the Father had given all things into his hands and that he had come from God and was going to God,*

*13:4 arose from the supper and laid aside his gar-
ments and took a towel and girded himself.*

*13:5 After that, he poured water into a basin and
began to wash the disciples' feet and to wipe them
with the towel with which he was girded.*

The earliest mention of foot washing in Scripture is in Genesis
18:1-5, when Abraham declared himself the slave of the LORD
and extended hospitality to the LORD and the angels traveling
with him. Foot washing was a great courtesy and normally the
work of a slave, yet here we find God's much-loved Son donning
the attire of a slave and performing the work of a slave. A hired
servant receives a salary and can quit, whereas a slave belongs
to an owner. Jesus, of course, was part of his Father and thus
belonged to him, but by taking on the role of a slave, he wanted
to demonstrate to his disciples that he was eternally bonded to
them, as he is eternally bonded to those who follow him today.

*13:6 Then he came to Simon Peter, and Peter said
unto him, Lord, dost thou wash my feet?*

Seeing Jesus in the role of a slave made Simon Peter extremely
uncomfortable. Not understanding Jesus' purpose, he was not
prepared to accept his actions without protest.

*13:7 Jesus answered and said unto him, What I
do thou dost not understand now, but thou shalt
understand afterwards.*

There are many things we shall never comprehend unless and
until Jesus opens our understanding.

*13:8 Peter said unto him, Thou shalt never wash my
feet. Jesus answered him, If I wash thee not, thou
shalt have no part with me.*

Peter blindly refused to accept his Lord in the role of a slave.

What he failed to realize was that Jesus was not simply offering cordial hospitality, he was demonstrating a principle that would prove to be absolutely essential to those who choose to follow him. Peter knew Jesus was the Master and that those who follow him are to serve him. However, unless Jesus serves us by cleansing every little detail with regard to our feet (that is, our walk with God), we will have no part with him.

13:9 *Simon Peter said unto him, Lord, not my feet only, but also my hands and my head.*

Many of us share Peter's tendency to go from one extreme to the other. If it was essential to have Jesus wash his feet, then Peter thought it would be even better to have him wash his hands and his head as well.

13:10 *Jesus said to him, He that is washed needs only to wash his feet because he is completely clean, and ye are clean, but not all.*

13:11 *For he knew who should betray him; therefore, said he, Ye are not all clean.*

Jesus knew Peter's hands (his desire and capacity to serve) were clean, as was his head (there were no thoughts of rebellion in Peter's mind). Jesus also knew that by now, Judas was so thoroughly unclean in spirit that the devil could plant whatever he wanted into Judas's heart and it would flourish. The other eleven disciples (and particularly Peter) would soon see, however, that there was a problem with their feet (that is, with their individual and collective walk) that could only be put right by Jesus cleansing them. All of us require this cleansing on a continual basis, and only constant and continual communion with Jesus and the Father by the Holy Spirit can accomplish it. The disciples would understand later.

13:12 *So after he had washed their feet and had*

*taken his garments and had sat down again, he said
unto them, Know ye what I have done to you?*

13:13 *Ye call me Master and Lord; and ye say well,
for so I am.*

13:14 *If I then, the Lord and the Master, have
washed your feet, ye also ought to wash one another's feet.*

13:15 *For I have given you an example that ye
should do as I have done to you.*

It is not even enough for us to receive constant input and cleansing from Jesus regarding our "feet," for we must also be willing
to serve one another and to receive service from one another.
The way to help cleanse (and be cleansed of) any imperfection
or uncleanness in the feet of any of us who are joined together
by the Spirit as we walk with God isn't to try to lord it over our
companions, but rather to act as a slave, meekly ministering or
serving according to the will of God.

13:16 *Verily, verily, I say unto you, The slave is not
greater than his lord; neither is the apostle greater
than he that sent him.*

13:17 *If ye know these things, ye shall be blessed if ye
do them.*

Just as every slave belongs to a lord or master, so every apostle
or missionary belongs to the one who sent him, who is greater
than he. It is the daily walk of life with our feet here on the
ground that will ultimately prove exactly who our lord and
master is and exactly who has sent us to go wherever we are
found and to carry out whatever we are doing.

13:18 *I speak not of you all; I know whom I have
chosen; but that the scripture may be fulfilled, He*

that eats bread with me has lifted up his heel against me,[64]

At this point, all the disciples were clean (even their feet) except Judas. He, of course, is the one who lifted up his unclean "heel" against Jesus. We know that *the steps of a good man are ordered by the LORD* (Psalm 37:23) and that if the Lord does *not* order our steps, we will go astray. Someone who uses their feet to "lift up their heel" against Jesus has gone so far astray as to be completely lost.

13:19 *now I tell you before it is done, so that, when it is come to pass, ye may believe that I AM.*

13:20 *Verily, verily, I say unto you, He that receives whomsoever I send receives me, and he that receives me receives him that sent me.*

As discussed earlier, I AM is the sacred name of God that describes the very nature of his eternal existence (Exodus 3:14), and in this sense, Jesus has the same name (nature) as his Father. Jesus, while remaining God, came to this world as a man, the only begotten Son of the Father, and if we receive him, we receive his Father as well. Jesus could look into Judas's heart and know what was about to happen – that Judas was about to not only reject him but betray him. Jesus prophesied this to the other eleven so as to strengthen their faith when they saw it come to pass, and he coupled this prophecy with one of the greatest truths of the Gospel: **The person who receives whomsoever Jesus sends receives Jesus, and the person who receives Jesus receives the Father who sent him.**

13:21 *When Jesus had thus said, he was troubled in*

---

64   These words are a quote from a messianic psalm of David: *Even the man of my peace, in whom I trusted, who ate of my bread, has lifted up his heel against me* (Psalm 41:9).

spirit and testified and said, Verily, verily, I say unto
you, that one of you shall betray me.

We know that *having loved his own who were in the world,* Jesus
loved them until the end (John 13:1). The fact that Judas would
betray him caused Jesus to be *troubled in spirit,* for Judas was
one of his disciples and Jesus had trusted him (Psalm 41:9). It is
those we trust (or have trusted) who have the greatest capacity
to betray us, because they have intimate, inside information
about us.

> 13:22 *Then the disciples looked one on another,*
> *doubting of whom he spoke.*

If it had been humanly possible to see this coming, the disciples would have known or quickly guessed the name of the
betrayer, but instead, they *looked one on another, doubting of*
whom he spoke.

> 13:23 *And one of his disciples, whom Jesus loved,*
> *was seated at the table beside Jesus.*

The disciple whom Jesus loved was undoubtedly John, who was
too modest to name himself here.

> 13:24 *Simon Peter therefore beckoned to this one*
> *that he should ask him who it was of whom he*
> *spoke.*

> 13:25 *He then, reclining on Jesus' breast, said unto*
> *him, Lord, who is it?*

> 13:26 *Jesus answered, He it is to whom I shall give*
> *a sop when I have dipped it. And when he had*
> *dipped the sop, he gave it to Judas Iscariot, the son*
> *of Simon.*

> 13:27 *And after the sop Satan entered into him.*

Then Jesus said unto him, That which thou shalt do,
do it more quickly.

First, the devil put it into Judas's heart to betray Jesus (John 13:2) and now, after Jesus having given Judas a "sop" – most likely a chunk of bread dipped in wine – *Satan entered into him.* Judas, partaking unworthily of the Last Supper, was filled with the devil himself. Even so, Jesus had the last word in the matter, letting Judas know he was fully aware of his planned betrayal.

13:28 *Now no one at the table understood for what*
purpose he spoke this unto him.

Judas was at the table when Satan entered into him. Therefore, in a certain sense, Satan was also at the table and was included among those who did not understand why Jesus spoke these words to Judas. Satan undoubtedly thought he was pulling off a masterpiece of deception and betrayal that would sink Jesus irrevocably, but in reality, it was the other way around. Satan had absolutely no understanding of the impending consequences for himself and his kingdom of darkness. The way of the cross is completely foreign to Satan's thinking.

13:29 *For some of them thought, because Judas had*
the bag, that Jesus had said unto him, Buy those
things that we need for the feast, or that he should
give something to the poor.

13:30 *He then having received the sop went immedi-*
ately out, and it was now night.

The stage was now set for the redemption of fallen humanity. Judas (with Satan possessing him) had now gone beyond the point of no return. *It was now night.*

13:31 *Therefore, when he was gone out,*[65] *Jesus said,*

---

65 Judas took himself out of the picture after giving himself over to evil motiva-
    tion. Everyone is motivated by something (internal or external), and those
    who are motivated by greed will never put their heart into anything unless it

Now is the Son of man clarified, and God is clarified in him.

13:32 If God is clarified in him, God shall also clarify him in himself and shall straightway clarify him.

Satan (along with the principalities and powers that had joined him in his rebellion against God) and Judas (along with the Jewish scribes, priests, and elders who had rejected Jesus) were locked into the pitch-black night of spiritual darkness, related to the evil desires of their own hearts that blinded them to the truth. Thus the light of God and the darkness of Satan were now clearly delineated and separated, and the loving intentions of the Father and the Son (which are intertwined just as the Father and Son are intertwined) would be clarified to everyone in the natural and supernatural realms.

With the departure of Judas, the wheels were set in motion for Jesus' death, and his subsequent resurrection would clarify to his disciples what the purpose of his life had been. The fact that Jesus was willing to die for us (and, as the Lamb of God from the foundation of the world, he had therefore been willing to give his life to redeem us from the beginning of the rebellion caused by Satan and Adam) would clarify the reality of God's nature in him. In turn, God would clarify that Jesus was not only his son but King of Kings and Lord of Lords in himself.

is to their direct benefit, for *the love of money is the root of all evil* (1 Timothy 6:10). This is why the intention and plan of Jesus and the Father were clarified only after Judas left. When miracles were flowing and multitudes congregated to seek Jesus, Judas had the benefit of being camouflaged among the other apostles, and no one could tell there was something radically wrong in his heart. Jesus was the only one who knew Judas was dipping into God's finances for his own gain. As long as this was going on, however, things would never be perfectly clear, because Judas's wrong motivation was blurring the picture. This is because people with the wrong motivation eventually lose the hope that is the anchor of our faith (Hebrews 6:18-19), and it is impossible for the love of God to flow in and through those who have neither faith nor hope. Unless we are demonstrating God's love, no one will be drawn to God by observing our example, for *whatsoever is not out of faith is sin* (Romans 14:23). Thus Judas's presence in the group was interfering with the clear picture of God's love.

He would *straightway clarify* Jesus with a name above all names and give him unlimited dominion and authority. Satan and his followers, who are *the princes of this age*, failed to see any of this coming (1 Corinthians 2:8).

> 13:33 *Little children,*[66] *yet a little while I am with you. Ye shall seek me; and as I said unto the Jews, Where I go, ye cannot come, so now I say to you.*

> 13:34 *A new commandment I give unto you, That ye love*[67] *one another; as I have loved you, that ye also love one another.*

> 13:35 *By this shall everyone know that ye are my disciples, if ye have love one to another.*

This is precisely what many people calling themselves Christians have failed to demonstrate over the centuries, whether they call themselves Catholic, Orthodox, Protestant, or any other subdivision or denomination. Over the course of the church age, many ugly wars have been fought in the name of God, and this has left a bad taste in the mouth of many onlookers out in the world. The truth is that it is not possible for us to love one another unless we truly love God, and our capacity to love will not function properly unless the life, presence, and love of Jesus dominates our hearts.

> 13:36 *Simon Peter said unto him, Lord, where*

---

66 Scripture denotes three levels of maturity: children, young people, and those who are mature fathers (or parents). Even though the disciples had been sent out with power and authority from Jesus, he addresses them here as *little children*. Those who are mature in Christ are dead to sin and do not seek to promote themselves, that is, they *live unto righteousness* (1 Peter 2:24).

67 Greek *agapao*. Essentially the same word as used in John 3:16, for God so *loved* the world. This is the verb form of the Greek noun *agape*, which is properly translated as "charity" in many English Bibles. It is quite distinct from the Greek word for brotherly love or affection (*phileos*). However, in English, unlike Greek, "charity" is never used as a verb, and thus English Bible translations are virtually forced to use the English verb "love" to translate both *agapao* and *phileos*, even though the two meanings are very different.

*goest thou? Jesus answered him, Where I go, thou
canst not follow me now; but thou shalt follow me
afterwards.*

*13:37 Peter said unto him, Lord, why cannot I follow
thee now? I will lay down my soul[68] for thy sake.*

*13:38 Jesus answered him, Wilt thou lay down thy
soul for my sake? Verily, verily, I say unto thee, The
cock shall not crow until thou hast denied me three
times.*

Jesus was on the way to the cross. Peter wanted to follow him,
but according to Jesus, as yet he was only a *little child* in the
faith; like all small children, Peter was still focused upon himself. He would be capable of initiating a sword fight to defend
Jesus, but as would soon be proven, in order to avoid going to
the cross, he would deny Jesus three times before the rooster
crowed. Jesus did, however, hold out some comfort to him by
adding, *but thou shalt follow me afterwards.*

John 14

*14:1 Let not your heart be troubled; ye believe in
God, believe also in me.*

*14:2 In my Father's house are many dwelling places;
if it were not so, I would have told you. I go to prepare a place for you.*

*14:3 And if I go and prepare a place for you, I will
come again and take you unto myself; that where I
am, there ye may be also.*

Peter was told that even though he could not follow where Jesus
was going, he would follow later (presumably at his own death

---

68   "Soul" and "life" are virtually the same word in Greek and in Hebrew. "Soul"
      is synonymous with our entire being.

when, according to tradition, he was crucified as Jesus had been). However, Jesus also links us being together with him to his second coming: *I will come again and take you unto myself.* Remember, pronouns beginning in *y* are always plural in Old English. Yes, it is possible for us to die as individuals and go to be with Jesus, but there is something corporate concerning the entire body of Christ that will not be completed until the second coming and the first resurrection.

> 14:4 *So that ye know where I go, and ye know the way.*

Where was Jesus going?

To his Father's house in the heavenly realm represented by the holy of holies. Jesus' death would rend the veil between the holy place and the holy of holies, and as high priest of the order of Melchisedec, Jesus would open the way for mankind to be reunited with God. Because Jesus is the way, he would mediate a new covenant.

> 14:5 *Thomas said unto him, Lord, we know not where thou goest; how, therefore, can we know the way?*

The disciples were clueless. They had only been to the outer court of the temple. They had not been granted a revelation of even the inner holy place of priestly ministry, let alone the holy of holies that represented the realm of the dwelling place of God.

> 14:6 *Jesus said unto him, I AM the way, the truth, and the life; no one comes unto the Father, but by me.*

> 14:7 *If ye had known me, ye should have known my Father also; and from now on ye know him and have seen him.*

Jesus came to reveal the Father and to bring fallen humanity back into communion with him. This can only be accomplished on God's terms, not on ours.

14:8 *Philip said unto him, Lord, show us the Father, and it will suffice us.*

14:9 *Jesus said unto him, Have I been such a long time with you, and yet thou hast not known me, Philip? He that has seen me has seen the Father; and how sayest thou then, Show us the Father?*

14:10 *Believest thou not that I am in the Father and the Father in me? The words that I speak unto you I speak not of myself; but the Father that dwells in me, he does the works.*

14:11 *Believe me that I am in the Father and the Father in me, or else believe me for the very works' sake.*

From an earthly perspective, Jesus was the temple of the Father, and the Father lived in him by the fullness of the Spirit. From a heavenly perspective, Jesus is in the Father as part of the Father's house (household) or family. God's plan of redemption accomplished in and through Jesus is designed to bring us into the very family (or house) of God. Now, as a result of what Jesus accomplished, we are the temple, and God no longer dwells in houses (or temples) made of hands. Jesus is the beginning and the end. He is the chief foundation stone (Isaiah 28:16; 1 Corinthians 3:11). Likewise, he is the head of the corner of God's new and final temple built of living stones (Psalm 118:22), a temple that will not be full and complete until after the second coming. This is where we will dwell with Jesus and the Father, and they with us. Jesus is now seated at the right hand of the Father, with all power and authority, preparing the place where all of us will live together with him as he mediates the new covenant and carefully shapes and molds each living stone of his new temple (1 Peter 2:4-10).

> 14:12 *Verily, verily, I say unto you, He that believes in me, the works that I do he shall do also; and greater works than these shall he do because I go unto my Father.*

What works could we do that would even be greater than the ones Jesus did while he was here on earth? He made the lame and the crippled whole. He made the blind see and the deaf hear. He even raised the dead. And yet Jesus promises we will do the same as he did – and more! By the Spirit, we shall minister healing to the soul. Those who are spiritually crippled and lame and unable to walk on the straight and narrow path with God will be healed. Those who are spiritually blind and deaf will be able to see God and hear his voice. Those who are spiritually dead in trespasses and sin will be raised up in resurrection life. These are among the greater works that shall be accomplished by the Spirit of God operating in us and through us.

> 14:13 *And whatsoever ye shall ask the Father in my name, that will I do, that the Father may be glorified in the Son.*

> 14:14 *If ye ask any thing in my name, I will do it.*

Jesus' name is linked to his nature, which in turn is linked to his Father's nature. If we in the body of Christ operate in the nature of God, with Jesus as our only head, then Jesus will do anything we ask in his name. He will not, of course, do anything that is contrary to the name or nature of the Father, and those who ask for the desires of their own corrupt and fallen nature and then tack Jesus' name onto the end of their prayer are deluding themselves.

> 14:15 *If ye love me, keep my commandments;*

If we really love Jesus, our love will motivate us to keep his commandments.

> 14:16 *and I will ask the Father, and he shall give you another Comforter, that he may abide with you for ever,*

> 14:17 *even the Spirit of truth, whom the world cannot receive because it does not see him, or know him; but ye know him, for he dwells with you and shall be in you.*

The Comforter is the Holy Spirit and comes forth from the Father at the petition of the Son. Jesus desires that the Comforter will abide with us forever. At this time, the *Spirit of truth* (the Comforter) dwelt in fullness in Jesus and therefore dwelt **with** the disciples. In a few days, however, the Comforter would be **in** the disciples.

> 14:18 *I will not leave you orphans; I will come to you.*

Jesus dwells in us by the Holy Spirit, and it is by the Spirit that we may live, putting to death the deeds of the flesh. By the Spirit we may know that we have been adopted by the Father as sons of God, and thus as brothers and sisters in Christ (Romans 8:13-16).

> 14:19 *Yet a little while, and the world shall see me no more, but ye shall see me; because I live, ye shall live also.*

After Jesus' death and resurrection, he did not appear unto the world, but he did appear to the disciples. The world has not seen him since, nor can the world see the Comforter. In fact, *the friendship of the world is enmity with God* (James 4:4). It is Jesus' life that makes it possible for us to live (Romans 5:10). The Holy Spirit is sent so that we may partake of the life of Jesus (John 14:18).

> 14:20 *At that day ye shall know that I am in my*
> *Father, and ye in me, and I in you.*

What is *that day*?

It is the prophesied day of the Lord, when Jesus returns.

> 14:21 *He that has my commandments and keeps*
> *them, he it is that loves me; and he that loves me*
> *shall be loved of my Father, and I will love him and*
> *will manifest myself to him.*

Jesus' commandment is that we love one another even as he loved us.[69] If we truly love Jesus, we will love one another, we will be loved by the Father, and Jesus will love us and will manifest himself to us.

> 14:22 *Judas, not Iscariot, said unto him, Lord, how*
> *is it that thou wilt manifest thyself unto us and not*
> *unto the world?*

Jesus will manifest himself unto us by the Holy Spirit, whom the world cannot see.

> 14:23 *Jesus answered and said unto him, He who*
> *loves me will keep my words, and my Father will*
> *love him, and we will come unto him and dwell with*
> *him.*

> 14:24 *He that does not love me does not keep my*
> *words, and the word which ye have heard is not*
> *mine, but of the Father who sent me.*

Jesus' words are very different from the doctrines of men, which are so often hotly fought over. His words have little to do with religious ritual or dogma but much to do with repentance and a complete change of heart. Jesus' words are linked to the way

---

69   It's amazing how much conflict and strife continue among those who, despite calling themselves people of God, do not love one another as Jesus loved us. Nevertheless, there are many places all over the earth where people clearly love both Jesus and one another (1 Peter 4:8-9).

of the cross. They are Spirit and they are life (John 6:63). Jesus'
words come from the Father who sent him.

> 14:25 *I have spoken these things unto you, being yet
> present with you.*

> 14:26 *But the Comforter, which is the Holy Spirit,
> whom the Father will send in my name, he shall
> teach you all things and bring to your remembrance
> all the things that I have said unto you.*

There is no limit to what the Holy Spirit can teach us. He shall
teach us *all things* and bring to our remembrance *all the things*
that Jesus said unto his disciples. What a promise![70]

> 14:27 *Peace I leave with you, my peace I give unto
> you; not as the world gives, give I unto you. Let not
> your heart be troubled, neither let it be afraid.*

> 14:28 *Ye have heard how I said unto you, I go away
> and come again unto you. If ye loved me, ye would
> rejoice because I said, I go unto the Father; for my
> Father is greater than I.*

Jesus is able to give us peace that passes understanding, peace
that will endure even in the midst of severe trials and tribulations. The disciples were filled with apprehension because they
perceived a looming crisis, even as Jesus was declaring peace
unto them while questioning their love. They were about to
enter a crisis in which the love of man would not prove sufficient. *In charity* (the *agape*[71] love of God) *there is no fear; but
charity that is perfect casts out fear* (1 John 4:18a).

---

70   Paul writes that *after ye believed, ye were sealed with that Holy Spirit of the
     promise, which is the earnest of our inheritance* (Ephesians 1:13b-14a). He
     refers to the same "earnest" in 2 Corinthians 1:22 and 5:5. If the experience of
     Christians over the past two thousand years of the church age is the earnest of
     our inheritance, what will the fullness of the Spirit be like?

71   There are several words in the original text that are translated into modern
     English as, *love,* in English. One is *agape,* translated by the early reformers as
     charity. The Greek word, *phileos,* is also translated as, *love.*

14:29 *And now I have told you before it comes to pass, that when it is come to pass, ye might believe.*

14:30 *Hereafter I will not talk much with you, for the prince of this world comes and has nothing in me.*

Satan planned to have the very Jews who were supposed to be God's chosen people judge Jesus according to the law that God had given Moses, find him guilty of a criminal offense, and sentence him to death. Satan was convinced that if he could legally have Jesus killed in this manner, he could claim victory in his rebellion against God. Since no one had ever been able to keep the law perfectly up until that point, Satan thought Jesus didn't stand a chance. It never once occurred to him that Jesus would be motivated to die voluntarily on behalf of fallen humanity. But Jesus was aware of Satan's plan and told his disciples in advance that *the prince of this world comes and has nothing in me.*

14:31 *But that the world may know that I love the Father; and as the Father gave me commandment, even so I do. Arise, let us go from here.*

Jesus came to do his Father's will, not his own. He acknowledged that Satan was the prince of this world, but he also knew Satan had no legal right to take him hostage by death, because Jesus was not *of* this world and had never acted according to the ways of this world. Jesus was completely confident that he had said and done only what the Father had ordained for him.

The above discourse appears to have taken place in the upper room that was the scene of the Last Supper. Jesus wanted to demonstrate his love for his Father to the entire world, and so even though he knew what lay ahead, he chose to continue along the way of the cross.

Let us pray

Dear Heavenly Father, we ask that our love for the Lord Jesus will be so intense that we will desire to love one another even as he has loved us. We ask for the indwelling fullness of the Holy Spirit so we can love one another as never before. May the world then see that we truly love you with all our heart, with all our mind, and with all our soul. We ask this in the name of our Lord Jesus Christ. Amen.

Chapter 14

The Comforter is the Key

I believe chapters 13, 14, 15, 16, and 17 of the gospel of John contain a most important message filled with extraordinarily great and precious promises. As noted in the introduction to Part I of this book, chapters 5, 6, and 7 of Matthew, widely known as the Sermon on the Mount, have also been called the Little Gospel, or the Magna Carta of the Kingdom of Heaven. In those chapters, Jesus describes how his kingdom will function. But here in the latter part of the gospel of John, we find the explanation and secret that is essential knowledge for everyone who will be part of that kingdom.

What Jesus tells us in these chapters must be implemented, however, or there will be no glorious kingdom. In Matthew 6, the disciples wanted Jesus to teach them to pray, and he did. We call it the Lord's Prayer. In contrast, John 17 contains Jesus' prayer of intercession for us, spoken as he was about to enter into his new role as high priest of the order of Melchisedec to mediate the new covenant in our favor: "mediate" in the sense that if we enter into what Jesus asks of us, he assures us that we may ask whatever we will of the Father in his name, and our request will be granted (John 14:13; 15:16; 16:23-24).

Jesus' intercessory petition has no risk of failure, for the Father delights in answering his Son's prayers. Nevertheless, for us there is still a risk. We may be among the those who will enjoy the blessing and the privileges the Lord outlines in John 17, or as individuals we may be excluded from this group. If we do not allow the Lord to use us to accomplish what he has in mind (as described in the latter half of this chapter), he will use someone else to achieve the same object, because the Father will not reject Jesus' last earthly desire and request. For many are called but few are chosen, and the time of fulfillment is at hand.

John 15

15:1 *I AM the true vine, and my Father is the husbandman.*

Jesus is *the true vine* and his Father is *the husbandman*. They are two completely different persons, yet here again Jesus applies God's sacred name (I AM) to himself.

15:2 *Every branch in me that does not bear fruit he shall take away; and every one that bears fruit, he shall purge that they may bring forth more fruit.*

Note that judgment and discipline are the province of the Father, the husbandman, who will take away every branch (even of the true vine) that does not bear fruit and will purge the branches that do bear fruit, so they will bring forth yet more fruit.

15:3 *Now ye are clean through the word which I have spoken unto you.*

When we receive the word Jesus speaks unto us, we are cleansed. For instance, when he told the woman caught in adultery to *go and sin no more*, she was given a real, substantive opportunity to embrace his word and be clean.

15:4 *Abide in me, and I in you. As the branch*

> *cannot bear fruit of itself, except it abides in the*
> *vine, no more can ye, except ye abide in me.*

Unless we stay connected to Jesus, it is impossible for us to bear good fruit.

What is the fruit Jesus is talking about?

Godly character. Specifically, *the fruit of the Spirit is this: Charity, joy, peace, tolerance, gentleness, goodness, faith, meekness, temperance* (Galatians 5:22-23a). *For the fruit of the Spirit is in all goodness and righteousness and truth* (Ephesians 5:9). Jesus and his Father want to bring forth fruit in us that will be a blessing to those around us.

> *15:5 I AM the vine, ye are the branches: he that*
> *abides in me, and I in him, the same brings forth*
> *much fruit; for without me ye can do nothing.*

> *15:6 He who does not abide in me shall be cast forth*
> *as an unsound branch and shall wither, and they*
> *are gathered and cast into the fire and are burned.*

Jesus is the true vine, but it is possible for a branch of that vine to be cast forth as unsound. Should that happen, the branch will wither, and eventually it will be gathered, cast into the fire, and burned. The evidence that we truly abide in Jesus and he abides in us is the fruit that is produced (see Matthew 7:15-20 for a parallel passage).

> *15:7 If ye abide in me and my words abide in you, ye*
> *shall ask what ye will, and it shall be done unto you.*

> *15:8 In this is my Father clarified, in that ye bear*
> *much fruit; and in this manner ye shall be my*
> *disciples.*

If we abide in Jesus and his words abide in us, not only will we bear good fruit, we will also be able to ask what we will and it

shall be done unto us. Bearing good fruit and receiving what
we ask for will clarify the Father – that is, make his nature
clear – as his plan and purpose are revealed in and through us
for the entire world to see.

We are branches that need to be connected directly to Jesus
so his life can flow through us. There is no room here for an
intermediating clergy that would place itself between the people
and God. Jesus is the only mediator of the new covenant. Those
who practice true ministry will join the people to Jesus, not
to themselves.

> 15:9 *As the Father has loved me, so I have loved you;*
> *abide in my love.*

Judas chose not to abide in Jesus' love. When Judas left the
room to betray him, Jesus was *troubled in spirit* (John 13:21).
Jesus and his Father will not allow anyone to pluck us out of his
hand (John 10:28-29), but we are always free to leave, for *where
that Spirit of the Lord is, there is liberty* (2 Corinthians 3:17).

> 15:10 *If ye keep my commandments, ye shall abide*
> *in my love, even as I have kept my Father's com-*
> *mandments and abide in his love.*

It is the very nature of Jesus to love his Father and to keep his
Father's commandments. If we abide in Jesus, his divine life and
nature will flow in and through us, and we will delight in his
commandments. Jesus did not really even have to overtly petition
his Father in order to make his requests known. Sometimes he
prayed as a demonstration to his disciples, but his communion
with his Father is beyond our mortal comprehension. When
Jesus showed mercy to someone, it was not only because his
own nature was merciful but also because he could sense the
feelings of his Father's heart. Jesus desires to place his nature
inside of us. Then, no matter what the emergency or need, our
response will be the same as his.

This can only happen if our hearts are clean, however. Then we will abide in Jesus and he in us, and the Father will approve of the fruit we produce. Even so, the Father will purge us so that we produce yet more fruit of an even better quality.

> 15:11 *These things I have spoken unto you that my joy may abide in you and that your joy might be fulfilled.*

The only way that the joy of Jesus may abide in us and that our joy might be fulfilled, is for us to produce fruit of righteousness that is approved by the Father. We will never be fulfilled or truly satisfied with anything less. In the Sermon on the Mount at the beginning of his earthly ministry, Jesus declared, *Blessed are those who hunger and thirst for righteousness, for they shall be satisfied* (Matthew 5:6).

I wouldn't exchange my vocation in Christ for anything in the world. Following Jesus is tremendously exciting, and I find it deeply fulfilling and rewarding to witness what he does in and through those he chooses. What the Lord does with me he can do with anyone, because there is no limit to what he can accomplish, and he is no respecter of persons (Acts 10:34-35). As the world around us grows worse and worse, as ever-increasing darkness descends on vast sectors of humanity, it is reassuring and uplifting to witness the fruit Jesus is producing in the lives of those who genuinely love one another. Despite the bleakness and desolation in the world, there is cause for much joy.

> 15:12 *This is my commandment, That ye love one another as I have loved you.*

Jesus only gave us one new commandment, and it is one that's quite simple and easy to understand. No special course of study is needed. In order to fulfill it, the only requirement is that we be filled with the Holy Spirit. On the other hand, over time the church has been invaded by complicated doctrines dreamt up by men and devils (Proverbs 18:1), the understanding of which requires many years of intellectual training. And the church's history demonstrates that even when such doctrines are implemented, the love of God does not automatically flow.

> 15:13 *Greater love has no man than this, that a man lay down his soul for his friends.*

> 15:14 *Ye are my friends if ye do whatsoever I command you.*

Jesus commands us to love one another. If we do whatever Jesus commands, we are his friends. What is more, he does not order us to do anything he was not prepared to do himself while on the earth. In fact, he was willing to even *lay down his soul for his friends.* The Greek word translated as "soul" is not *bios*, the word for biological life. It is *pneumos*, the word that also means breath. *Pneumos* is a word that describes a person's very being. In other words, Jesus put everything on the line for us. He did this not only to redeem us but also to set an example for us to follow.

> 15:15 *From now on I do not call you slaves, for the slave does not know what his lord does; but I have called you friends, for all things that I have heard of my Father I have made known unto you.*

> 15:16 *Ye have not chosen me, but I have chosen you and ordained you, that ye should go and bring forth fruit, and that your fruit should remain; that whatever ye shall ask of the Father in my name, he may give it unto you.*

> 15:17 *This I command you, that ye love one another.*

This is the fourth time Jesus repeats his commandment that we are to love one another. The fact that he repeats it several times means it is of absolute and imperative importance.

Jesus chose his disciples carefully, and he selected only those who were willing to leave everything and follow him. There are other Scriptures that are addressed to *whosoever will come* (Mark 8:34) and that make it clear God accepts those who have *a contrite heart* (Psalm 51:17). Here, however, the point is that Jesus has chosen and ordained his disciples for a purpose: that they should bring forth long-lasting fruit. To aid them in this mission, whatever they ask of the Father in Jesus' name may be given unto them.

The fruit Jesus wants to bring forth that should remain is godly character in us and in those we serve, according to the love of God flowing in us and through us. Those who ask the Father for the fleeting things of this world to satisfy their own lust are completely missing the point of prayer.

Near the beginning of his ministry, Jesus advised his listeners to *take no thought, saying, What shall we eat? or, What shall we drink? or, With what shall we be clothed? (For the Gentiles seek after all these things.) For your heavenly Father knows that ye have need of all these things. But seek ye first the kingdom of God and his righteousness, and all these things shall be added unto you* (Matthew 6:31-33).

And later he challenged them, *If ye then, being evil, know how to give good gifts unto your children, how much more shall your Father who is in the heavens give good things to those that ask him?* (Matthew 7:11).

If we ask our heavenly Father for good things, he will give us good things. So instead of attempting to use Jesus' promises like an Aladdin's lamp to satisfy our selfish cravings or puff up our ego, let's ask him to produce the fruit of the Holy Spirit in us. Let's ask him for wisdom and understanding; for victory over the flesh, over sin, over the world, and over the devil; and for supernatural love that will reach the lost and win over even our enemies.

15:18 *If the world hates you, ye know that it hated
me before it hated you.*

15:19 *If ye were of the world, the world would love*[72]
*its own; but because ye are not of the world, but
I have chosen you out of the world, therefore the
world hates you.*

What is the world?

The world is different from the earth. God created the heavens and the earth, and the earth belongs to him (Exodus 9:29; 19:5; 1 Corinthians 10:26). The world, on the other hand, is primarily a system. The Greek word for it is *cosmos*, and it relates to a way of doing things that is diametrically opposed to the way God does them. Satan founded the world system. As you might expect, given that Satan is the father of lies, his system is based on lies, and the consequence of following those lies is sin and death. We mentioned earlier that Satan is the prince of this world. Since it is not possible for anyone to serve two masters, we cannot be the world's friend and God's friend at the same time. And because the world is the domain of Satan, it will hate anyone who is a friend of God.

15:20 *Remember the word that I said unto you, The
slave is not greater than his lord. If they have persecuted me, they will also persecute you; if they have
kept my word, they will keep yours also.*[73]

15:21 *But they will do all these things unto you for
my name's sake, because they do not know him that
sent me.*

Since the world hates Jesus, it will also hate and persecute those

---

72 Greek *phileo*.

73 If we are a friend of the Lord, if we have a clean, pure heart because the Father has purged and cleansed us, and if we are bringing forth the fruit of the Spirit of God, then we can speak and our word will be taken into account by those who keep Jesus' word, because it will be the Lord speaking through us.

who belong to him. Remember that slaves have an owner, and slavery was holding us in bondage under Satan's kingdom of darkness. Because Jesus paid the price that redeemed us from slavery to the flesh and to sin, we belong to him. However, where the Spirit of the Lord is, there is liberty. Jesus wants us to keep his commandments voluntarily so we can be his friends. And his commandment is that we love one another. When Jesus reveals his intimate plans and secrets to us, he isn't sharing them with servants or with slaves, he is sharing them with his friends. When we become friends of Jesus, his friends are our friends and his enemies our enemies.

> 15:22 *If I had not come and spoken unto them, they would not have sin; but now they have no excuse for their sin.*

> 15:23 *He that hates me hates my Father also.*

> 15:24 *If I had not done among them works which no other man has done, they would not have sin; but now they have seen them and hate both me and my Father.*

The Greek word *hamartia*, translated three times as "sin" in the above passage, does not mean (as commonly interpreted) "to miss the mark." It means "to intentionally shoot at the wrong target." When Jesus came and spoke to those who were friends of this world, the confrontation between light and darkness was clear and left them with no excuse (or cloak) for their sin. For this, they hated him, so they turned their fire on him (they shot at the wrong target) in response. If Jesus *had not done among them works which no other man has done, they would not have sin* (their hatred of his miraculous works would not have led them to shoot at the wrong target by persecuting him).[74]

---

74 For further clarification of the use of the word *hamartia* and how its

15:25 But this comes to pass that the word might be fulfilled that is written in their law, They hated me without a cause.[75]

15:26 But when the Comforter is come, whom I will send unto you from the Father, even the Spirit of truth, which proceeds from the Father, he shall testify of me;

15:27 and ye also shall bear witness because ye have been with me from the beginning.[76]

Many people may begin to receive a profound witness regarding the things of God through another person. They may hear a message on the radio or at a meeting or from someone who speaks to them personally. Preaching that is anointed by the Spirit of truth may open their understanding, and they may even hear truth that does not seem to be overtly included in the message. This may help lead them into direct communion with the Lord Jesus and his Father, for if the messenger they encounter has truly been sent and commissioned by God, then a wonderfully simple law comes into effect: if the messenger is received, Jesus is received, and if Jesus is received, the Father is also received. This is how the character and nature of God that is manifest in us may be multiplied into others.

God has exalted him [Jesus] with his right hand as Prince and Saviour, to give repentance to Israel and forgiveness of sins. And we are his witnesses of these

---

misinterpretation has caused serious misunderstanding and confusion, see commentary on 1 John at the end of this volume.

75 The full quote reads: *They compassed me about with words of hatred and fought against me without a cause* (Psalm 109:3). The entire Psalm is messianic and clearly indicates what will happen to Satan and Judas and their associates, who all decided to sit there and take potshots at the wrong target(s).

76 From the beginning of what? From the beginning of the gospel, from the beginning of Jesus public ministry (Mark 1:1).

things, and so is also the Holy Spirit, whom God has given to those that persuade him (Acts 5:31-32).

What must we persuade God of, in order to be given the Holy Spirit?

That we love and trust Jesus; that we desire to love one another; that we submit to the authority of God; and that we wish to be corrected and brought to genuine repentance of anything that displeases God.

How do we persuade him of our sincerity in this?

We can begin by receiving those whom Jesus sends as his witnesses.

Without faith it is impossible to please God (Hebrews 11:6a). Without the Holy Spirit, we will not be connected to Jesus, the true vine. And unless we stay connected to Jesus, it will be impossible for the Father to cleanse and purge us so we will bear fruit in abundance.

If we walk with the Lord Jesus, we will have his peace, which is not like the peace the world gives. We will have his presence inside of us, by the Spirit. We will be his friends, and he will share intimate secrets with us regarding him and his Father. Those who are of the world, however, will hate and persecute us just as they did him. Remember, the worst persecutors of Jesus were from a religious realm that had been absorbed, contaminated, and taken over by the prince of this world, and such people will be eager to persecute us as well.

John 16

16:1 *These things I have spoken unto you that ye should not be offended.*

16:2 *They shall put you out of the synagogues, and the hour will even come when whosoever kills you will think that he does God service.*

16:3 And they will do these things unto you because they do not know the Father, nor me.

Now, almost two thousand years later, many millions of Christians have been martyred, and most of the killing has been at the hands of people who thought they were serving God, even though they were clearly demonstrating that they did not really know Jesus or his Father.

16:4 But I have told you these things that when that hour shall come, ye may remember that I told you of them. And I did not say these things unto you at the beginning because I was with you.

16:5 But now I go unto him that sent me, and none of you asks me, Where goest thou?

16:6 But because I have said these things unto you, sorrow has filled your heart.

The disciples did not understand God's plan or his purpose. They did not comprehend what was about to happen with the coming of the Holy Spirit, and I am convinced there are many people in the earth today who name the name of God, yet find themselves in the same type of confusion.

16:7 Nevertheless I tell you the truth: It is expedient for you that I go away; for if I do not go away, the Comforter will not come unto you; but if I depart, I will send him unto you.

Why?

Jesus' death, resurrection, and ascension would prove to be expedient and indeed essential for many reasons. It would be important for him to win such a significant victory over death and the devil, and it would also be important for him to send us the Comforter. This would enable the disciples (including us) to follow Jesus and walk in his victory by the power of the Holy Spirit as he mediates the new covenant, seated at the right hand of the Father with all power and authority. Jesus had to depart, however, for any of this to take place. He is now high priest after a new order, the order of Melchisedec, meaning "king of righteousness" (Hebrews 5:6), and in this new role he was able to send the Comforter to us.

16:8 *And when he is come, he will reprove the world of sin and of righteousness and of judgment:*

In modern English, "to reprove" means "to reprimand" or "to censure," but in Old English it could mean "to convince or convict" as well as "to refute or disprove."[77] Thus the Holy Spirit will bring people under conviction and reveal their wrong motives.

Those in the world need to be brought under conviction with regard to their sin (Greek *hamartia*) as it concerns Jesus. The Holy Spirit provides the light of truth whose beams can show those who are in error not only that they are intentionally shooting at the wrong target but also reveal the serious consequences ahead if they continue in sin.

In addition, those who are in the world need to be brought under conviction with regard to their misunderstanding of righteousness (which is the same word as "justice" in the Greek). The light of truth can show them that their goals and ambitions are earthly rather than spiritual and that their concept of both righteousness and justice has become perverted and needs to be reviewed and revamped.

The Holy Spirit will also bring them under conviction with regard to the judgment that is to come and the false judgment and condemnation they have heaped upon others. He will make

---

77 According to *Webster's Unabridged Dictionary*, to *reprove* implies "calmness and self-possession" (temperance) and a *reprimand* "proceeds from a person invested with authority."

plain to them both the imminent and the future consequences of their sin and their lack of righteousness and justice.

The role of the Holy Spirit is *to reprove the world of sin and of righteousness and of judgment.* (Our role, on the other hand, is *to love one another* even as Jesus has loved us.)

16:9 *of sin, because they do not believe in me;*

Those who do not believe in Jesus (who is the truth) will never have the right goals and will never shoot at the right target.

16:10 *of righteousness, because I go to my Father, and ye see me no more;*

When Jesus was here in person, he was the manifestation of the righteousness of the Father in the flesh. When he returns to the Father, it falls to the Holy Spirit to demonstrate righteousness to the world. The Holy Spirit, however, operates in and through people like us.

16:11 *of judgment, because the prince of this world is judged.*

The prince of this world was judged on his involvement in the events and circumstances surrounding Jesus' death and resurrection. And as the Holy Spirit operates in and through the genuine disciples of Jesus who make up the bride of Christ, the principalities and powers and the friends of this world continue to be judged.

16:12 *I have yet many things to say unto you, but ye cannot bear them now.*

16:13 *Howbeit when he, the Spirit of truth, is come, he will guide you into all truth, for he shall not speak of himself; but whatsoever he shall hear, that shall he speak, and he will cause you to know the things which are to come.*

Those who have the Holy Spirit have access to all truth and to all knowledge regarding the things that are yet to come. If we lack wisdom, we may ask the Lord and he will respond by the Spirit.

> 16:14 *He shall clarify me, for he shall take of that which is mine and shall cause you to know it.*

> 16:15 *All that the Father has is mine; therefore I said that he shall take of that which is mine and shall cause you to know it.*

This is not the dry, legalistic implementation of the letter of the law (which kills). The ministry of the Holy Spirit brings life to us and can affect everyone with whom we come into contact. When we are cleansed and moved by the Spirit of God, Jesus is clarified. Not only are others aware of his presence within us but they can clearly see his nature. And we have the potential to be brought into both the fullness of Jesus' victory and into a direct relationship with God, the Father.

> 16:16 *A little while, and ye shall not see me; and again, a little while, and ye shall see me, because I go to the Father.*

After his resurrection, Jesus would *go to the Father* prior to appearing to his disciples. We will look into this in more detail later (John 20:17).

> 16:17 *Then some of his disciples said among themselves, What is this that he says unto us, A little while, and ye shall not see me; and again, a little while, and ye shall see me; and, Because I go to the Father?*

> 16:18 *They said therefore, What is this that he says, A little while? we cannot understand what he says.*

The natural man finds it difficult, if not impossible, to grasp the things of the Spirit, and the disciples were no exception to that fact. After all, mere *flesh and blood cannot inherit the Kingdom of God* (1 Corinthians 15:50). Just a few weeks later, however, the same disciples who were now so confused would collectively – and effectively – witness for Jesus in the power of the Holy Spirit, a power that is described as the earnest or down payment of our inheritance (2 Corinthians 1:22; 5:5). Many people are drawn to the love of God and to the truth they see in us, and they will probably ask questions of us and of each other as they attempt to understand our witness. This issue can only be resolved, however, when each one develops their own personal relationship with Jesus and is baptized (immersed) by him into the Holy Spirit (the Comforter). This is the only path toward knowing the Father.

> 16:19 *Now Jesus knew that they were desirous to ask him and said unto them, Do ye enquire among yourselves of what I said, A little while, and ye shall not see me; and again, a little while, and ye shall see me?*

> 16:20 *Verily, verily, I say unto you, That ye shall weep and lament, and the world shall rejoice; but even though ye shall be sorrowful, your sorrow shall be turned into joy.*

> 16:21 *The woman, when she is in travail, has pain, because her hour is come; but as soon as she is delivered of the child, she remembers the anguish no more, for joy that a man is born into the world.*[78]

---

78 Revelation 12:1-5 seems to be a parallel passage. Jesus is the head of the new free-born man, and members have been added to the body of Christ throughout history with much travail and pain. Just as Jesus was *caught up unto God and to his throne,* so it will also be with the rest of us who will reign with Christ with *power over the Gentiles* (Revelation 2:26) and *rule all the Gentiles with a rod of iron* (Revelation 12:5).

> *16:22 And ye now therefore have sorrow; but I will*
> *see you again, and your heart shall rejoice, and no*
> *one shall take your joy from you.*

True joy is a fruit of the Spirit, and no one in this present world can take it from us or even diminish it.

> *16:23 And in that day ye shall ask me nothing.*
> *Verily, verily, I say unto you, Whatever ye shall ask*
> *the Father in my name, he will give you.*

> *16:24 Until now ye have asked nothing in my name;*
> *ask, and ye shall receive, that your joy may be*
> *fulfilled.*

The Father has many blessings that he longs to bestow on us, but we first have to ask him. Having asked, we will receive, and our joy will be fulfilled. One of the most important things we can ask for (and receive) is for the Father to send us the Comforter.

> *16:25 I have spoken these things unto you in prov-*
> *erbs, but the hour comes when I shall no longer*
> *speak unto you in proverbs, but I shall show you*
> *plainly of the Father.*

Proverbs and parables are essentially the same thing, both being forms of symbolic speech. *And he said unto them, Unto you it is given to know the mystery of the kingdom of God; but unto those that are without, all these things are done in parables* (Mark 4:11). Those who are privy to *the mystery of the kingdom of God* are those who will be given the Comforter, who will guide them *into all truth.* This is how Jesus will *show us plainly of the Father.*

> *16:26 In that day ye shall ask in my name, and I do*
> *not say unto you that I will ask the Father for you;*

> *16:27 for the Father himself loves you because ye*

have loved me and have believed that I came out
from God.

Jesus is the truth, and the Father loves those who love his Son. Those who genuinely seek the truth are really seeking Jesus, and those who love the truth really love Jesus, even though they may not know him by that name. Those who receive us and love us because God has sent us and we stand for the truth will also be loved by Jesus and the Father.

Some believe God loves us unconditionally in our unregenerate natural state, but this isn't exactly the case.[79] Translation and terminology have caused some confusion in this regard. As mentioned previously, there are several very different Greek words that have been translated as "love" in English. The Greek word *phileos*, for example, has to do with brotherly love. *Agape*, on the other hand, is the Greek noun that describes God's redemptive love, and *agapao* is its verb form. *Agape* is properly translated as "charity" in many of the older English Bibles; however, in English (unlike Greek), "charity" is not a verb, and thus in English Scriptures, there is no way to properly separate these two very different words in texts that use "love" as a verb.

When Scripture states that *God so loved the world*, the root word translated "loved" is *agapao*, not *phileos*. This means God decided to have charity (i.e., mercy) toward the world and sent his only begotten Son to die for us (John 3:16). It does not mean God is enamored of the world or the conduct of unregenerate sinners. *Agape* love, or charity, is not primarily an emotion. It is a decision involving sacrifice and is redemptive by its very

---

79 God is, of course, deeply concerned about the lost. However, in our unregenerate state as rebels, there is something in us that God definitely does not love and that is totally incompatible with his nature and presence. Therefore, if we were to stand before God in our natural state, we would be destroyed by his very presence. This is clearly represented in the OT by the veil between the holy place and the holy of holies, embroidered with the cherubim, as well as by the flaming sword placed by God so that man could not return to the Garden of Eden and to his direct presence. This incompatibility is why Jesus came to redeem us.

nature. God chose to give us his only Son, and Jesus chose to come here as a man and die for us. As humans, we lack the capacity to demonstrate *agape* love without God. This is why, if we are to produce good fruit and flow in the love of God, we must stay connected to Jesus, who is the vine. When he commands us to love one another, it is the Greek verb *agapao*, and we are therefore required to demonstrate sacrificial charity and mercy to one another, even if we doubt that the other person deserves it. In so doing, we extend God's redemption, healing, and restoration in the world. We are even asked to love (*agapao*) our enemies (Matthew 5:44; Luke 6:27).

John 16:27 above tells us *the Father himself **loves** you.* Here the Greek word *phileos* is used, indicating that the Father has a deep emotional attachment and affection for us. The implication is that he wholeheartedly approves of us. Jesus said this is *because ye have **loved** me and have believed that I came out from God.* Again, the word used is *phileos*, meaning we have demonstrated a deep emotional attachment and affection for Jesus and wholeheartedly approve of him.

> 16:28 *I came forth from the Father and am come into the world; again, I leave the world and go to the Father.*

> 16:29 *His disciples said unto him, Behold, now thou speakest plainly and speakest no proverb.*

> 16:30 *Now we understand that thou knowest all things and needest not that anyone should ask thee; by this we believe that thou didst come forth from God.*

The disciples were doing their best to make sense out of all that Jesus had been telling them. They wanted to encourage Jesus, and they desperately wanted to believe in him. They had left everything for his sake and had spent the past three and a half years faithfully following him. They confirmed that they understood Jesus knew all things and it was not their place to question him, even though he had said many things that were very hard for them to understand. They expressed confidence that they genuinely believed he did *come forth from God.* Yet Jesus responded with a very serious question.

16:31 *Jesus answered them, Do ye now believe?*

16:32 *Behold, the hour comes and is now come, that ye shall be scattered, each one to his own, and shall leave me alone; and yet I am not alone, because the Father is with me.*

Clearly, there was a discrepancy between what the disciples meant when they said they believed, and what Jesus meant when he asked, *Do ye now believe?* The disciples thought that to believe was to acknowledge what they saw to be the obvious facts of who Jesus was, where he had come from, and where he said he was going. This was a good start, but when Jesus asked whether they now believed, he meant much more than that. Were they willing to completely trust and depend on him, just as he totally depended upon his Father?

Jesus knew that soon, in a frantic attempt to save their own lives, these men would all scatter and leave him alone. However, in the weeks and months and years ahead, they would not only constantly remember his words, they would all repeatedly put their lives on the line for the cause of Jesus Christ and his gospel. The book of the Acts of the Apostles bears this out. The disciples, the apostles, and countless others throughout history would follow Jesus' example and go the way of the cross. Jesus summed it up like this:

16:33 *These things I have spoken unto you that in*

me ye might have peace. In the world ye shall have tribulation; but be of good cheer; I have overcome the world.

Jesus had called them out of the world, and he still calls people like us out of the world to follow him. In Jesus Christ we can have peace, even though the world will rage against us as it did against him. In the midst of trials and tribulations, we are to *be of good cheer* because Jesus has *overcome the world*, and in him we can also overcome and rejoice, no matter what the hardship (Matthew 5:10-12).

Let us pray

Heavenly Father, we desire to learn to ask according to Jesus' will and his name and his nature, and not according to our own will or our own life, so that your will may be done on earth even as it is in heaven. Amen.

Chapter 15

Jesus' High Priestly Prayer

John 17

17:1 Jesus spoke these words and lifted up his eyes to heaven and said, Father, the hour is come; clarify thy Son, that thy Son may also clarify thee,

Jesus did not bow his head and close his eyes, as we so often do. Instead, he lifted up his eyes to heaven and asked the Father to clarify him. The devil and his followers in the world had been questioning Jesus' motive and witness, and their attempt to smear him was also an attempt to smear the Father. Now, the hour had come to clarify exactly why Jesus had come to the earth and why the Father had sent him.

17:2 as thou hast given him power over all flesh, that he should give eternal life to as many as thou hast given him.

Jesus had not yet died for us, but it was already clear that the Father had *given him power over all flesh.* Even before his death and resurrection, Jesus forgave sins and promised eternal life, not just to a few people but to as many as the Father had given him.

*17:3 And this is life eternal, that they might know
thee the only true God and Jesus Christ, whom thou
hast sent.*

Here is Jesus' definition of eternal life. His prayer to his Father
was clearly designed to be overheard by his disciples at the
time and passed on to each subsequent generation of disciples.

*17:4 I have clarified thee on the earth; I have fin-
ished the work which thou didst give me to do.*

What was the work the Father had given Jesus to do?

It was to clarify the Father upon the earth. Until Jesus took
on the form of man, no one at any time had ever seen God the
Father. Now, those who had been with Jesus (with spiritual eyes
to see) had seen the Father, who dwelt in him by the fullness of
the Spirit. And soon it would be possible for Jesus to be present
in the disciples by the Spirit.

*17:5 And now, O Father, clarify thou me with thine
own self with that clarity which I had with thee
before the world was.*

Jesus is referring to the dazzling, brilliant clarity that he had with
the Father before Satan started the world system by deceiving
Eve and maneuvering Adam into rebellion against God. Jesus
and the Father created the heavens and the earth and the seas,
along with creatures that could live in each of these realms.
They were aware ahead of time of the possible consequences
of giving free will to men and to angels. The clarity Jesus had
with the Father *before the world was* included his willingness to
die for us, should the need arise and should the Father request
him to do so, for Jesus is the Lamb *slain from the foundation
of the world* (Revelation 13:8b).

*17:6 I have manifested thy name unto the men
which thou didst give me out of the world; thine they*

were, and thou didst give them me; and they have
kept thy word.

Jesus repeatedly pronounced the sacred name of God (I AM)
in relation to himself, and he manifested the eternal existence
of God while here in the flesh. He also manifested the name
(nature) of the Father to the men whom the Father gave him.
Note that here it also says the Father also gave Jesus unto the
men that he had given Jesus out of the world (*thou didst give*
them me). Jesus is the gift of salvation; Jesus is the gift of eternal life, and the Father is the giver. Jesus stresses that these
men belonged to the Father first, and he vouches for the fact
that after being given to him, they have continued to keep the
Father's word.

> 17:7 *Now they have known that all things whatso-*
> *ever thou hast given me are of thee.*

Everything God the Father has given Jesus belonged to the
Father and was his to give to the Son, and the disciples have
been made aware of this. Yet because Jesus and his Father are
one, if we are among those given to Jesus by the Father, we also
still belong to the Father.

> 17:8 *For I have given unto them the words which*
> *thou gavest me; and they have received them and*
> *have known surely that I came out from thee, and*
> *they have believed that thou didst send me.*

Here Jesus is bearing witness and confirming that the disciples have received the words the Father gave him, that they
know for a certainty that he came out from the Father, and
that they believe the Father sent him. As Jesus' prayer continues, it becomes evident that he desires to bring them into an
even higher realm of faith by placing the Comforter inside of
each disciple, though in his prayer he does not mention the
Comforter by name.

*17:9 I pray for them; I do not pray for the world,
but for those whom thou hast given me; for they are
thine.*

*17:10 And all my things are thine, and thine are
mine; and I have been clarified in them.*

Jesus isn't praying for those who are in rebellion out in the world
but only for those whom the Father has given him. Everyone
and everything that belongs to Jesus belongs to the Father and
vice versa. This includes the disciples, of course, and Jesus
declares that he has been clarified in them. Quite a statement!
If we belong to Jesus and to the Father, then we will clarify
Jesus to those around us by our words and deeds and attitude.

*17:11 And now I am no longer in the world, but
these are in the world, and I come to thee. Holy
Father, those whom thou hast given me, keep them
in thy name, that they may be one, as we are.*

If the Father does not keep us in his name (in his nature), we
will not be kept. Among the Psalms collected by King David,
who was an example of the coming Messiah being both prophet
and priest, we find these assertions: *Unless the LORD had been
my help, my soul would have quickly dwelt with the dead* (Psalm
94:17); *Unless the LORD builds the house, they labour in vain
that build it; unless the LORD keeps the city, the watchmen watch
in vain* (Psalm 127:1).

*17:12 While I was with them in the world, I kept
them in thy name; those that thou gavest me I have
kept, and none of them is lost, but the son of perdition, that the scripture might be fulfilled.*

Jesus kept the disciples in the Father's name while he was here,
and he could certify to his Father that *none of them is lost, but
the son of perdition.* The disciples he was able to keep were those

who belonged to God, but *the son of perdition* was an entirely different matter. Jesus was obviously aware that according to Scripture, someone close to him would betray him (Psalm 41:9), but nevertheless when it had become evident earlier that this person was Judas, he was *troubled in spirit* (John 13:21). When Judas had arrived at the Last Supper, he already had in his possession the thirty pieces of silver for which he had sold Jesus. Even knowing of his betrayal, Jesus washed Judas's feet along with the feet of the other disciples, but it was to no avail because Judas was not clean (John 13:10).

> 17:13 *And now I come to thee; and these things I speak in the world that they might have my joy fulfilled in themselves.*

Jesus would soon be in heaven with his Father, but he didn't wait to speak these things until he could do so from his throne there. He spoke them while he was still *in the world* so that his disciples (including disciples like us) might have his joy fulfilled in them.

> 17:14 *I have given them thy word, and the world has hated them because they are not of the world, even as I am not of the world.*

> 17:15 *I do not pray that thou should take them out of the world, but that thou should keep them from the evil.*

Jesus would not be asking the Father to keep his disciples (including us) from *the evil*, even while we are still in the world, if this were not possible.

> 17:16 *They are not of the world, even as I am not of the world.*

> 17:17 *Sanctify them in thy truth; thy word is the truth.*

To be "sanctified" is to be separated out and dedicated to the exclusive service of God. The Father will set us apart as vessels of honor in his truth. The word of the Father is the truth, just as Jesus is the truth, for Jesus is the living Word of God. Therefore, we are to be sanctified in Jesus as members of the universal body of Christ.

> 17:18 *As thou hast sent me into the world, even so have I also sent them into the world.*

> 17:19 *And for their sakes I sanctify myself, that they also might be sanctified in the truth.*

Jesus, as our high priest after the order of Melchisedec, sanctified himself for our sake, setting himself apart to serve and minister exclusively unto God so we might *also be sanctified in the truth.*

> 17:20 *Neither do I pray for these alone, but also for those who shall believe in me through their word;*

Here, Jesus doubles down and makes it perfectly clear that he is praying not just for the eleven disciples who were with him at the time but also for *those who shall believe in me through their word.* We are included.

> 17:21 *that they all may be one; as thou, Father, art in me, and I in thee, that they also may be one in us, that the world may believe that thou hast sent me.*

Jesus, as High Priest and as the only mediator of the new covenant in which God will write his laws on the tablets of our hearts and in our minds, asks the Father that all of his disciples may be one, even as he and his Father are one. This is so the world may believe that God the Father really did send Jesus. So far, the history of the church has been a mixed bag. There have been some excellent examples of love and unity among those who belong to the body of Christ, but there have also been many disasters. Today, there are innumerable sects, denominations, and divisions among groups and among individuals claiming to be followers of Jesus Christ, but it is evident that most of the world still does not believe.

Jesus told his disciples (including us) to ask the Father what we will in his name and it will be granted, and our joy will then be complete. If even our own petitions to the Father will be taken into account and granted, what will happen regarding the petitions of Jesus, his only begotten Son? Even though we have not yet seen the fullness of the Father's response to Jesus' prayer, we can know with absolute certainty that the time will come when all of his disciples will be as one. For this to happen, each individual son (or daughter) must submit to the chastening and discipline of Father God (Proverbs 3:12). The time will come (it is not far off) when the tares (the sons of the Evil One) will be removed from among the wheat (the sons of God), as Judas was removed from among the disciples.

> 17:22 *And the clarity which thou gavest me I have given them, that they may be one, even as we are one:*

Clarity relates to light and transparency and glory. The clarity the Father gave to Jesus has in turn been given to us that we might be as one, and the darkness will never be able to overpower the light and clarity of Jesus Christ, whom the Father has given to us. Rest assured that one way or another, Jesus' request will be granted.

> 17:23 *I in them, and thou in me, that they may be perfect in one and that the world may know that thou hast sent me and hast loved[80] them as thou hast loved me.*

---

80   The Greek word translated twice as "loved" in the above verse is *agape*, and this is also used in verses 24 and 26.

When we, Jesus' disciples and followers, are *perfect in one*, then the world will know that the Father has sent Jesus and has loved us even as he has loved Jesus.

Exactly when will this happen?

We already discussed the living parable of the resurrection of Lazarus (meaning "without help"), which is an example of the promised first resurrection (Revelation 20:4-6). And we know it took place prior to Jesus' triumphal entry, which is an example of his second coming. We also know Jesus will return for a bride *not having spot or wrinkle or any such thing* and *that she should be holy and without blemish* (Ephesians 5:27).

It seems to me that in order for Jesus' bride to be perfect and holy, without blemish or spot or wrinkle or any such thing, at least two major events will take place: (1) the body of Christ will come to maturity, which will allow God to send the fullness of the Spirit instead of the earnest that we have been experiencing up until now, and (2) at some point, the first resurrection will occur in response to Jesus' voice, at which time his bride will be complete here upon the earth and ready to be caught up and meet him in the air.[81]

The effect of a mature body of Christ under the full, unlimited anointing of the Spirit (John 3:34), followed by (or coupled with) the first resurrection, will set the stage for Jesus' physical return. This will convince the world that God the Father really did send Jesus and that the mature, many-membered body of Christ grew out of his handful of disciples. Satan and his minions will cower in fear, desperately seeking to hide

---

81   *For if we believe that Jesus died and rose again, even so those who sleep in Jesus will God also bring with him. For this, we say unto you by the word of the Lord, that we who are alive and remain unto the coming of the Lord shall not precede those who are asleep. For the Lord himself shall descend from heaven with a shout, with the voice of the archangel, and with the trumpet of God; and the dead in Christ shall rise first; then we who are alive and remain shall be caught up together with them in the clouds, to meet the Lord in the air, and so shall we ever be with the Lord* (1 Thessalonians 4:14-17).

themselves in the caves and among the rocks of the mountains (Revelation 6:15-17).

> 17:24 *Father, I will that they also, whom thou hast given me, be with me where I am, that they may behold my clarity, which thou hast given me, for thou hast loved me from before the foundation of the world.*

Those who are clean and pure because they have been purged, disciplined, and cleansed by the Father will be transformed when they come face to face with the clarity of Jesus (2 Corinthians 3:18). The man of sin, however, will be revealed, consumed, and removed. *And then shall that Wicked one be revealed, whom the Lord shall consume with the Spirit of his mouth and remove with the clarity of his coming* (2 Thessalonians 2:8). This is true of Satan, but it also applies to all of his followers.

> 17:25 *O righteous[82] Father, the world has not known thee; but I have known thee, and these have known that thou hast sent me.*

Even before the Comforter (that is, the indwelling presence of the Holy Spirit) was made available to every believer, Jesus' disciples fully accepted that the Father had sent him, and knowing from where he really came, they had received him wholeheartedly. The scribes and Pharisees and priests, however, claimed they did not know from whence he came. When the love of Jesus flows in and through us, it causes many in the world around us to receive us and to accept that we also have been sent by God, and this acceptance will intensify as the time of the end draws near.

> 17:26 *And I have manifested unto them thy name and will manifest it still, that the love with which thou hast loved me may be in them, and I in them.*

---

82   Remember, in the Greek, "righteous" is the same word as "just."

Jesus manifested the name (nature) of the Father while he was here on earth, and he will (and does) manifest it still by the Holy Spirit as he operates in and through people like us, so that both Christ and the *agape* love of God the Father will be in us.

Let us pray

Heavenly Father, we join with our Lord Jesus Christ in his petition that we (as disciples and followers of Jesus and part of his royal priesthood sanctified unto you) may be as one, even as Jesus is one with you, so the world may know that you have sent Jesus and that you have loved us even as you have loved him. Amen.

Chapter 16

From the Garden of Gethsemane to the Garden at Golgotha

John 18

18:1 *When Jesus had spoken these things, he went forth with his disciples over the brook Cedron, where there was a garden, into which he entered, and his disciples.*

C edron" is the same as "Kidron," which means "turbid." This marked the point of no return as Jesus continued along the way of the cross. In both Jesus' last message to his disciples and his prayer to his Father, clarity was a major theme. In order to clarify his name and his Father's name, he must cross the murky brook named Cedron. Jesus' decision to go all the way to the cross for us would cut through the turbid, religious, self-righteous smoke screen that Satan and his followers had been spewing.

18:2 *And Judas also, who betrayed him, knew the place: for Jesus gathered there often with his disciples.*

Jesus knew that once he crossed the Cedron and entered the garden on the other side of the brook, there would be no turning back, because Judas and his lynch mob would lying in wait for him.

> 18:3 *Judas then, taking a company of soldiers and ministers of the high priests and of the Pharisees, came there with lanterns and torches and weapons.*

Judas appeared suddenly, leading a company of Roman soldiers and ministers (servants) of the high priests and of the Pharisees. Throughout church history, many of Satan's henchmen have, like Judas, used a combination of secular and religious power to hunt down, persecute, and kill the true followers of Jesus Christ. It seems they prefer to operate at night *with lanterns and torches and weapons* of this world.

> 18:4 *Jesus therefore, knowing all the things that should come upon him, went forth, and said unto them, Whom seek ye?*

> 18:5 *They answered him, Jesus of Nazareth. Jesus said unto them, I AM. And Judas also, who betrayed him, stood with them.*

> 18:6 *And when he said unto them, I AM, they went backward and fell to the ground.*

> 18:7 *Then he asked them again, Whom seek ye? And they said, Jesus of Nazareth.*

> 18:8 *Jesus answered, I have told you that I AM; if, therefore, ye seek me, let these go away,*

> 18:9 *that the word might be fulfilled, which he spoke, Of those whom thou gavest me I have lost none.*

Jesus didn't want any of his remaining disciples to be captured and killed by the lynch mob before his death, resurrection, and ascension that would trigger the coming of the Holy Spirit. In accordance with the desire of his Father, he had called, trained, and prepared the disciples for this series of events, and he did not want to lose any of them.

> 18:10 *Then Simon Peter, having a sword, drew it and smote the high priest's slave and cut off his right ear. The slave's name was Malchus.*

"Malchus" means "counselor," and he was *the high priest's slave*, that is, the personal property of the high priest. Therefore Malchus's right ear belonged to the high priest, and in a certain sense, Simon Peter had just cut off the ear with which the high priest was supposed to hear from God for the entire nation. The right ear symbolizes the high priest's God-given position and authority, which would now be cut off and revoked, as a new high priest of the order of Melchisedec was to be sanctified and instituted forever. Simon Peter's sword is symbolic of the word of God that Jesus left with his disciples. Even though Jesus, the living Word, would be returning to his Father, his word would continue to operate in and through us by *the sword of the Spirit, which is the word of God* (Ephesians 6:17).

> 18:11 *Then Jesus said unto Peter, Put up thy sword into the sheath; the cup which my Father has given me, shall I not drink it?*

Luke gives us another account of the same event:

> *And while he yet spoke, behold a multitude, and he that was called Judas, one of the twelve, went before them and drew near unto Jesus to kiss him. But Jesus said unto him, Judas, betrayest thou the Son of man with a kiss? When those who were about him saw what would follow, they said unto him, Lord,*

shall we smite with the sword? And one of them
smote the slave of the prince of the priests and cut
off his right ear. And Jesus answered and said, Suffer
ye thus far. And he touched his ear and healed him.
(Luke 22:47-51)

Some of the disciples suddenly realized what was about to happen and asked Jesus if they should *smite with the sword*. By the time Jesus answered, Simon Peter had already cut off the right ear of the high priest's slave. Jesus' answer was, *Suffer ye thus far*. In other words, he seemed to authorize Peter's actions up to this point but no further. Jesus then healed Malchus. This incident was, therefore, not about a personal issue with Malchus but rather a living parable of what the slave represented.

In yet another gospel account, Jesus said to Peter, *Put up again thy sword into its place, for all those that take the sword shall perish by the sword* (Matthew 26:52). Jesus allowed Peter and Malchus to engage in a spiritual object lesson, but he did not want Peter to kill anyone or to set a precedent for Jesus' followers (then or in the future) to rely on natural weapons.[83]

18:12 *Then the company of soldiers and the tribune*[84]
and the ministers of the Jews took Jesus and bound
him

18:13 *and led him away to Annas first, for he was*
father-in-law to Caiaphas, who was the high priest

---

83 *For though we walk in the flesh, we do not war after the flesh (For the weapons of our warfare are not carnal, but mighty through God for the destruction of strong holds), casting down reasonings and every high thing that exalts itself against the knowledge of God and leading captive every thought into the obedience of the Christ and having a readiness to avenge all disobedience, when your obedience is fulfilled* (2 Corinthians 10:3-6).

84 The Roman tribune was most likely the highest-ranking Roman military officer in Jerusalem and would undoubtedly have had a number of centurions under his command. His presence is an indicator that this was not just any random group of soldiers; it shows that Jesus' betrayal and capture were orchestrated from the top. The high priests and the Pharisees had involved the Romans at the very highest level, well in advance, to make sure nothing would go wrong with their nefarious plot to betray and kill Jesus.

of that year and he sent him bound unto Caiaphas,
the high priest.

"Annas" means "grace of the LORD" and "Caiaphas" means "dell" or "depression" (i.e., a hollow in the terrain). Annas and Caiaphas apparently took turns being the high priest (Luke 3:2; Acts 4:6). They presented themselves as being representatives of the grace or favor of the LORD, but they really represented a new low or depression of corrupt religious power.

18:14 *Now Caiaphas was he who had given the*
counsel to the Jews that it was expedient that one
man should die for the people.

Caiaphas gave this counsel after the resurrection of Lazarus (John 11:45-53). We can also infer that the high priests were of the sect of the Sadducees, who *say that there is no resurrection, neither angel, nor spirit; but the Pharisees confess both* (Acts 23:8). While there is evidence that some of the Pharisees eventually became legalistic believers (Acts 15:5), and some of them even defended Paul at his trial many years later (Acts 23:9), the same is not true of the Sadducees.

The Sadducees did not change their position even after the irrefutable resurrection of Lazarus. Instead, they doubled down on it by deciding that Jesus must be killed, and Caiaphas gave unwittingly prophetic *counsel to the Jews that it was expedient that one man should die for the people.* Caiaphas subsequently lost his "right ear" to the sword of Simon Peter, and the Levitical line of high priests soon came to an end, with the priesthood being transposed to Jesus Christ of the order of Melchisedec,[85] *who is not made according to the law of a carnal commandment, but by the virtue of an indissoluble life.* Jesus *continues forever* and *has the intransmissible priesthood* (Psalm 110:4; Hebrews 7).

18:15 *And Simon Peter followed Jesus, and so did*

---

85   In the OT, Melchisedec, is spelled, Melchizedek.

> *another disciple; that disciple was known unto the high priest and went in with Jesus into the palace of the high priest.*
>
> *18:16 But Peter stood at the door without. Then that other disciple, who was known unto the high priest, went out and spoke unto her that kept the door and brought in Peter.*

The other unnamed disciple mentioned above was undoubtedly the apostle John, who did not want to appear as a protagonist in his own narrative.

> *18:17 Then the damsel that kept the door said unto Peter, Art not thou also one of this man's disciples? He said, I am not.*
>
> *18:18 And the slaves and servants stood there, who had made a fire of coals, for it was cold, and they warmed themselves; and Peter stood with them and warmed himself.*

Peter was cold and wanted to warm himself physically, but he did not want to venture into the fire of trial and tribulation beside Jesus. Instinctively, without premeditation, he denied Jesus to protect his own life. In a sudden crisis, the instinct to save our own lives first and foremost is a common human weakness, and many of us have yielded to it in one way or another.

> *18:19 The high priest then asked Jesus of his disciples and of his doctrine.*

Religious inquisitors are always concerned about the correctness (or otherwise) of our doctrine and always demand a list of our associates. God, on the other hand, judges us according to our fruit. He looks at our character and attitude and how these have affected others. Although right doctrine is obviously significant, the fruit that our life demonstrates is even more important to God. We will exhibit either the rotten, poisonous fruit of the life of fallen Adam or the righteous, wholesome fruit of the life of Jesus Christ.

> 18:20 *Jesus answered him, I spoke openly to the world; I always taught in the synagogue and in the temple, where all the Jews gather; and I have said nothing in secret.*

> 18:21 *Why dost thou ask me? Ask those who heard me what I have said unto them; behold, they know what I said.*

> 18:22 *And when he had thus spoken, one of the servants who stood by struck Jesus with the palm of his hand, saying, Answerest thou the high priest so?*

The attitude of the high priest and his servants was extremely arrogant. Several decades later, the apostle Paul encountered this same sort of attitude when he addressed the high priest at a similar inquisition (Acts 23:2).[86]

> 18:23 *Jesus answered him, If I have spoken evil, bear witness of the evil, but if well, why dost thou smite me?*

> 18:24 *Thus Annas sent him bound unto Caiaphas the high priest.*

Annas had no reply to Jesus' question. Jesus had never spoken any evil, and thus it was impossible for anyone to bear witness of it.

> 18:25 *And Simon Peter stood and warmed himself.*

---

86 Paul's situation had an interesting twist. When Jesus was put on trial, the Roman tribune (a top ranking military commander) who was present supported the Jewish high priests. By the time Paul was put on trial, however, the Jews had made such a continuous display of their uncontrolled anger at the Roman occupation that the tribunal (or tribune) who attended the proceedings sided with his fellow Roman, Paul, and protected him from the Jews (Acts 23:10-35).

*They said therefore unto him, Art not thou also one
of his disciples? He denied it and said, I am not.*

*18:26 One of the slaves of the high priest, kinsman of
the one whose ear Peter had cut off, said, Did I not
see thee in the garden with him?*

*18:27 Peter then denied again, and immediately the
cock crew.*

The cock crowed, announcing a new day was dawning, and
Simon Peter suddenly realized he had just denied Jesus three
times. At that moment, the new day did not look very promising
for Simon Peter and the rest of the disciples. Before the day was
over, however, the tables would turn completely, and it would
be Satan and his principalities and powers of wickedness that
would go down to a stunning defeat.

*18:28 Then led they Jesus from Caiaphas unto
the hall of judgment, and it was early; and they
themselves did not go into the judgment hall, lest
they should be defiled, but that they might eat the
passover.*

The high priests and the Pharisees and their servants did not
go into Pilate's[87] Roman hall of judgment, because they did not
want to be ceremonially defiled and unable to eat the Passover.
It did not even cross their self-righteous minds that spiritually,
they were already defiled, having not only refused the baptism
offered by John but also rejected, maligned, and persecuted
Jesus at every turn.

*18:29 Pilate then went out unto them and said,
What accusation bring ye against this man?*

18:30 They answered and said unto him, If he were

---

87 Pontius Pilate was the Roman governor of Judea and had been in that post since
the time of John the Baptist (Luke 3:1).

> *not a malefactor, we would not have delivered him*
> *up unto thee.*

A central tenet of Roman law is that the accused has a right to face his accusers and attempt to refute their accusations. The Jews wanted Pilate to skip this part of the trial and condemn Jesus to death without any direct testimony or evidence.

> 18:31 *Then Pilate said unto them, Take him, and*
> *judge him according to your law. The Jews therefore*
> *said unto him, It is not lawful for us to put anyone*
> *to death;*

> 18:32 *that the saying of Jesus might be fulfilled,*
> *which he spoke, signifying what death he should die.*

The Jews could have taken Jesus out and stoned him (as they were accustomed to doing, whether this was kosher with the Romans or not). Here, their apparently pious statement that it was *not lawful for us to put anyone to death*, when they had already blatantly disregarded Roman law, would help ensure that Jesus was indeed crucified by the Roman soldiers. This, in turn, would fulfill the prophetic sayings of Jesus and the prophets.

> 18:33 *Then Pilate entered into the judgment hall*
> *again and called Jesus and said unto him, Art thou*
> *the King of the Jews?*

> 18:34 *Jesus answered him, Sayest thou this thing of*
> *thyself, or did others tell it unto thee of me?*

The name "Pilate" could mean "armed with a javelin." Pilate began his attack by asking if Jesus really was *the King of the Jews*. Jesus turned this around and put the onus back on Pilate by asking a question in his turn: Did Pilate have a genuine query regarding the gospel of Jesus Christ or was he allowing others to put words in his mouth?

> 18:35 *Pilate answered, Am I a Jew? Thine own*
> *nation and the chief priests have delivered thee unto*
> *me; what hast thou done?*

Pilate knew all along that Jesus was not really a criminal and that the Jews were attacking him out of spite and envy (Matthew 27:18; Mark 15:10).

> 18:36 *Jesus answered, My kingdom is not of this*
> *world; if my kingdom were of this world, then my*
> *servants would fight, that I should not be delivered*
> *to the Jews; now, therefore, my kingdom is not from*
> *here.*

When Jesus said, *My kingdom is not of this world*, the text uses the Greek word *cosmos*, which means a system or way of doing things. Satan is the founder of the world system, which is based on lies (Genesis 3:1-5). Jesus, however, refused to compete on this level because *friendship of the world is enmity with God* (James 4:4). Jesus came *that through death he might destroy him that had the empire of death, that is, the devil, and deliver those who through fear of death were all their lifetime subject to slavery* (Hebrews 2:14b-15).

Jesus came so we might be reconciled to God by his death and saved by his life (Romans 5:10). His purpose was to reign in the heart of every believer (Luke 17:20-21) and eventually reign over and judge all the Gentiles (Romans 15:12; Isaiah 11:10-12; 42:1).

> 18:37 *Pilate therefore said unto him, Art thou a king*
> *then? Jesus answered, Thou sayest that I AM king.*
> *To this end I was born, and for this cause I came*
> *into the world, that I should bear witness unto the*
> *truth. Every one that is of the truth hears my voice.*
>
> 18:38 *Pilate said unto him, What is truth?...*

Jesus came to declare the name (nature) of his Father. When he answered, *Thou sayest that I AM king*, he was confirming that even Pilate, the Roman governor, recognized this. The truth, in person, was standing there front and center when Pilate, even as he was about to give in to the lies of the Jews, asked, *What is truth?*

> 18:38 … *And when he had said this, he went out again unto the Jews, and said unto them, I find no fault at all in him.*

> 18:39 *But ye have a custom, that I should release unto you one at the passover; will ye therefore that I release unto you the King of the Jews?*

> 18:40 *Then they all cried again, saying, Not this man, but Barabbas. Now Barabbas was a robber.*

Pilate was struggling with his conscience. He knew Jesus was innocent and that the Jewish leaders were accusing him out of envy, so he made a direct appeal to the people, referencing their custom or tradition that a prisoner should be released at Passover, a time when they celebrated that the firstborn of every Jewish household had been spared because the blood of a lamb had been applied to the doorposts. Pilate asked the nation if they wanted him to release Jesus, but the crowd picked Barabbas (whose name means "son of Abba," that is, "son of Father"). The enraged mob not only wanted Jesus to be crucified, they also wanted Barabbas, the robber, to be released.

Bear in mind that the Jews were a people who, in the eyes of the world, represented God, a people who prided themselves on keeping the law of God, including the feast of the Passover, when Jews and their proselytes came from all over the world to worship at the temple in Jerusalem. Yet here they all were, demanding that Jesus, the Son of God, their Messiah, be crucified and that Pilate instead release Barabbas, a representative of the fallen, dishonest line of Adam.

John 19

> 19:1 *Then Pilate, therefore, took Jesus and scourged him.*

The Romans were prone to scourge people as standard practice in order to examine them and find out more information. Pilate may have done this as a matter of routine, or he may have had other motivation. Perhaps he thought that if the Roman soldiers scourged and ridiculed Jesus, the people would feel sorry for him and want him released. Whatever Pilate's reasoning, he definitely played a role in fulfilling Scripture (Isaiah 53:5).

> 19:2 *And the soldiers platted a crown of thorns and put it on his head, and they put a purple robe on him*
>
> 19:3 *and said, Hail, King of the Jews! and they smote him with their hands.*

From where do thorns come?

They are a result of the curse, which in turn is a result of sin and rebellion (Genesis 3:17-18). The devil and his followers desperately wanted the curse to reign over Jesus. They thought that if he could be legally condemned, then the power of death would be sufficient to hold him. Purple has long been the color that represents royalty. The purple robe could have been provided by Herod (Luke 23:11).

> 19:4 *Pilate therefore went forth again and said unto them, Behold, I bring him forth to you, that ye may know that I find no fault in him.*
>
> 19:5 *Then Jesus came forth, wearing the crown of*

> thorns and the purple robe. And Pilate said unto
> them, Behold the man!
>
> 19:6 When the princes of the priests and the ser-
> vants saw him, they cried out, saying, crucify him,
> crucify him.[88] Pilate said unto them, Take him, and
> crucify him, for I find no fault in him.

This is the third time Pilate told the Jews *I find no fault in him*,
in the face of their overwhelming and repeated desire to have
Jesus crucified.

> 19:7 The Jews answered him, We have a law, and by
> our law he ought to die because he made himself the
> Son of God.
>
> 19:8 Therefore when Pilate heard that word, he was
> the more afraid
>
> 19:9 and went again into the judgment hall and said
> unto Jesus, Where art thou from? But Jesus gave
> him no answer.

If Pilate was now *more afraid*, he must have been afraid from
early on.

> 19:10 Then Pilate said unto him, Speakest thou not
> unto me? knowest thou not that I have power to cru-
> cify thee[89] and have power to release thee?
>
> 19:11 Jesus answered, Thou could have no power at
> all against me, unless it were given thee from above;
> therefore he that delivered me unto thee has the
> greater sin.
>
> 19:12 And from then on Pilate sought to release
> him,...

---

88 Greek verb *stauroo* – "to fasten to a stake or pale."
89 Greek *stauroo* – thus, "hang thee on a stake."

Not only was Pilate now completely convinced Jesus was innocent, he was also very fearful that Jesus might really be who he claimed to be. So if *Pilate sought to release him*, why did he not do so?

> 19:12 ... *but the Jews cried out, saying, If thou let this man go, thou art not Caesar's friend; whosoever makes himself a king speaks against Caesar.*

> 19:13 *Therefore when Pilate heard that word, he brought Jesus forth and sat down in the judgment seat in a place that is called the Pavement, but in the Hebrew, Gabbatha.*[90]

In the end, Pilate proved to be more afraid of the people and of Caesar than of God.

> 19:14 *And it was the preparation of the passover and about the sixth hour;*[91] *then he said unto the Jews, Behold your King!*

> 19:15 *But they cried out, Away with him, away with him, crucify him. Pilate said unto them, Shall I crucify your King? The high priests answered, We have no king but Caesar.*

Pilate made one last appeal to the people who were still insisting that Jesus be crucified. The shocking answer from the high priests that they had *no king but Caesar* not only denied Jesus as their king and Messiah but revealed that they identified as subjects of the pagan Caesar, who was considered by the Romans to be a god. Pilate must have felt he had no alternative.

> 19:16 *So that then, he delivered him unto them to be crucified. And they took Jesus and led him away.*

---

90   *Gabbatha* means "elevated place."

91   It was about noon on the day of preparation for the Passover, thus the thirteenth day of the first month. This day had begun at sundown the previous evening and would expire in about six more hours.

> 19:17 *And he, bearing his cross, went forth into a*
> *place called the place of a skull, which is called in*
> *the Hebrew, Golgotha,*
>
> 19:18 *where they crucified him and two others with*
> *him, one on either side and Jesus in the middle.*

The place of a skull is the place where human thoughts end. The evil thoughts of the men who called for Christ's crucifixion, the prophetic thought of the high priest who said it was *expedient for us that one man should die for the people, and not that the whole nation be lost* (John 11:49-53), went no further than this place of execution. That high priest's statement was certainly true from God's perspective, but not in the way the man intended. Within thirty-seven years or so of Jesus being sentenced to death, there was virtually nothing left of Jerusalem or its temple.

The thoughts of men do not lead to life but rather to death. Fallen man has been able to come up with marvelous plans, weapons, and techniques for destruction, but he has never been able to give life. (He may think he gives life to his children, but that life comes from God, not man.) He has never been able to cleanse society on his own. His greatest thoughts end in a mere "skull" at the time and place of his death, where there is apparently no hope.

The Lord, however, can bring us beyond death and the grave, because he is the one who invented the law of the seed. *Verily, verily, I say unto you, Except the grain of wheat falls into the ground and dies, it abides alone; but if it dies, it brings forth much fruit* (John 12:24). Jesus came to plant his life in death so it could be multiplied into us.

> 19:19 *And Pilate also wrote a title and put it*
> *above the cross. And the writing was, JESUS OF*
> *NAZARETH THE KING OF THE JEWS.*

19:20 *And many of the Jews read this title, for the place where Jesus was crucified was near to the city; and it was written in Hebrew and Greek and Latin.*

19:21 *Then the high priests of the Jews said to Pilate, Write not, The King of the Jews, but that he said, I AM King of the Jews.*

I AM is the sacred name of God. The fact that Jesus kept pronouncing this name was one of the main reasons for the Jews' condemnation of him (Mark 14:61-64; Luke 22:66-71). They considered this to be blasphemous behavior and wanted Pilate to include the forbidden name in Jesus' epitaph above the cross.

19:22 *Pilate answered, What I have written I have written.*

Pilate's refusal is further evidence that he had become convinced Jesus really was the king of the Jews.

19:23 *Then the soldiers, when they had crucified Jesus, took his garments and made four parts (to each soldier a part); and also his coat: now the coat was without seam, woven from the top throughout.*

19:24 *They said therefore among themselves, Let us not rend it, but cast lots for it, whose it shall be; that the scripture might be fulfilled, which says, They parted my garments among them, and for my raiment they did cast lots. These things therefore the soldiers did.*

This was prophesied by David in Psalm 22:18. The phrase "cast lots" appears in only twenty-two Scriptures, and it normally has to do with dividing up an inheritance or the spoils of battle. Jesus' seamless coat was symbolic of his covering. I wonder what happened to the "lucky" soldier who won the lottery and received that coat!

> 19:25 *Now there stood by the cross[92] of Jesus his mother and his mother's sister, Mary the wife of Cleophas, and Mary Magdalene.*
>
> 19:26 *When Jesus therefore saw his mother and the disciple standing by, whom he loved, he said unto his mother, Woman, behold thy son!*
>
> 19:27 *Then he said to the disciple, Behold thy mother! And from that hour that disciple took her unto his own home.*

There were three women all named Mary standing at the foot of the cross, along with the disciple that Jesus loved (John). John clearly loved Jesus in return, because he appears to have been the only disciple who risked being at the cross, in a place of obvious danger, when Jesus died. The three women named Mary, together with John the beloved, are a beautiful symbol of the special people of God who are destined to become the bride of Christ. "Mary" means "bitter" and is linked with myrrh, a bitter spice that has a lovely fragrance and is symbolic of the way of the cross; "Cleophas" means "all glory"; "Magdalene" means "inhabitant of a tower." The way of the cross is really the way to all glory, and by it the people of God will be secured in the name (nature) of the Lord, like the inhabitants of a strong tower (Proverbs 18:10).

> 19:28 *After this, Jesus knowing that all things were now accomplished, that the scripture might be fulfilled, said, I thirst.*
>
> 19:29 *Now there was set a vessel full of vinegar, and they filled a sponge with vinegar and put it upon hyssop and put it to his mouth.*

---

92   Greek *stauros* – stake.

> 19:30 *When Jesus therefore had received the vinegar,*
> *he said, It is finished, and he bowed his head and*
> *gave the Spirit.*

In the midst of his suffering and pain, Jesus was keeping track of all the prophecies that must be fulfilled. There was one detail left, mentioned in Psalm 69:21, *They also gave me gall for my food; and in my thirst they gave me vinegar to drink.* Remembering this, Jesus said *I thirst,* and received a vinegar-filled sponge that the Roman soldiers put upon a stalk of the plant known as hyssop. Like myrrh, this aromatic plant with its pungent taste is linked to the way of the cross and to redemption. Hyssop was used at Passover to apply the blood to the doorposts of the house (Exodus 12:22). *And almost all things are by the law purged with blood, and without shedding of blood there is no remission* (Hebrews 9:22).

After Jesus received the vinegar, he said simply, *It is finished.* His work of redemption was now complete. *He bowed his head and gave the Spirit.* Jesus' enemies did not take his life; Jesus gave his life for us (John 10:18). By this sacrifice, he made the Holy Spirit available to us.

> 19:31 *The Jews therefore, because it was the prepa-*
> *ration, that the bodies should not remain upon the*
> *cross[93] on the sabbath day (for that sabbath day was*
> *a high day)[94] besought Pilate that their legs might be*
> *broken and that they might be taken away.*

> 19:32 *Then the soldiers came and broke the legs of*
> *the first and of the other who were crucified with*
> *him.*

---

93 Greek *stauros* – stake.

94 The Passover, celebrated on the fourteenth day of the first month *between the two evenings* (Leviticus 23:5), was considered a High Sabbath, and due to the lunar calendar, there was a one in seven possibility of it falling on any given day of the week.

> 19:33 *But when they came to Jesus and saw that he was dead already, they did not break his legs,*
>
> 19:34 *but one of the soldiers with a spear pierced his side, and forthwith blood and water came out.*

Eve was made from that which God took from the side of Adam after causing him to fall into a *"deep sleep"* (Genesis 2:21-22). When one of the soldiers pierced Jesus' side after his death, *blood and water came out.* According to Scripture, the life of the flesh is in the blood,[95] and water symbolizes the word of God.[96] The literal blood and water that flowed from Jesus' riven side (from below his heart) after his death are symbolic of God's redemptive provision to form Jesus' bride.[97] The water represents the Word of God, and the blood is representative of Jesus' life. Jesus is the living Word of God, and he desires for his word to come alive in our hearts (as symbolized by the women and John, who were watching all of this transpire).

> 19:35 *And he that saw it gives testimony, and his testimony is true, and he knows that he says the truth, that ye also might believe.*

In this sense and context, to *believe* is not the modern concept or head knowledge of believing the historical facts. Rather, to believe is to trust and depend on Jesus Christ instead of anything

---

95 *For the soul (or life) of the flesh is in the blood, and I have given it to you to reconcile your persons (or souls) upon the altar; therefore the same blood reconciles the person* (Leviticus 17:11).

96 *Husbands, love your wives even as the Christ also loved the congregation* [Greek *ekklesia*, meaning "called-out ones"] *and gave himself for her, that he might sanctify and cleanse her in the washing of water by the word, that he might present her glorious for himself, a congregation, not having spot or wrinkle or any such thing, but that she should be holy and without blemish* (Ephesians 5:25-27).

97 *And so it is written, The first man Adam was made a living soul; the last Adam was made a life-giving Spirit. Howbeit the spiritual is not first, but the natural; and afterward, that which is spiritual. The first man is of the earth, earthy; the second man is the Lord of heaven. As is the earthy, such are those also that are earthy; and as is the heavenly, such also are those that are heavenly* (1 Corinthians 15:45-48).

or anyone else. In this sense, we are to believe in our hearts, not primarily in our minds (Romans 10:9).

Later, John would go on to write:

> *This is Jesus, the Christ, who came by water and blood; not by water only, but by water and blood. And the Spirit is he that bears witness, because the Spirit is the truth. For there are three that bear witness in heaven, the Father, the Word, and the Holy Spirit; and these three are one. And there are three that bear witness on earth, the Spirit and the water and the blood; and these three agree in one. If we receive the witness of men, the witness of God is greater: for this is the witness of God which he has testified of his Son.* (1 John 5:6-9)

With regard to *the witness of men*, the law is clear: *One witness shall not be valid against a man for any iniquity or for any sin, in any sin which he should commit. At the mouth of two witnesses or at the mouth of three witnesses, shall the matter be established* (Deuteronomy 19:15).

But John goes beyond this, describing *three that bear witness in heaven* and *three that bear witness on earth*. When Jesus died, all three who bear witness on earth were present. Jesus *gave the Spirit*, and then the *blood and water came out* of his side. This mighty river of God (the life and word flowing from Jesus' heart) continues to flow by the Spirit to wash away the filth of the fallen race of Adam in all those who truly believe. After Jesus' ascension, the three who bear witness in heaven are also together: the Father, the Word (Jesus is the living Word of God), and the Spirit. The Spirit bears witness both on earth and in heaven.

Returning to John 19:

> 19:36 *For these things were done that the scripture*

should be fulfilled, A bone of him shall not be broken.[98]

When the children of Israel celebrated the first Passover on their way out of Egypt, they were ordered to eat of the lamb *in one house* and to not *break a bone thereof* (Exodus 12:46). Jesus' death brings everything together (Jew and Gentile) in Christ in *one house*. It also brings man here on earth back into fellowship with God in heaven by the Spirit. In God's plan of redemption, blood must be spilt and the flesh must be dealt with, but the "bones" representing God's original design, structure, and plan are not to be broken.

> *19:37 And again another scripture says, They shall look on him whom they pierced.*

There were undoubtedly some who passed by and observed what happened on the day that Jesus was pierced and died (although most Jews were probably busy at home killing their own Passover lambs at the time he was being sacrificed). The fullness of this prophecy, however, is yet to come, when the book of Zechariah is completely fulfilled at Jesus' second coming: *And I will pour upon the house of David and upon the inhabitants of Jerusalem the Spirit of grace and of prayer, and they shall look upon me whom they have pierced, and they shall mourn over him as one mourns for his only son, afflicting themselves over him as one afflicts himself over his firstborn* (Zechariah 12:10).

> *19:38 After these things, Joseph of Arimathaea, being a disciple of Jesus but secretly for fear of the Jews, besought Pilate that he might take away the body of Jesus, and Pilate gave him leave. He came therefore and took the body of Jesus.*

Jesus' natural step-father, who was named Joseph, had undoubtedly passed away by the time of Jesus' ministry, so it is interesting

---

98   Psalm 34:20.

to see that after Jesus' death, God the Father provided another Joseph to fulfill the role that would have fallen to Jesus' earthly father. "Arimatheaea" means "high place."

> 19:39 *Then Nicodemus came also, who at the first came to Jesus by night, and brought a mixture of myrrh and aloes, about one hundred pounds.*

Nicodemus is mentioned five times in Scripture (all of them in text written by John). At first he came by night (John 3:1-4), and Jesus told him that he needed to be "born again." Then he had a question about how to be born of the Spirit (John 3:9). Later, Nicodemus stood up for Jesus and was rebuked by the Pharisees (John 7:50-52). Apparently, when the Sanhedrin met at midnight to condemn Jesus, they excluded Nicodemus, who at some point became aware of the situation and showed up to help bury Jesus, bringing with him one hundred pounds of myrrh and aloes, which must have cost a small fortune. This (John 19:39) is the fifth and final mention of his name. Interestingly, aloes (a tree with aromatic wood) are also mentioned in only five Scriptures. Five is a number related to mercy and grace. One hundred symbolizes the plan of God,[99] and myrrh, as we have already mentioned, has to do with the way of the cross.[100]

---

99 Abraham was one hundred years old when Isaac (another symbol of Jesus Christ) was born, Noah spent one hundred years building the ark (a symbol of redemption), and so on.

100 Aloes are first mentioned when Baalam was forced to prophesy the truth regarding the people of God when King Balak, their mortal enemy, hired him to curse Israel: *How beautiful are thy tents, O Jacob, and thy habitations, O Israel! As the valleys are they spread forth, as gardens by the river's side, as the trees of lign aloes which the LORD has planted, and as cedars beside the waters. From his branches he shall distil waters, and his seed shall be in many waters, and his king shall be higher than Agag, and his kingdom shall be exalted* (Numbers 24:5-7). Agag, meaning, covered (or the roof), is a symbol of the arrogant, natural, carnal man that is at enmity with God.
God brought him forth out of Egypt; he has, as it were, the strength of a unicorn; he shall eat up the Gentiles his enemies and shall break their bones and pierce them through with his arrows (Numbers 24:8).
God's people are like trees of lign aloes with the strength of a unicorn (rhinoceros) that shall eat up the Gentiles (those who are not in a proper covenant with God and who have uncircumcised hearts) and *shall break their bones*. None of Jesus' bones were allowed to be broken.

The Jews and the high priests spent quite a bit of time cursing Jesus and even in the midst of their unrighteousness swore allegiance to Caesar. On the other hand:

> *Thy throne, O God, is eternal and for ever, the rod of righteousness is the sceptre of thy kingdom. Thou lovest righteousness, and hatest wickedness; therefore God, thy God, has anointed thee with the oil of gladness above thy fellows. All thy garments smell of myrrh and aloes and cassia, out of the ivory palaces, by which they have made thee glad.* (Psalm 45:6-8)

Even at his death, Jesus "garments" smelled of myrrh and aloes and his body never entered into corruption (Psalm 16:10; Acts 2:27-31). If we follow Jesus along the way of the cross as part of the body of Christ, the same will spiritually be true of us. If we die to our own way, to sin and to the control of the flesh, we will be clothed in the linen clothes of Jesus' righteousness and as we learn to obey him in the power of the Holy Spirit the fragrance of myrrh and aloes and cassia (true worship) will be most evident as we experience the true joy of the Lord.

> *19:40 And they took the body of Jesus and wound it in linen clothes with the spices, as is the manner of the Jews to bury.*
>
> *19:41 Now in the place where he was crucified there was a garden, and in the garden a new sepulchre, in which no one had yet been laid.*
>
> *19:42 Therefore they laid Jesus there because of the Jews' preparation day, for the sepulchre was near.*

The problem of mankind began in a garden, so it is only fitting that the solution should also transpire in a garden.

He couched, he lay down as a lion and as a great lion; who shall awaken him? Blessed is he that blesses thee, and cursed is he that curses thee (Numbers 24:9).

The fact that *in the place where he was crucified there was a garden* is symbolic of something even more wonderful. The real garden of God cannot be seen with our carnal eyes, for it exists in the spiritual realm. When Jesus entered God's garden on leaving this world, the veil in the temple was rent from top to bottom, symbolizing that Jesus' sacrifice had torn apart, once and for all, the barrier that had been separating mankind from God. However, the torn veil exposed the holy of holies to the view of the common man – signifying that God was now accessible to man through Jesus Christ rather than through the Levitical priesthood – which so horrified the Jewish priests that they lost no time in sewing it back up. The legalistic religion of mankind continues to prefer precepts and values formulaically applied by man instead of communion with God in the realm of the throne room of his heavenly "ivory palaces." God's plan is to have a royal priesthood, a priesthood of all believers who, through the life of Jesus Christ, have access to the Father's throne, of which Solomon's resplendent ivory-and-gold throne was but an earthly example (2 Chronicles 9:17).

The Lord Jesus Christ is now the only mediator of a new covenant in which the commandments of God are written, not on tablets of stone, but on something far more precious. For he has promised, *I will give my law in their souls and write it in their hearts* (Jeremiah 31:31-34).

Let us pray

Lord Jesus, we offer you thanks for giving your life for us, for doing something that continues to go beyond our capacity to understand. We do, however, desire to be part of that great river of God that flows from your throne into the spiritually sterile desert of the seemingly good intentions of the people of God, and on into the sea of lost humanity. May we swim in the river of your resurrection life and live. May we become an extension of your love and mercy and grace.

May your death be our death, to the flesh and to sin. May your life fill, cleanse, regenerate, and transform our entire being by the Holy Spirit. Amen.

Chapter 17

From the Fear of the Jews
to the Joy of the Lord

The Jews had developed quite a bit of expertise in managing dead bodies from a religious point of view (in fact, under the law, they were all dead in trespasses and sin). Their customs included anointing the body of the deceased with aromatic spices in a vain attempt to ward off decomposition. Many religious congregations today are the spiritual equivalent of corpses, still using religious rites and rituals to try to stave off the stench of corruption.

The body of Lazarus had been anointed in the usual manner after he died, yet by the fourth day even his sister Martha thought that if his tomb was opened, the bad odor would be overwhelming. Mary Magdalene and the disciples did not want this to be the case with Jesus. Having already been forced to hastily entomb his body on the late afternoon of the day of preparation and wait the entire day of the Passover, they were anxious to go and anoint his corpse before decomposition set in.

John 20

20:1 The first of the sabbaths,[101] *Mary Magdalene*
came early, when it was yet dark, unto the sepulchre
and saw the stone taken away from the sepulchre.

Why was Mary Magdalene the first one to arrive at the empty
tomb?

Mary Magdalene was one of Jesus' most devoted followers,
being one of a group of women who not only traveled with
him and the disciples but also supplied his needs (Luke 8:2-3).
Before meeting Jesus, she had been profoundly troubled, but
he had transformed her life by casting seven demons out of her.
The term "seven demons" denotes a person who is completely
possessed by demonic forces. Although we are not told what
form this total possession took in Mary's case (she has tradi-
tionally been associated with the nameless woman of ill repute
who washed Jesus' feet with her tears and dried them with her
hair before anointing them with expensive lotion[102]), many of
us know someone who seems to have fallen into the clutches
of the Enemy, someone who feels hopeless and helpless, unable
to even imagine a way to escape their particular demon. Mary
Magdalene proved that no matter what we have been or what
we have done when the Enemy controlled us, Jesus can save us
and give us a new life and great reason to hope. She is symbolic

---

101 This phrase is used seven times in the New Testament according to the Jubilee
Bible translation (this is the fifth usage). Its meaning is set in the law of Moses
as the first *holy convocation* or "Sabbath" of the Feast of Unleavened Bread
that began the day after Passover and ended with the second *holy convocation*
seven days later (Leviticus 23:5-8). Therefore the *first of the sabbaths* began
at sundown on what to us would have been the previous day. Parts of three
different days would have passed: (1) Whatever hours were left on the day of
preparation after Jesus was laid in the *new sepulchre* prior to sundown, (2) the
entire twenty-four hours of the day of Passover, beginning at sundown, and (3)
the hours of darkness from the time of the sundown that ended the Passover
to the point at which *Mary Magdalene came early, when it was yet dark, unto
the sepulchre and saw the stone taken away.*

102 Jesus demonstrated to Simon the Pharisee that the person who had been forgiven the most would be the one who would love him the most (Luke 7:36-50).

of all the people of God who were once completely enslaved in the tower or fortress of the Enemy but who are now rescued, redeemed, and forgiven to become the inhabitants of the strong tower of the Lord ("Magdalene" means "inhabitant of a tower"). For the *name of the LORD is a strong tower: the righteous shall run into it, and be raised up* (Proverbs 18:10).

> 20:2 *Then she ran and came to Simon Peter and to the other disciple, whom Jesus loved, and said unto them, They have taken away the Lord out of the sepulchre, and we know not where they have laid him.*

Mary Magdalene was planning to anoint Jesus' dead body (Mark 16:1), but her purpose was frustrated when she found an empty sepulchre. The same is true for those who even today visit what they consider to be holy sites where Jesus or his apostles (or countless saints and martyrs) are reported to have died. There is nothing of eternal value for us to worship or anoint at any of those tombs, because Jesus is now alive and sitting at the right hand of the Father.[103]

> 20:3 *Peter therefore went forth, and that other disciple, and came to the sepulchre.*
>
> 20:4 *So they both ran together, and the other disciple outran Peter and came first to the sepulchre.*
>
> 20:5 *And he, stooping down and looking in, saw the linen clothes lying; yet he did not go in.*
>
> 20:6 *Then came Simon Peter following him and went into the sepulchre and saw the linen clothes lying*
>
> 20:7 *and the napkin, that had been placed over his*

---

103 Remember that *the souls of those that had been slain because of the word of God and for the testimony which they held* are described as being under the heavenly altar, not in Hades (Revelation 6:9).

*head, not lying with the linen clothes, but wrapped
together in a place by itself.*

Jesus is the head of the body of Christ, and therefore Peter and
John found that the "napkin" *that had been placed over his head*
was *not lying with the* "linen clothes" but was *wrapped together
in a place by itself.*[104]

> 20:8 *Then that other disciple, who came first to the
> sepulchre, went in also and he saw and believed.*
>
> 20:9 *For as yet they did not know the scripture, that
> he must rise again from the dead.*
>
> 20:10 *Then the disciples went away again unto their
> own.*

Jesus' resurrection, through prophesied, had been a closely kept
secret that the devil and his followers did not understand until
it was too late. When Lazarus was resurrected, he was restored
in his normal body (which would continue to decay and eventually die) and had to be loosed from his grave clothes. Jesus'
resurrection, however, was a complete transformation, after
which he was able to move freely between the natural and the
spiritual realms. Having conquered death, Jesus will never die,
and therefore he is our source for eternal life and resurrection.
An interesting detail is that although his grave clothes were
found in the empty tomb, the following verses make it obvious
Jesus was not naked after he left the sepulchre.[105]

> 20:11 *But Mary stood outside near the sepulchre
> weeping, and as she wept, she stooped down and
> looked into the sepulchre*

---

104 *And he is the head of the body, the congregation* [Greek *ekklesia* – meaning
   "called-out ones"], *who is the beginning, the firstborn from the dead, that in all
   things he might have the preeminence* (Colossians 1:18).

105 And if we are chosen to participate in the first resurrection, I'm sure we will
   not be naked either (2 Corinthians 5:1-11; Revelation 16:15; 20:4-6).

> 20:12 *and saw two angels in white sitting, the one at the head and the other at the feet, where the body of Jesus had been placed.*

> 20:13 *And they said unto her, Woman, why dost thou weep? She said unto them, Because they have taken away my Lord, and I know not where they have laid him.*

Mary was so distraught that she didn't even realize that she was speaking with angels. Neither did the angels blurt out that the Lord was resurrected – it was necessary that the Lord reveal himself to Mary, as he still does to people today (John 6:44).

> 20:14 *And when she had said this, she turned around and saw Jesus standing there and did not know that it was Jesus.*

Mary did not recognize Jesus after the resurrection. She was still focused on seeking a dead body to put back in the tomb.

> 20:15 *Jesus said unto her, Woman, why dost thou weep? whom seekest thou? She, supposing him to be the gardener, said unto him, Lord, if thou didst carry him off, tell me where thou hast laid him, and I will take him away.*

In a certain sense Jesus really is the gardener, and his "garden" includes the fertile ground of our hearts and souls if we believe in him.

> 20:16 *Jesus said unto her, Mary! Turning herself around, she said unto him, Rabboni, which is to say, Master.*

Even though Mary failed to recognize Jesus by his appearance, she soon identified his voice (John 10:27) and turned around. Not only did she turn herself around physically, at this point she also turned herself around metaphorically, walking away from the rites and rituals of dead religion and freeing herself to obey the resurrected, living Christ.

> 20:17 *Jesus said unto her, Touch me not,*[106] *for I have not yet ascended to my Father; but go to my brethren and say unto them, I ascend unto my Father and your Father, and to my God and your God.*

> 20:18 *Mary Magdalene came giving the news to the disciples, That I have seen the Lord, and he spoke these things unto me.*

Peter and John witnessed the empty sepulchre, and John records (20:8) that when he saw the scene inside the sepulchre, he believed. Two angels also observed the empty tomb. However, Scripture makes it clear that the first person to see Jesus and speak with him after his resurrection was Mary Magdalene.

> 20:19 *Then the same day at evening, being the first of the sabbaths, when the doors were shut where the disciples were assembled for fear of the Jews, Jesus came and stood in the midst and said unto them, Peace be unto you.*

This was the same day at evening, prior to sundown on the first of the Sabbaths, which was the first day of the seven-day Feast of Unleavened Bread. Jesus wants his people to be a new lump of dough, without the leaven (sin) of unrighteousness or of the Pharisees or of Herod (1 Corinthians 5:6-7; Galatians 5:9). This is why he has provided us with the Holy Spirit.

> 20:20 *And having said this, he showed them his*

---

106 Note that Jesus did not allow a touchy-feely emotional encounter with Mary Magdalene, while at the same time she received the honor of being the first person to see him after his resurrection and handled the occasion with all due respect for her Lord.

hands and his side. Then the disciples were glad
when they saw the Lord.

The disciples went from experiencing *fear of the Jews* to feeling *glad when they saw the Lord.* The presence of the Lord brings joy to his disciples.

20:21 *Then Jesus said to them again, Peace be unto*
you; as my Father has sent me, even so send I you.

Jesus had just spent the day ascending victoriously above all heavens to the throne of his Father, leading captivity captive. He was commissioned from the throne of the Father with all power and all authority in heaven and in earth (Matthew 28:18), and now the disciples were being sent in like manner. Those who are sent on such a mission are called apostles. On this very special day of his resurrection and triumph, Jesus twice declared to his disciples, *Peace be unto you.*

20:22 *And when he had said this, he breathed on*
them and said unto them, Receive ye the Holy Spirit;

20:23 *unto those whose sins ye release, they shall be*
released; and unto those whose sins ye retain, they
shall be retained.

This is when the disciples (who were being sent as apostles) received the Holy Spirit by the very breath of Jesus, at his command (the Greek word *emphusao* – meaning "to breathe on," also has connotations of germinating or sprouting). They received the Holy Spirit at the beginning of the Feast of Unleavened Bread, but the outpouring, bubbling over, or infilling of the Holy Spirit did not take place until fifty days later on the feast of Pentecost. In the meantime, something new was definitely germinating and sprouting within the apostles. I find this very interesting and worthy of meditation.[107]

107 Another factor to consider was that on the day of Pentecost, the believers of the "upper room" *were all with one accord in one place* (Acts 2:1).

It is also well worth noting that the promise that *unto those whose sins ye release, they shall be released; and unto those whose sins ye retain, they shall be retained* is given in context to those who have been truly sent by Jesus (with the full authority of the Father) and who have received the Holy Spirit by the very breath of God. By the Holy Spirit we may have victory over sin, conquest over the flesh, forgiveness of sin, removal of guilt, and the continued presence of the Lord Jesus Christ in our hearts every hour of our lives – a presence that is cause for great and abundant joy and is likewise our continual strength (Nehemiah 8:10; Psalm 48:1-3; 1 Thessalonians 1:6).

> 20:24 *But Thomas, one of the twelve, called Didymus, was not with them when Jesus came.*

> 20:25 *The other disciples, therefore, said unto him, We have seen the Lord. But he said unto them, Unless I shall see in his hands the print of the nails and put my finger into the print of the nails and thrust my hand into his side, I will not believe.*

Thomas had been with Jesus for years and had not only observed many miracles (including the resurrection of Lazarus) but had also been sent out by Jesus with power to cast out demons and heal the sick. However, he may have been so profoundly shaken by Judas's betrayal of Jesus and the subsequent trial and crucifixion that he was overcome by unbelief.

> 20:26 *And again eight days later, his disciples were within and Thomas with them; then Jesus came, the doors being shut, and stood in the midst and said, Peace be unto you.*

This is the third time after his resurrection that Jesus commanded, *Peace be unto you*. The peace that he declares to his disciples is internal and will remain no matter what may be going on in the world outside. The peace he declares is not a negotiated peace. Rather, Jesus imposes his peace. It goes along with his presence.

> 20:27 *Then he said to Thomas, Reach here thy finger and behold my hands and reach here thy hand and thrust it into my side and be not unbelieving, but faithful.*

> 20:28 *And Thomas answered and said unto him, My Lord and my God.*

Jesus was forbearing with Thomas, as he is with all who seek the truth. He is pleased to resolve the doubts of any who genuinely desire to be his disciples.

> 20:29 *Jesus said unto him, Thomas, because thou hast seen me, thou hast believed; blessed are those that have not seen and yet have believed.*

This blessing is for us if we believe the witnesses Jesus has provided and receive him into our hearts.

> 20:30 *And Jesus truly did many other signs in the presence of his disciples, which are not written in this book;*

> 20:31 *but these are written that ye might believe that Jesus is the Christ, the Son of God, and that believing ye might have life in his name.*

Let us pray

Lord, we are completely overwhelmed by the magnitude of your love, grace, and mercy toward us. The least we can offer in return is to believe on you and place our hearts, souls, minds, and all that we have securely into your hands as we humbly request that you use your unlimited power and authority to make the new covenant a brilliant reality in our lives. Amen.

Chapter 18

Come and Dine

John 21

*21:1 After these things Jesus manifested himself
again to the disciples at the sea of Tiberias, and he
manifested himself in this manner:*

This is the second reference in the gospel of John to the sea
of Tiberias (which is another name for the sea of Galilee),
named for the Roman emperor Tiberius (the name having to do
with the Tiber River of Rome). Jesus called his disciples to be
fishers of men (Matthew 4:19; Mark 1:17); he knew they would
eventually evangelize many Gentiles from the Roman Empire,
of which the fish of the sea of Tiberias are symbolic.

*21:2 Simon Peter and Thomas, called Didymus,
and Nathanael of Cana in Galilee and the sons of
Zebedee and two other of his disciples were together.*

Seven disciples are mentioned, but the number actually symbolizes all the disciples.

21:3 Simon Peter said unto them, I am going fishing.

> *They said unto him, Let us also go with thee. They*
> *went forth and entered into a ship immediately, and*
> *that night they caught nothing.*

And so it is with most of us. Our natural efforts to evangelize and to be fishers of men for Jesus are unproductive at best.

> 21:4 *But when the morning was now come, Jesus*
> *stood on the shore, but the disciples did not under-*
> *stand that it was Jesus.*

> 21:5 *Then Jesus said unto them, Children, have ye*
> *any food? They answered him, No.*

The use of the Greek word *paidion* (meaning "half-grown children") denotes the immaturity of the disciples. Many of them were professional fishermen, and when the Lord had called them approximately three and a half years before, they had left everything to follow him (Luke 5:1-11). Now, here they were, back on a fishing boat in a position that was outwardly very similar to their situation when Jesus had first called them, but strange things had been happening, and they were not sure what to do. They knew Jesus had died on the cross, yet he had appeared unto them twice after his death. His physical appearance had changed dramatically, however, and it was difficult for them to recognize him with certainty, save for the scars in his hands and feet and side.

> 21:6 *And he said unto them, Cast the net on the*
> *right hand side of the ship, and ye shall find. They*
> *cast therefore, and now they were not able to draw it*
> *for the multitude of fishes.*

The right-hand side is the side of power and authority, which operates in accordance with the living word of God (Jesus).

> 21:7 *Therefore that disciple whom Jesus loved said*
> *unto Peter, It is the Lord. Now when Simon Peter*

> *heard that it was the Lord, he girt his fisher's coat*
> *unto him (for he was naked) and cast himself into*
> *the sea.*

They were far enough out to sea where it may have been difficult for them to discern the tone of Jesus' voice. It was only when they witnessed the power of his word that the disciples realized the stranger was Jesus. Simon Peter had been fishing naked all night, with no covering (that is, with no specific word from the Lord). Now, surprised by Jesus, *he girt his fisher's coat unto him*, securing his old, smelly "professional" coat tightly around his body to cover his nakedness before he *cast himself into the sea.*

> 21:8 *And the other disciples came in the little ship*
> *(for they were not far from land, but as it were two*
> *hundred cubits), dragging the net with the fishes.*

Two hundred cubits is about three hundred feet. The number two hundred is linked to gifts, to grace, and to the bearing of fruit. Here the disciples, even with their natural gifting as fishermen, bore no fruit (caught no acceptable fish) until they received a direct, precise instruction from the Lord. Jesus had called them to leave everything behind, including their nets and boats, and to follow him. Now he had found them about two hundred cubits out into the sea of Tiberias after apparently forgetting, or ignoring, his call on their lives. Fortunately for the disciples, two hundred cubits proved to still be within the limits of Jesus' grace.

> 21:9 *As soon then as they were come to land, they*
> *saw a fire of coals there, and a fish laid thereon, and*
> *bread.*

Regardless of the miraculous catch they had just made by obeying his word, Jesus already had bread and a fish prepared for them to eat. Jesus Christ himself is provision for our every need, and he is accompanied by the fire of God to purify us and cleanse us of every wrong desire.

> 21:10 *Jesus said unto them, Bring of the fish which ye have now caught.*

> 21:11 *Simon Peter went up and drew the net to land full of great fishes, one hundred and fifty-three; and being so many, yet the net was not broken.*

One hundred and fifty-three is a significant number in Scripture.[108] For example, the word "Zion," meaning "sustained" or "lifted up" (such as a fortress being raised), occurs one hundred and fifty-three times, as does the word "Sabbath(s)." Zion is symbolic of where God dwells (and of where he desires for us to dwell with him), and if we dwell in peace with God, we will be in his Sabbath (rest). The word "perfect" or "perfection" in its various forms also occurs one hundred and fifty-three times in the Jubilee Bible.[109] First, however, we must be "fished" into the kingdom of God and laid upon the "fire of coals" of his altar until every impurity in us is consumed.

> 21:12 *Jesus said unto them, Come and dine. And none of the disciples dared to ask him, Who art thou? knowing that it was the Lord.*

> 21:13 *Jesus then came and took the bread and gave them, and the fish likewise.*

> 21:14 *This was now the third time that Jesus manifested himself to his disciples, after he was risen from the dead.*

---

108 One hundred and fifty-three is fifty-one times three. Fifty-one is a number that has to do with being cleansed and purified of sin, iniquity, and rebellion (see Psalm 51), and three relates to fruitfulness. Therefore three times fifty-one is the result of us being cleansed and purified so God can make us fruitful and multiply us.

109 See the Appendix for the one hundred and fifty-three verses in which the word "perfect" or "perfection" occurs in the Jubilee Bible translation.

In the gospel of John, Jesus' last command to the seven disciples (really to all of his disciples, including us) was and is, *Come and dine.* Earlier in this gospel, he announced, *I AM the bread of life* (John 6:35, 48). Elsewhere in Scripture, Moses prophesied that *man does not live by bread alone, but by every word that proceeds out of the mouth of the LORD shall man live* (Deuteronomy 8:3b). However, now that God has also become man, Jesus is one of us. If we are symbolized as "fish," then so is he. And when he invites us to come and dine, we may now partake not only of the word of God but also of Jesus himself. His last didactic lesson to his disciples may be summed up as follows: "If you desire to live by the Spirit and to enter into the fruitful resurrection life that I now represent, then you may not only feed on what I say, you may also feed on what I AM." This is the meaning of the symbolic fish on the fire of coals. If Jesus did not shy away from the way of the cross, why should we?

> 21:15 *So when they had dined, Jesus said to Simon Peter, Simon, son of Jonas, lovest thou me more than these?...*

Jesus and Simon Peter and the other disciples had just dined (literally and symbolically) on the fish and bread that Jesus had prepared along with some of the one hundred and fifty-three fish the disciples had just caught. When Jesus posed this question to Simon Peter, he called him by his formal name of Simon, son of Jonas. "Simon" means the same as "Simeon," that is, "hearkening" (hearing and obeying). "Jonas" means "dove." Having gotten Peter's undivided attention by the use of this formality, Jesus asked him, *Lovest thou me more than these?*

What, exactly, did Jesus mean by *these?*

Was he referring to the other disciples? Was he asking Peter if he loved[110] Jesus more than he loved John and Thomas and the others?

I don't know for sure, but I doubt that Jesus would do this. I think it much more likely that by using the word *these*, Jesus was referring to the ship and the nets and the physical fish and the wet and smelly "fisher's coat" Peter was still wearing. After all, it was Peter who had said (in verse 3), *I am going fishing*, and it was the others who had responded, *Let us also go with thee.*

Without hesitation, Peter replied:

> 21:15 ... *He said unto him, Yes, Lord, thou knowest that I love thee....*

Instead of repeating the Greek verb *agapao* that Jesus had employed, Peter switched the terminology around and used the Greek noun *phileos* or "brotherly love," implying a strong emotional bond and affection.

> 21:15 ... *He [Jesus] said unto him, Feed my lambs.*[111]

> 21:16 *He said to him again the second time, Simon, son of Jonas, lovest thou me? He said unto him, Yes, Lord thou knowest that I love thee. He said unto him, Feed my sheep.*

In his second repetition of the basic question to Peter, Jesus continued to use the Greek word *agapao* and Peter again responded with *phileos*, affirming his deep affection, approval, and emotional attachment to Jesus, who answered with, *Feed my sheep*, using the word for mature sheep that hear his voice and will not follow anyone else (John 10:3, 27).

---

110 In this question, Jesus used the Greek word *agapao*, which implies a choice from the heart.

111 Jesus loves children, and here he uses the word for lamb in the diminutive (a lambkin). This Greek word, *arnion*, is used twenty-nine times in the Book of Revelation and thus is closely linked to Jesus himself. This instance in John 21:15 is the only time it is plural, making it a clear reference to Jesus' followers, who must enter his kingdom as little children. This reference brings the word's total usage by John to thirty times in Scripture.

> *17 He said unto him the third time, Simon, son of*
> *Jonas, lovest thou me? Peter was grieved because he*
> *said unto him the third time, Lovest thou me?...*

The third time, Jesus switched words and used same the Greek word (*phileos*) that Peter had been using in his responses. This grieved Peter, not only because it was the third time of asking but because to him this seemed to question his love and affection on an even deeper level.

> *21:17 ... And he said, Lord, thou knowest all things;*
> *thou knowest that I love thee. Jesus said unto him,*
> *Feed my sheep.*

When Peter said, *Lord, thou knowest all things*, he had to have been thinking about the occasion, just a few days before, when he had so confidently assured Jesus that he (Peter) was willing to die for him and would never forsake him – only to find himself denying Jesus three times in a single night before the rooster crowed.

Now it was dawning on Peter that in and through all of this, Jesus was giving him the opportunity to make up for the three times Peter had denied him on the day of crucifixion. Not only this, but after the day of Pentecost it would soon become clear that Peter was Jesus' choice to be the lead apostle to continue his work of bringing the gospel to the Jewish nation, as well as caring for and feeding the Jewish believers, just as Paul would be Jesus' choice to be the lead apostle to the Gentiles (Galatians 2:8).

Then Jesus went on to say something that, in Peter's understanding, must have clinched the fact that Peter was definitely restored to his favor, even if the second half of the sentence may not have seemed to be very good news to anyone other than Peter.

> *21:18 Verily, verily, I say unto thee, When thou wast*
> *young, thou didst gird thyself and walk where thou*

wouldest, but when thou shalt be old, thou shalt stretch forth thy hands, and another shall gird thee and carry thee where thou wouldest not.

21:19 This he spoke, signifying by what death he should clarify God. And when he had spoken this, he said unto him, Follow me.

Jesus' words made it clear to Peter that he would become mature in Christ and follow him in the way of the cross. Jesus told Peter that when he was "young" or immature, *thou didst gird thyself and walk where thou wouldest.* Peter was accustomed to going wherever he desired and "covering himself" as he deemed necessary. However, when Peter became mature or "old," *thou shalt stretch forth thy hands,* meaning that he would no longer seek to govern himself and would stretch forth his hands to the Lord for assistance. Then *another shall gird thee and carry thee where thou wouldest not.* That is, Peter would be girded (covered) by the Holy Spirit, who would conduct and even carry him along the way of the cross that he had refused to enter into on his own. This is a worthy example and lesson for all of us.

History proves that after this, Peter never wavered. He spent a long life of faithful service to Jesus Christ for which eventually, as Jesus prophesied here, he was crucified. "Peter" means "a small rock or stone." Jesus had prophesied early on that Peter would be called "Cephas," meaning "a (monumental) stone or pillar" (John 1:42). Sure enough, after this encounter near the end of the gospel of John, there are five Scripture references in which Peter is referred to as Cephas (1 Corinthians 1:12; 3:22; 9:5; 15:5; and Galatians 2:9). Remember that the number five can be symbolic of God's mercy and grace.

21:20 Then Peter, turning about, saw the disciple whom Jesus loved following, who also leaned on his breast at supper, and said, Lord, which is he that betrays thee?

It seems Jesus had been walking along the beach with Peter when all of a sudden Peter turned and saw that John was following them.

> 21:21 *Peter seeing him said to Jesus, Lord, and what shall this man do?*

> 21:22 *Jesus said unto him, If I will that he tarry until I come, what is that to thee? follow thou me.*[112]

Peter, overcome with curiosity (another trait common to all of us), wanted to know about John's future, so he asked Jesus, *and what shall this man do?*

Consider what John had already done. After the disciples all scattered and fled from the garden of Gethsemane on the night Jesus was betrayed and arrested, John was the first to recover, and seemingly he was the only one who recovered quickly enough to be present at the trial. John was also the only disciple recorded as being present at the foot of the cross when Jesus died. This behavior placed John in grave danger of being killed along with Jesus. In fact, John is described in Scripture as one *who bore witness of the word of God and of the testimony of Jesus Christ* (Revelation 1:2). The word used here for "witness" is the Greek word *martus*, which also means "martyr" (someone willing to lay down their life for the truth). This is the same word used to describe Jesus in Revelation 1:5.

John was a living martyr. According to tradition and history, he was the only one of Jesus' original disciples to die a natural death. In God's book, however, John was a martyr because he willingly and repeatedly exposed himself to great danger in order to bear witness of the word of God and the testimony of

---

112 Scripture records five times when Peter was specifically told, *Follow me.* This is the fourth occasion. Jesus' initial call to Peter and Andrew is recorded twice (Matthew 4:19; Mark 1:17). After Peter's denial of Jesus, there are these two instances when Jesus repeats his call to Peter (John 21:19,22). And in the book of Acts, when the Angel of the Lord breaks Peter out of prison, he is again told, *Follow me* (Acts 12:8).

Jesus Christ. When making his determinations, God looks at the intention of the heart.

> 21:23 *Then this saying went abroad among the*
> *brethren that that disciple should not die; yet Jesus*
> *did not say unto him, He shall not die, but, If I will*
> *that he tarry until I come, what is that to thee?*

In effect, Jesus answered the question about what would happen to John by telling Peter it was none of his business. Peter was to leave his curiosity aside and concentrate on following Jesus. This is good advice for us all.

> 21:24 *This is the disciple who testifies of these things*
> *and wrote these things, and we know that his testi-*
> *mony is true.*

The disciple *who testifies of these things and wrote these things* is, of course, John.

> 21:25 *And there are also many other things which*
> *Jesus did, which, if they should be written every one,*
> *I think that even the world*[113] *itself could not contain*
> *the books that should be written. Amen.*

Let us pray

Lord, we thank you for your love, tenderness, and concern for your disciples. We thank you for the table you have prepared for us, even in the midst of our enemies, as we bear witness to your word and to your testimony. We desire to come and dine so we may be nurtured by what you say and by what you are. Amen.

---

113 The word "world" here is the Greek word *cosmos*, meaning a system or arrangement. In other words, if everything Jesus did was written down and turned into books, although there would be room enough to house them all, the system of this world would not be able to cope with the effect of these books. Even so, if we are found among the believers who will spend all eternity with Jesus, at the proper time, we will have the opportunity to look into these and many other things of great interest to those who understand the way of the cross.

Part II

The Universal Epistles of John

Introduction to Part II

Many seem to think that if they can hear the voice of God, this is sufficient in itself. Hearing and responding to the voice of God is a great beginning, but Scripture is clear that it is essential for us to be able to see by the Spirit from God's perspective. Jesus said, *Blessed are the pure in heart, for they shall see God* (Matthew 5:8).

Therefore, unless our hearts are pure and clean, we will be troubled by darkness and shadows, easily deceived, and unable to clearly discern and understand spiritual things, even if we think we can hear the voice of God.

The apostle John demonstrated his ability to see with great clarity into the spiritual realm when he wrote the book of Revelation. This is his first universal epistle, and in it John assumes that even "little children" in Christ are "born again" into the life and light of God and have the ability to perceive the difference between light and darkness. He also assumes that every genuine believer has the indwelling presence of the Holy Spirit, referred to in this epistle as *the anointing*.

John is described four times in Scripture as "the disciple whom Jesus loved," yet we can see from his writing that he also grew into a very deep and mature relationship with God the Father. May this wonderful example challenge and encourage all of us to know the Father and to come to maturity in Christ.

Chapter 19

That Your Joy May Be Fulfilled

1 John 1

1:1 *That which was from the beginning, which we have heard, which we have seen with our eyes, which we have looked upon, and our hands have handled, of the Word of life*

1:2 *(for the life is manifested, and we also saw it and bear witness and show unto you that eternal life, which was with the Father and appeared unto us);*

J esus *was* (that is, he eternally existed) *from the beginning. And he is before all things, and by him all things consist* (Colossians 1:17). When Jesus Christ was here as a man, the Father dwelt in him bodily by the Spirit, and so John and the other disciples were not only able to hear and see and look upon and handle Jesus, *the Word of life*, they were also able to *bear witness and show* us *that eternal life, which was with the Father and appeared* unto them. This is because just as the Father dwelt in Jesus and thus his life was manifest in and through the Son, now Jesus dwelt in John and in the other disciples, which in turn made his life manifest so John could *show unto you* (the reader) *that eternal life.*

> 1:3 *that which we have seen and heard we declare unto you, that ye also may have communion with us; and truly our communion is with the Father and with his Son Jesus Christ.*

Here the Father is clearly differentiated from the Son, and John desires that we may have communion (intimate fellowship) with both, just as he does.

> 1:4 *And these things write we unto you, that your joy may be fulfilled.*

The psalmist summed it up this way: *Happy are the people that know how to enter into joy; they shall walk, O LORD, in the light of thy countenance* (Psalm 89:15).

> 1:5 *This then is the promise which we have heard of him and declare unto you, That God is light, and in him is no darkness at all.*

This ties in with the promise God made to David, *as he promised to give a light to him and to his sons for ever* (2 Chronicles 21:7). The promised gift is Jesus Christ, who said, *I AM the light of the world; he that follows me shall not walk in darkness but shall have the light of life* (John 8:12). Jesus' life is *the light of men* (John 1:4).

> 1:6 *If we say that we have fellowship with him and walk in darkness, we lie, and do not the truth;*

God wants us to not only speak the truth but to *do* the truth. Those who claim to have fellowship with him and yet continue to walk in darkness are lying.

> 1:7 *But if we walk in the light, as he is in the light, we have communion with him in the midst of us,*

*and the blood of Jesus Christ, his Son cleanses us
from all sin.*

God is light, and thus *if we walk in the light* we must walk with
God. Scripture also states that *God is a Spirit* (John 4:24) and
that *no man has seen God at any time* (John 1:18). With the
advent of Jesus Christ, witnesses like John here upon the earth
were able to testify that *we have looked upon, and our hands
have handled, of the Word of life.*

We cannot *have fellowship with him* (with God the Father)
and walk in darkness. To think otherwise is a lie. It is when *we
walk in the light, as he is in the light* that *we have communion
with him in the midst of us, and the blood of Jesus Christ his
Son cleanses us from all sin.*

God is light, and in him there is no darkness at all. However,
he also desires to appear in us. He longs to reign from our
hearts, and this is why he gives the promised light. He will not
accept darkness in our heart. If we are to become his temple
and he is to reign in us, then he requires that we be completely
cleansed. This cleansing, however, will only happen if we walk
in the light, in communion with him who will be found in our
midst as we walk in accordance with his Word.[114] That is when
the blood[115] *of Jesus Christ, his Son,* will cleanse us *from all sin.*

1:8 *If we say that we have no sin, we deceive ourselves, and there is no truth in us.*

What is *all sin*?

The Greek word translated as "sin" in this passage is *hamartia*,
from the root word *hamartano*, defined by many as meaning
"to commit an offense" or "to miss the mark." As explained
earlier, *hamartia* is definitely an offense, but it does not just

---

114 Remember that the Lord Jesus Christ is the living Word of God (John 1:1).
115 Remember that according to Scripture, life is in the blood (Leviticus 17:11).
Consider this in the light of the following verse: *For if, when we were enemies,
we were reconciled with God by the death of his Son, much more, now reconciled,
we shall be saved by his life* (Romans 5:10).

mean "to miss the mark," it means "to shoot at the wrong target." An archer who shot at the wrong target in a competition (and even more so in a war) would be committing a sin or offense even if he hit the bull's-eye. This is why all of us in our natural state *have sinned and are made destitute of the glory of God* (Romans 3:23).

Thus when John writes that *the blood of Jesus Christ cleanses us from **all sin**,* he means it cleanses us from all of our attempts to go our own way, or any way that is not the way of God. From that point on, our only ambition must be to follow him.

All of us are guilty of going our own way instead of God's way. *All we like sheep have become lost; we have turned each one to his own way; and the LORD transposed in him the iniquity of us all* (Isaiah 53:6).

> 1:9 *If we confess our sins, he is faithful and just*
> *to forgive us our sins and to cleanse us from all*
> *unrighteousness.*

In this passage, the one who *is faithful and just to forgive us our sins and to cleanse us from all unrighteousness* is clearly God the Father. This isn't just about confessing our sins and being forgiven because God is *faithful and just* and therefore is not satisfied until he can *cleanse us from all unrighteousness.* God certainly wants us to be forgiven and clean, but he desires this not just for his sake but for ours.

> 1:10 *If we say that we have not sinned, we make him*
> *a liar, and his word is not in us.*

If we say that we have not sinned, that we have not been guilty of committing offenses by going our own way and seeking our own pleasure (shooting at the wrong goals or targets), *we make him a liar, and his word* (Jesus) *is not in us.*

1 John 2

2:1 My little children, I write these things unto you, that ye sin not; and if anyone has sinned, we have an Advocate before the Father, Jesus, the righteous Christ;

2:2 and he is the reconciliation for our sins, and not for ours only, but also for the sins of the whole world.

Reconciliation does not mean that we go through some kind of mediation process in which we meet God at a point halfway between our "mortal" sins and our "venial" ones. When *he is the reconciliation for our sins* our past is blotted out and forgiven and our future is secured. This means coming into a clean state where our will and desires are lined up straight with God as our hearts are transformed from the inside out, for God never changes. We are the ones who have to be lined back up (reconciled) with him. *Jesus, the righteous*[116] *Christ*, is the reconciliation not only for our individual sins (our *hamartia*) but also for the sins of the whole world. The world (corporately as well as individually) is shooting at the wrong targets and causing untold damage, because not only do the inhabitants of the world go their own way and aim at that wrong target, but they also defame, persecute, and even kill those who follow Christ. Jesus is the only way for anyone to be reconciled to God, and there is no limit to the number of people he can reconcile in this way.[117] He is the reconciliation *for the sins of the whole world.*

2:3 And in this we do know that we have known him if we keep his commandments.

---

116   In the Greek, the word *dikaios*, translated here as "righteous," also means "just."

117   Jesus' death can justify and reconcile an unlimited number of people to God. If we are truly dead in Christ; if we are dead to trespasses and sin then no legal charges can be brought against a dead person.

Keeping Jesus' commandments is beyond the power of the natural man, so if we have been granted the strength (by grace) to keep them, we can be certain that we know him. Our actions will demonstrate whether or not we are shooting at the right targets.

> 2:4 *He that says, I have known him, and does not keep his commandments, is a liar, and the truth is not in him.*

> 2:5 *But whosoever keeps his word, in him verily is the charity of God perfected: hereby know we that we are in him.*

If Jesus resides in our hearts by the Holy Spirit, then the truth is in us, the Word of God is in us, the hand of God will circumcise our hearts, and all our sins will be dealt with. We will no longer have the wrong goals. Instead, the desire of our hearts will be to keep his commandments and do his will. The *charity of God* is to be perfected in us as we keep his word. Aiming at the right goals can be looked on as a form of target practice.

> 2:6 *He that says he abides in him ought himself also so to walk, even as he walked.*

How did Jesus walk?

Jesus walked in communion with his Father. He did and said what the Father indicated. His heart was always in tune with the heart of his Father. If Jesus felt compassion and reached out and had mercy on someone, it was because the Father also felt compassion for that person.

> 2:7 *Brethren, I write no new commandment unto you, but an old commandment which ye have had from the beginning. The old commandment is the word which ye have heard from the beginning.*

Regarding the "old commandment" (the word we have heard from the beginning), the law and the prophets can be summed up as follows: *Jesus said unto him, Thou shalt love the Lord thy God with all thy heart and with all thy soul and with all thy mind. This is the first and great commandment. And the second is like unto it, Thou shalt love thy neighbour as thyself. On these two commandments hang all the law and the prophets* (Matthew 22:37-40).

> 2:8 *Again, a new commandment I write unto you, which is the truth in him and in you, because the darkness is past, and the true light now shines.*

Remember that Jesus said: *A new commandment I give unto you, That ye love one another; as I have loved you, that ye also love one another. By this shall everyone know that ye are my disciples, if ye have love one to another* (John 13:34-35).

If we keep Jesus' new commandment, our actions will demonstrate the truth in him and the truth in us, and *everyone* will know that we are his disciples. The only way for the truth to be in us is if we are filled with the Holy Spirit. If we reject the truth in Jesus and his truth in us and instead rely on memorized doctrine (religious indoctrination) about him, although we may think that we stand in the light, we will remain in darkness.

Virtually everything recorded in the Scriptures has to do with Jesus and comes from him. All of scripture was written by the inspiration of the Spirit of God. However, if anyone attempts to distill doctrines, principles, and values to apply at their own discretion (or at the discretion of others) separate and apart from Christ, they will remain deceived and in darkness even while claiming to be in the light.

> 2:9 *He that says he is in the light and hates his brother is still in darkness.*

What about the infighting that takes place between Christians of different denominations or different doctrinal views? What about the factions and divisions that bring about church splits? What about family problems, even divorce, among Christians?

That these things happen is undeniable, but in the next two verses, John divides putative believers into two basic categories, into one of which we each must fall.

> 2:10 *He that loves his brother abides in the light,*
> *and there is no occasion of stumbling in him.*

The Greek word translated here as "love" is *agapao* – meaning to decide from the heart to show mercy and charity, whether the other person deserves it or not.

> 2:11 *But he that hates his brother is in darkness and*
> *walks in darkness and does not know where he goes,*
> *because that darkness hath blinded his eyes.*

Jesus said, *And if the blind lead the blind, both shall fall into a pit* (Matthew 15:14b). What pit is he talking about? The bottomless pit of the insatiable desires of the carnal natural man. If we hate our brother, the darkness of our hate will blind us to the danger that lies in our path, and once we fall into this pit, we find ourselves in fierce and even violent competition for the limited resources of this world, with hatred against anyone who might challenge our claims.

> 2:12 *I write unto you, little children, that your sins*
> *are forgiven you for his name's sake.*

> 2:13 *I write unto you, fathers, that ye have known*
> *him that is from the beginning. I write unto you,*
> *young men, that ye have overcome the wicked one....*

John is writing to those of all three levels of spiritual maturity. Those who have been born again and are still *little children* can rest assured that their *sins are forgiven*. Those who are mature in Christ and are fathers in the faith are reminded that they have known *him that is from the beginning* (they have a trajectory of knowing God the Father). Yet it is the *young men* who, collectively, *have overcome the wicked one.*

Under the old covenant, the stages of maturity were child (up to twelve years old), young people (from twelve to thirty), and then fathers or parents (someone who had achieved the maturity necessary to enter into ministry or to receive an inheritance). John changes the order of this sequence and then doubles down on the new order.

> 2:13 ... *I write unto you, little children, that ye have known the Father.*

> 2:14 *I have written unto you, fathers, that ye have known him that is from the beginning. I have written unto you, young men, that ye*[118] *are strong and the word of God abides in you, and ye have overcome the wicked one.*

The *little children* are those who know Father God. They understand that he will not only provide for them but will also correct them and discipline them so he may bless them.

The *fathers* are those who have established a strong and intimate relationship with God the Father and can be used by God to reach others. It is the plan of God to bring us quickly into this level of maturity because Jesus Christ is mature (same word in Greek as "perfect"), and he desires to reign and rule from the depths of our hearts. Maturity in Christ need not take decades if we simply yield to Jesus Christ in every matter that arises, and it is no longer a matter of male or female.

It is now the desire of God, as laid out here by John, to take us quickly from immature "children" in the faith to mature "fathers" capable of sharing our faith and seeing it multiplied

---

118   Remember that in Old English (which accurately reflects the pronouns of the Hebrew and Greek of the original Scriptures), "thee" and "thou" are always singular and "ye" and "you" are always plural. This is also true of possessive determiners such as "thy," always singular, and "your," always plural.

into others under the lordship of Jesus Christ, and then to virile "young people" who *are strong*, in whom *the word of God abides*, and who corporately *have overcome the wicked one*. The goal of our faith is not that we should be spiritual greybeards doddering around in "old age" with the help of a cane, but that we should all (male and female) be eternally young and virile, in the prime of our life with God, and in the midst of the overcoming company of the body of Jesus Christ.

> 2:15 *Love not the world neither the things that are in the world. If anyone loves the world, the charity of the Father is not in him.*

Love of the world is directly antagonistic to the charity or love of the Father. We can have one or the other, not both.

> 2:16 *For all that is in the world, the lust of the flesh and the lust of the eyes and the pride of life, is not of the Father, but is of the world.*

> 2:17 *And the world passes away and the lust thereof, but he that does the will of God abides for ever.*

Everything *that is in the world*, including *the lust of the flesh and the lust of the eyes and the pride of life*, is a false target that those who sin (those who aim at the wrong targets) are attempting to hit in order to win worldly prizes. The wrong targets will eventually pass away, but *he that does the will of God abides for ever.*

> 2:18 *Little children, it is the last hour, and as ye have heard that the antichrist comes, likewise there are also beginning to be many antichrists, by which we know that it is the last time.*

An antichrist[119] is a false Christ. Jesus specifically told the

---

119 In Greek, the prefix anti-, such as in antichrist, does not mean the opposite of Christ. It means a false or counterfeit Christ.

disciples to watch out for false Christs (Matthew 24:24; Mark 13:22). The fact that John mentions it is *the last hour* and *the last time* most likely means that this epistle was written near the time of the siege and destruction of Jerusalem. Jesus' Olivet Discourse, recorded in Matthew 24, Mark 13, and Luke 21 was, as you remember, his response to several questions from the disciples triggered by his statement regarding the temple buildings: *There shall not be left here one stone upon another that shall not be thrown down. And as he sat upon the mount of Olives, the disciples came unto him privately, saying, Tell us, when shall these things be? and what shall be the sign of thy coming and of the end of the age?* (Matthew 24:2b-3).

Jesus answered the questions in a way that used the signs and events signaling the impending destruction of Jerusalem and the temple (at the end of the age of the law) as an example in type and shadow of what will happen in the time leading up to his second coming (at the end of the age of grace), due to take place approximately two thousand years later. (Bear in mind that the events regarding the end of the age of the law in about AD 67 to AD 70 were localized to Jerusalem and Judea. The events leading up to the second coming will be worldwide.)

According to the Jewish historian Josephus, the tragic events leading into what he called the "Jewish Wars" involved several false messiahs (false Christs or antichrists) who helped trigger the Roman invasion, occasioning significant bloodshed (even among Jewish factions) and a major fire that among other things destroyed the temple grain reserves long before the Romans breached the city. What about today?

> 2:19 *They went out from us, but they were not of us; for if they had been of us, they would no doubt have continued with us; but this happened that it might be made manifest that they were not all of us.*

John states that these antichrists *went out from us, but they were not of us.*

What does this tell us about the time that we are in now, when Jesus' return is imminent?

> 2:20 *But ye have the anointing of the Holy One, and ye know all things.*

The *anointing of the Holy One* is the indwelling presence of the Holy Spirit. This is the only way that, when everything that can be shaken will be shaken, we will be able to *know all things* and respond appropriately according to the will of God.

As the time of Jesus' return rapidly approaches, it is of paramount importance that our hearts be so clean and pure that we can hearken to (that is, hear and obey; be led by) the Spirit and have keen spiritual vision and discernment.

> *See that you do not refuse him that speaks. For if those who refused him that spoke on earth did not escape, much less shall we escape, if we turn away from him that speaks from the heavens, whose voice then shook the earth; but now he has promised, saying, Yet even once, I shall shake not the earth only, but also the heaven. And this word, Yet even once, signifies the removing of those things that are shaken, as of things that are made, that those things which cannot be shaken may remain. Therefore, receiving a kingdom which cannot be moved, let us hold fast to the grace, by which we serve God, pleasing him with reverence and godly fear: for our God is a consuming fire.* (Hebrews 12:25-29)

The Jews who refused to hear and obey Jesus did not escape. Only the believers who were in tune with the Holy Spirit were spared, and even they were scattered. Nevertheless, they witnessed for Jesus throughout the known world and literally *turned the world upside down* (Acts 17:6). When Jesus returns in glory and the first resurrection takes place, the very foundations of this world will be destroyed and its kingdoms will fall (Revelation 11:15).

As Peter tells us: *The Lord is not late concerning his promise, as some count lateness, but is patient with us, not willing that any should perish, but that all should come to repentance* (2 Peter 3:9). God has granted time for repentance. There is, however, a limit to his patience.

> But the day of the Lord will come as a thief in the night, in which the heavens shall pass away with a great noise, and the elements, burning, shall be dissolved, and the earth and the works that are in it shall be burned up. Seeing then that all these things shall be dissolved, what manner of persons ought ye to be in all holy conversation and godliness, waiting for and desiring earnestly for the coming of the day of God, in which the heavens being on fire shall be dissolved, and the elements[120] shall melt with fervent heat? (2 Peter 3:10-12)

The coming day of God need not take us unaware. Now is the time for us to get ready and remain that way. The best preparation we can make is to keep our hearts upon the altar of God and allow him to cleanse and purify us as he sees fit.

Returning to 1 John 2:

> 2:21 I have not written unto you as if ye ignore the truth, but as unto those that know it, and that no lie is of the truth.

> 2:22 Who is a liar but he that denies that Jesus is the Christ? This same is antichrist, who denies the Father and the Son.

---

120 The elements of the world are defined in Galatians 4:3,9 and Colossians 2:8,20.

The word "Christ" in Greek means the same as "Messiah" in Hebrew. To deny that Jesus is the Christ is not only to refuse to believe that a historical Jesus existed, it is to refuse to give him his rightful place of authority in our lives and in our midst. Jesus Christ is our Sovereign Lord and King as well as our Redeemer. We must never deny him our wholehearted allegiance and obedience.

> 2:23 *Whosoever denies the Son, the same does not have the Father. Whosoever confesses the Son, has the Father also.*

What does it mean to confess the Son?

Matthew records Jesus as saying: *Whosoever therefore shall confess me before men, him will I also confess before my Father who is in the heavens. But whosoever shall deny me before men, him will I also deny before my Father who is in the heavens* (Matthew 10:32-33).

According to the gospel of Luke, Jesus said: *Also I say unto you, Whosoever shall confess me before men, him shall the Son of man also confess before the angels of God; but he that denies me before men shall be denied before the angels of God* (Luke 12:8-9).

Believing in Jesus is not necessarily the same as confessing him. John tells us: *Nevertheless, even among the princes many believed in him, but because of the Pharisees they did not confess him, lest they should be put out of the synagogue; for they loved the glory of men more than the glory of God* (John 12:42-43).

To "confess the Son" means to take a public stand for Jesus. This implies words and deeds.

> 2:24 *Let that therefore abide in you, which ye have heard from the beginning. For if that which ye have heard from the beginning shall abide in you, ye also shall continue to abide in the Son and in the Father.*

What is that which we *have heard from the beginning* of our walk with God?

The Word of life.

Jesus is the Word of life, and if we let him abide in us as we continue to hear and obey him, we shall also *continue to abide in the Son and in the Father.*

> 2:25 *And this is the promise that he has promised us, even eternal life.*

Eternal life is *the promise* and is immutably linked to Jesus Christ. The Holy Spirit (the anointing) is the down payment, or earnest, of our promised inheritance in Christ. As the apostle Paul wrote to the Corinthians: *For all the promises of God are yes in him, and in him Amen, by us for the glory of God. Now he who confirms us with you unto Christ and has anointed us is God; who has also sealed us and given the earnest of the Spirit in our hearts* (2 Corinthians 1:20-22).

God's plan is to bring us into the fullness of our inheritance in Christ. This requires our cooperation so that we do not deviate from that which we *have heard from the beginning.*

Paul wrote to the Ephesians along similar lines:

> [God] *having made known unto us the mystery of his will, according to his good pleasure which he has purposed in himself, that in the dispensation of the fulfillment of the times he might restore all things by the Christ, both those which are in heaven and those which are on earth, in him in whom likewise we have obtained an inheritance, having had the way marked out beforehand according to the purpose of him who works all things after the counsel of his own will, so that we should be to the praise of his glory, those of us who first trusted in the Christ.*
> (Ephesians 1:9-12)

The apostles, including John and Peter and Paul, were among those *who first trusted in the Christ*. (In fact, everywhere the gospel has spread, there have always been *those who first trusted in the Christ*.)

We have received the apostles' testimony through the written word of the Scriptures and through the anointed preaching of the gospel by contemporary preachers. We have also had the opportunity to observe the witness and testimony of genuine believers and followers of Jesus Christ in our own time (as did those to whom Paul was writing).

Paul continued: *In whom ye also trusted, hearing the word of truth, the gospel of your saving health; in whom also after ye believed, ye were sealed with that Holy Spirit of the promise* (Ephesians 1:13).

This is what we *have heard from the beginning*: the witness of the inspired writers of the Scriptures and the inner witness and power of *that Holy Spirit of the promise* after we believed and were sealed.

Paul concluded his description with these words: *which is the earnest of our inheritance unto the redemption of the purchased possession, unto the praise of his glory* (Ephesians 1:14).

We are *the purchased possession*. We belong to Jesus, who paid for us with his blood, and our redemption is *unto the praise of his glory*.

Returning again to 1 John 2:

> 2:26 *These things I have written unto you concerning those that seduce you.*

John is concerned for the "little children" to whom he is writing. Inspired by God, he is concerned that some of them might be seduced – that is, deceived – into letting down their guard.

> 2:27 *But the anointing which ye have received of him abides in you, and ye do not need that anyone teach*

*you; but as the same anointing teaches you of all
things and is truth, and is no lie; and even as it has
taught you, abide ye in him.*

False teachers and those with a spirit of antichrist want to make
us dependent upon them and upon their doctrines, dogmas,
and church order, instead of abiding in Jesus Christ according
to the anointing with which we have been sealed. The anointing (the Holy Spirit) will teach us *of all things and is truth, and
is no lie.* If Jesus Christ and his Father live in our hearts by the
Holy Spirit and we have communion with them and experience their thoughts and feelings (John 16:13-15), why would
we want to follow anyone else?

True ministers of God help join people to Jesus Christ and
encourage them to follow him and abide in him and love one
another. Let's face it: loving our fellow humans isn't always
easy. Can anyone other than God teach us to love one another
the way Jesus loved us?

*2:28 And now, little children, abide in him; that,
when he shall appear, we may have confidence and
not be ashamed before him at his coming.*

*2:29 If ye know that he is righteous, also know that
any one that does righteousness is born of him.*

Remember that "righteousness" and "justice" are the same word
in the Greek and in Hebrew. This is not about dogmas or rituals
or sects (which are, in effect, private kingdoms). *Any one that
does righteousness* (justice) *is born of him* (Jesus). And anyone
that is born of him is, by definition, our brother (or sister) in
Christ. We are to love one another as Jesus loved us. As we do
so in the power of the Holy Spirit, we will find that our joy is
complete. Then we will *have confidence and not be ashamed
before him at his coming.*

Let us pray

Heavenly Father, we ask that you may keep your mighty hand upon us. Please examine our hearts, expose anything that is not to your liking, and deal with it according to your will. May your love, charity, and mercy flow through us to everyone around us so that our joy may be complete. Amen.

Chapter 20

Born of God

1 John 3

In modern times, this has possibly been one of the most misunderstood chapters in the Bible, because over the past century or more, many people have defined key terminology in this passage improperly and have therefore misinterpreted the text.

> 3:1 *Behold, what charity the Father has given us,*
> *that we should be called the sons of God; therefore*
> *the world does not know us, because it does not*
> *know him.*

Sons of God reflect, at least in some degree, the nature of their Father. Sons of God belong to the family of God, being brothers and sisters of Jesus Christ. As sons of God, our goal is to come to maturity in Christ. Achieving this goal is not only important to us, it is also very important to our heavenly Father.

> 3:2 *Beloved, now we are the sons of God, and it is*
> *not yet made manifest what we shall be; but we*
> *know that if he shall appear, we shall be like him; for*
> *we shall see him as he is.*

If God shall appear, *we shall be like him*. This is all in the future tense. Jesus appeared here on earth as a man, but at his return, he will appear as the Lord of heaven. *The first man is of the earth, earthy; the second man is the Lord of heaven. As is the earthy, such are those also that are earthy; and as is the heavenly, such also are those that are heavenly. And as we have borne the image of the earthy, we shall also bear the image of the heavenly* (1 Corinthians 15:47-49).

Although all of us begin our time here on earth in the image of Adam, God's plan is for us to be transformed into the image of the Lord Jesus Christ. In order for this to happen, we must be purified, and this is a matter of the heart. Remember Jesus said, *Blessed are the pure in heart, for they shall see God.*

3:3 *And every one that has this hope in him purifies himself, even as he is pure.*

How can we purify ourselves at all, let alone purify ourselves to such an extent that we will be pure *even as he is pure?*

The Jewish purification rituals involved sacrifice and blood and water. *And almost all things are by the law purged with blood, and without shedding of blood there is no remission. So that it was necessary that the figures of the heavenly things should be purified with these, but the heavenly things themselves with better sacrifices than these* (Hebrews 9:22-23).

The *better sacrifices than these* are the sacrifice of Jesus Christ and our willingness to sacrifice our own way and our own life as we follow Jesus on the way of the cross until we become living sacrifices and are transformed as his pure life comes forth in us (Romans 12:1-2).

3:4 *Whosoever commits sin transgresses also the law: for sin is the transgression of the law.*

Whosoever commits sin (Greek *hamartia*) by "shooting at the wrong targets" (with wrong desires, goals, and ambitions) *transgresses also the law.* God's commandments are law. Under the old covenant, the Ten Commandments were written on tablets of stone. In the new covenant, God's commandments are placed within our very being by the nature of Christ.

> *But this is the covenant that I will make with the house of Israel after those days, said the LORD, I will give my law in their souls and write it in their hearts and will be their God, and they shall be my people. And they shall no longer teach every man his neighbour and every man his brother, saying, Know the LORD, for they shall all know me, from the least of them unto the greatest of them, said the LORD, for I will forgive their iniquity, and I will remember their sin no more.* (Jeremiah 31:33-34)

> *And I will make an eternal covenant with them, that I will not turn away from doing them good, and I will put my fear in their hearts that they shall not depart from me.* (Jeremiah 32:40)

If Jesus truly lives and reigns in and from our hearts, then the fear of God will be in our hearts. Remember, *the fear of the LORD is the beginning of wisdom* (Psalm 111:10; Proverbs 9:10).[121]

> *3:5 And ye know that he appeared to take away our sins, and there is no sin in him.*

Jesus, by his very nature, does not "shoot at wrong targets." *There is no sin in him.* Jesus is incorruptible, and if we have received the word of life, the seed he has planted in us is incorruptible.

Simon Peter put it this way: *Having purified your souls in the obedience of the truth, by the Spirit, in unfeigned brotherly love, love one another with a pure heart fervently, being born*

---

121 The fear of the Lord is not terror. It is a very strong and healthy respect.

again, not of corruptible seed, but of incorruptible, by the word of God, which lives and abides for ever (1 Peter 1:22-23).

> *3:6 Whosoever abides in him does not sin: whosoever sins has not seen him or known him.*

Whosoever abides in Jesus does not shoot at wrong targets. Those who have the wrong goals and ambitions have *not seen him or known him.*

> *3:7 Little children, let no one deceive you; he that does righteousness is righteous, even as he also is righteous.*

> *3:8 He that commits sin is of the devil; for the devil sins from the beginning. For this purpose the Son of God appeared, that he might undo the works of the devil.*

> *3:9 Whosoever is born of God does not commit sin; for his seed remains in him; and he cannot sin, because he is born of God.*

History is littered with the wreckage caused by those who have failed to understand the above passage. If the definition of sin (*hamartia*) is believed to be "to miss the mark," then it is inevitable that this Scripture will be seriously misunderstood. For example, many people seem to think these verses must apply to some future dispensation. Others have used the text to justify extreme views on sanctification and even "sinless perfection." The true explanation, however, is very simple: The person who commits *hamartia* (who shoots at wrong targets) is of the devil, regardless of whether they hit the bull's-eye or miss the mark.

How is your outlook on people likely to be affected if you think that anyone who misses the mark is of the devil? What about someone who fails to get a perfect score on a math test or any other test? Or someone who is forgetful or who succumbs to some common fault or failure tied to our limited human condition? What if, in order to not be *of the devil*, everyone was required not just to shoot at the right target but to score a bull's-eye with every shot? How many of us could possibly meet such a standard?

God looks at the intention of the heart. Those who are *born of God* have right desires and right goals. They will always intentionally shoot at the right target, even if they only hit the bull's-eye occasionally at first. Their joy is to please God.

We all need "target practice." We are exhorted and encouraged in this endeavor by those who have given us good examples, such as Paul, who declared, *I press toward the mark for the prize of the high calling of God in Christ Jesus* (Philippians 3:14).

> 3:9 *Whosoever is born of God does not commit sin; for his seed remains in him; and he cannot sin, because he is born of God.*

Some parse the phrase "born of God" and claim that since this is impossible in our present age or dispensation, the text must therefore be referring to something that will happen in the future. I disagree. I think Scripture is very clear that being born of God is exactly the same as being "born again." But what if you mistakenly thought that just because you were born again that therefore it would now be impossible for you to ever miss the mark?

Whosoever is born of God does not shoot at wrong targets. Why not? Because when God is in charge of our life, the first thing he changes in our being is our heart. God circumcises our heart, taking a scalpel to the power of the flesh to control us and corrupt us with its wrong desires and goals. As we follow Jesus, we will encounter plenty of opportunity for target practice along the way to improve our aim, but at least our heart will be set on shooting at the right target, even in the presence of numerous incoming fiery darts from the enemy (Ephesians 6:16).

If we stumble or fall, it matters which way we were heading when we went down. Were we struggling against great trials yet still intending to do the right thing and follow Jesus? Or did we turn our back on him and return to the world? *For a just man falls seven times and rises up again, but the wicked shall fall into evil* (Proverbs 24:16).

> 3:10 *In this the sons of God are manifest, and the sons of the devil: whosoever does not righteousness and that loves not his brother is not of God.*

Jesus explained, *Ye shall know them by their fruits* (Matthew 7:16). *For the fruit of the Spirit is in all goodness and righteousness and truth* (Ephesians 5:9).

> 3:11 *For this is the message that ye heard from the beginning, That we should love one another.*

> 3:12 *Not as Cain, who was of the wicked one and killed his brother. And why did he kill him? Because his own works were evil, and his brother's righteous.*

> 3:13 *Marvel not, my brethren, if the world hates you.*

The devil is referred to as the "prince of this world" three times in the gospel of John, and Scripture tells us that the kingdoms of the world are all under his control (Matthew 4:8-9; Luke 4:5-6). The devil is the father of lies and a murderer (John 8:44). He and his followers hate those who are righteous.

> 3:14 *We know that we are passed from death unto life, in that we love the brethren. He that does not love his brother abides in death.*

> 3:15 *Whosoever hates his brother is a murderer and*

ye know that no murderer has eternal life abiding in him.

That verse calls to mind the words of Jesus: *Ye have heard that it was said to the ancients, Thou shalt not commit murder, and whosoever shall commit murder shall be guilty of the judgment; but I say unto you, That whosoever is angry with his brother out of control shall be in danger of the judgment* (Matthew 5:21-22a).

3:16 *In this we have known the charity of God because he laid down his life for us; we also ought to lay down our lives for the brethren.*

Compare 1 John 3:16 to the well-known John 3:16: *For God so loved the world that he gave his only begotten Son, that whosoever believes in him should not perish but have eternal life.*

How can we know if we have come into the reality of John 3:16? How can we be sure that we have eternal life?

We know that we are passed from death unto life, in that we love the brethren (1 John 3:14).

Therefore, if *we have known the charity* (of the love) *of God because he laid down his life for us,* then *we also ought to lay down our lives for the brethren.*

John tells us that Jesus said, *Greater love has no man than this, that a man lay down his soul* [that is, his life] *for his friends* (John 15:13).

Jesus' new commandment is not just about having warm fuzzy feelings and kind words for all of our brothers and sisters in Christ. It also goes well beyond loving our neighbor as our self. If we keep Jesus' commandment in the power of the Holy Spirit, we will soon find ourselves pouring out our very soul on behalf of our "brother," even to the point of being willing to lay down our life.

3:17 *But whosoever has this world's goods and sees*

*his brother have need and shuts up his bowels of
compassion from him, how does the charity of God
abide in him?*

*3:18 My little children, let us not love in word nei-
ther in tongue, but in deed and in truth.*

*3:19 And in this we know that we are of the truth
and have our hearts certified before him.*

What does it mean to *have our hearts certified* before God? It
simply means that we will have a clean conscience. Our conscience will be *void of offense* (Acts 24:16).

*3:20 And if our heart condemns us, God is greater
than our heart and knows all things.*

Our heart may tell us that we have violated our conscience in
the past, but *God is greater than our heart and knows all things.*
He knows exactly how to deal with our situation, if we let him.

*3:21 Beloved, if our heart does not condemn us, then
we have confidence in God;*

*3:22 and whatsoever we ask, we receive of him
because we keep his commandments and do those
things that are pleasing in his sight.*

If our heart does not condemn us (and remember that John's
words are directed to those who are *beloved*), *then we have
confidence **in** God.* This is the realm of answered prayer. If we
have *confidence in God*, then we have faith in him, and *without
faith it is impossible to please God* (Hebrews 11:6). Faith is not
just believing in God (although that's a good start). Having
faith means believing God,[122] trusting him, and depending on

---

122 Abraham, a father of faith, didn't just believe in God. *Abraham believed God,
and it was counted unto him as righteousness* (Romans 4:3). He believed God
and **obeyed** him such as when he left Ur of the Chaldees and traveled to the
promised land and when he offered his son Isaac, etc.

him to do for us what we cannot do for ourselves (this involves grace as well as faith), as our hearts are transformed and we delight to *keep his commandments and do those things that are pleasing in his sight.*

> 3:23 *And this is his commandment, That we should believe on the name of his Son Jesus Christ, and love one another, as he has commanded us.*

If we respond to the light and truth of God and embrace his commandment with faith, then he will provide us with the grace that will enable us to *believe on the name of his Son Jesus Christ, and love one another, as he has commanded us.* Our own works (apart from Christ) are not acceptable to God, but the work of his Son is. God desires to work both in us and through us. First, he will work in us to circumcise and cleanse our hearts, and then he will work through us as his love flows out of our hearts toward others.

> 3:24 *And he that keeps his commandments dwells in him, and he in him. And in this we know that he abides in us, by the Spirit which he has given us.*

It is very important for us to invite Jesus and the Father to come and live in our hearts and give us the Holy Spirit. But God also wants us to dwell in him. If we make room for him to live in *our* hearts so that we may keep his commandments, he will also have a special place for us in *his* heart, and we are given this wonderful promise: *he that keeps his commandments dwells in him, and he in him.*

How can we really know if God the Father abides in us? *By the Spirit which he has given us.*

Let us pray

Heavenly Father, we ask that we may understand this message in our hearts and in our minds; that the word of your truth will penetrate and permeate our soul until we are pure and clean; that our hearts will be circumcised and transformed until your love flows in and through us. May we keep your commandment to believe on your Son Jesus Christ and love one another, so we may dwell in you and you in us. May we receive the gift of the Holy Spirit. Amen.

Chapter 21

Sons of God

1 John 4

4:1 Beloved, do not believe every spirit, but try the spirits whether they are of God because many false prophets are gone out into the world.

There are spirits operating out of *many false prophets* and trying to compete with the Holy Spirit that God has given us. These spirits are supernatural but not holy, and we are warned not to believe them. They will deny any possibility of personal victory in Christ over sin and the flesh.

4:2 In this know ye the Spirit of God: Every spirit that confesses that Jesus Christ, is come in flesh is of God:

4:3 And every spirit that does not confess that Jesus Christ, is come in flesh is not of God: and this is that spirit of antichrist, of which ye have heard that it should come, and that now it is already in the world.

*Every spirit that confesses that Jesus Christ, **is come** in flesh is of God.* Putting this phrase into modern English is virtually impossible because English has no equivalent to the Greek present continuous tense. The old English *is come* is probably as close as we can get, since it indicates not only that Jesus came in the past but that he continues to come and be present *in flesh.* Jesus can come and live in us and put our flesh under his control by the Spirit. As Paul wrote to the church in Rome: *So then, those that are carnal cannot please God. But ye are not in the flesh, but in the Spirit, because the Spirit of God dwells in you. Now if anyone does not have the Spirit of Christ, that person is not of him ... For if ye live according to the flesh, ye shall die; but if through the Spirit ye mortify the deeds of the body, ye shall live. For all that are led by the Spirit of God, the same are sons of God* (Romans 8:8-10, 13-14).

What does John mean in verses 2 and 3?

The spirit of antichrist won't necessarily begin by denying a historical Jesus or even by denying that Jesus was God incarnate in mortal man. The events that took place almost two thousand years ago may not be of immediate concern to counterfeit spirits or false Christs (false anointings), even though these beings will eventually attempt to subvert, pervert, and eradicate anything having to do with the true God. *Every spirit that does not confess*[123] *that Jesus Christ is come in flesh is antichrist.*

Therefore, every spirit that does not demonstrate the authentic presence of Jesus Christ coming in flesh (including in *our* flesh) is antichrist.

Just as a great seal has historically been used to impress a symbol on softened wax, thus not only sealing the document in question but authenticating that its contents are authorized

---

123 Greek *homologeo*, precursor of our English words, *homologate* and *homologous*, defined in *Webster's Unabridged Dictionary* respectively as, "to agree," and as "having the same relative position, proportion, value, structure, character, etc." as another entity)

by the monarch, so every spirit that comes from God will bear the seal (image) of Jesus' values, character, and word. Without that authentication, it is a false and antichrist spirit and is not to be believed or trusted. *This is that spirit of antichrist, of which ye have heard that it should come, and that now it is already in the world.* The coming of the *spirit of antichrist* was prophesied by Jesus in Matthew 24:24 and Mark 13:22, and that spirit was already in the world when John wrote this epistle sometime during the latter half of the first century.

Returning to 1 John:

> 4:4 *Ye are of God, little children, and have overcome them because greater is he that is in you than he that is in the world.*

> 4:5 *They are of the world; therefore, they speak of the world, and the world hears them.*

The false prophets who operate with a spirit of antichrist are of the world. They preach that we can have all that the world has to offer and heaven as well, *and the world hears them.* They know nothing of the narrow way, of sacrifice, of the way of the cross. Yet even *little children* who are born of God have overcome these false prophets *because greater is he that is in you than he that is in the world.*

> 4:6 *We are of God; he that knows God hears us; he that is not of God does not hear us. By this we know the spirit of truth and the spirit of error.*

This still applies today. If we are of God, there will be some who will hear us and some who will not. The spirit of truth operates in those who know God, and the spirit of error operates in those who are not of God and refuse to hear us.

> 4:7 *Beloved, let us love one another, for charity*[124] *is*

---

124 In the Jubilee Bible translation, the Greek noun *agape* is translated as "charity," in accordance with the scholarship of most early Reformation Bible translations.

of God. Anyone that loves is born of God and knows God.

The *agape* love of God is unalterably linked to his own person and character, and is charity. ***Anyone*** *that loves* (Greek *agapao*) *is born of God and knows God.* This type of love is born of sacrifice and is redemptive by its very nature: *God so loved the world that he gave his only begotten Son.* God decided to have charity or mercy on the world by giving his only begotten Son, not because he approved of the world or had warm, fuzzy feelings toward it but because he wanted to make a sacrificially loving offer to the world's inhabitants: that *whosoever believes in him should not perish but have eternal life.*

4:8 *He that does not love does not know God, for God is charity.*

Charity – the supernatural, sacrificial, redemptive love of God – is not difficult to discern when demonstrated in word and deed.

4:9 *In this was the charity of God demonstrated in us, in that God sent his only begotten Son into the world, that we might live through him.*

God's plan and purpose in sending his only begotten Son is not only to offer us eternal life but also to have *the charity of God* (the love of God) *demonstrated in us.* Jesus said that when

---

However, the verb form of *agape* (which is *agapao*) does not have a direct English equivalent. Our word "charity" (and even our word "mercy") is never used as a verb. Therefore, English Bible translations are virtually forced to use the word "love" to translate two very different Greek words: (1) *agapao*, which relates to the unique love of God that is basically a decision from the heart to show charity and mercy and does not necessarily denote a strong emotional attachment to, or approval of, those being loved; and (2) *phileos*, which is used when describing brotherly love (human affection) and which does imply approval and strong emotional attachment to those being loved. According to Scripture, God is *agape*, not *phileos* (and in spite of what some people seem to assume, *phileos* certainly is not God). *Agape* can be unilateral, but *phileos* (at least in its basic human form) seems to demand reciprocity or something in return. It is when God's *agape* love flows in and through us that we are capable of *phileos* in the highest sense. As an example of this, I recommend reading Jesus' letter to the angel of the congregation at Philadelphia, the city of brotherly love (Revelation 3:7-13).

this happens, the world will know that he was truly sent by the Father and that the Father has loved us even as he has loved Jesus (John 17:23).

> 4:10 *In this does the charity consist, not because we had loved God, but because he loved us and has sent his Son to be the reconciliation for our sins.*

The charity or love that God extended to us even while we were enemies and sinners began unilaterally, from him to us, and was clearly demonstrated when Jesus came and died for us. *The reconciliation for our sins* is directly tied to Jesus' shed blood and physical death. *Without the shedding of blood there is no remission* (Hebrews 9:22b).

As Paul puts it in his letter to the Roman believers: *For if, when we were enemies, we were reconciled with God by the death of his Son, much more, now reconciled, we shall be saved by his life* (Romans 5:10).

Jesus' death becomes our death when we identify with him and become *dead to sins* (Romans 6:2; 1 Peter 2:24). This is similar to the circumcision of the heart that takes place when God, by his word and his Spirit, cuts from our heart the control of the flesh and destroys the source of our wrong goals and wrong targets (Romans 2:29; Colossians 2:11; Philippians 3:3).

It is very clear that *we were reconciled with God by the **death** of his Son.* Becoming *reconciled* means having our past blotted out, no matter how sordid it may have been, and being lined back up straight with God. Jesus accomplished this when he died for us on the cross as a once-and-for-all sacrifice. And if we are dead and hidden in Christ, dead to sins, dead to our past, well, who can accuse a dead person of anything? Therefore, now reconciled with God, dead to sins (dead to the *hamartia* of shooting at wrong targets), and free from the guilt of our past, *we shall be saved by his life.* God's *agape* love and the presence of his life will engulf our entire being by the Spirit, bringing health and salvation and restoration and purification to our soul.

> 4:11 *Beloved, if God so loved us, we also ought to love one another.*

Not only shall we be saved by his life, but as his life and love flow in and through us, others will be blessed, those in the world will notice, and some will be saved.

> 4:12 *No one has seen God at any time. If we love one another, God abides in us, and his charity is completed in us.*

Those who are in the world cannot see God. *If we love one another,* however, *God abides in us,* and those who are lost, out in the world, will be able to see God in us. When this happens, *his charity is completed in us.*

> 4:13 *In this we know that we abide in him, and he in us, in that he has given us of his Spirit.*

Chapter 3 of 1 John ends with these words: *And in this we know that he abides in us, by the Spirit which he has given us.* It is the Spirit that will witness to us that we are truly the children of Father God and that he abides in us (Romans 8:14-16). Another indicator is this: *If we love one another, God abides in us, and his charity is completed in us.* When this happens, the Spirit will also let us *know that we abide in him* and that God the Father has a special place in his heart for us.

> 4:14 *And we have seen and do testify that the Father sent the Son to be the Saviour of the world.*

John and the other apostles saw and testified *that the Father sent the Son to be the Saviour of the world.* However, even though many have been saved out of the world, Jesus' prayer recorded in John 17 has still not been completely fulfilled. At that time, he petitioned his Father with this request:

*Neither do I pray for these alone, but also for those
who shall believe in me through their word; that they
all may be one; as thou, Father, art in me, and I in
thee, that they also may be one in us, that the world
may believe that thou hast sent me. And the clarity
which thou gavest me I have given them, that they
may be one, even as we are one: I in them, and thou
in me, that they may be perfect in one and that the
world may know that thou hast sent me and hast
loved them as thou hast loved me.* (John 17:20-23)

The followers of Jesus Christ remain divided into sects and
denominations, and private kingdoms continue to abound.
Nevertheless, Jesus' prayer that all of his followers will *be perfect in one*, even as he and the Father are one, will ultimately be
answered and completely fulfilled, and we are called to be part
of this. Jesus is in us and the Father is in him that we *may be
perfect*[125] *in one and that the world may know* what, in general,
it does not currently acknowledge, namely that the Father sent
Jesus and has loved Jesus' followers even as he has loved Jesus.

4:15 *Whosoever shall confess that Jesus is the Son of
God, God abides in him, and he in God.*

Whosoever shall confess[126] and show forth *that Jesus is the Son
of God* will prove *that God abides in him, and he in God.*

4:16 *And we have known and believed the charity that God has in us. God is charity, and he that
abides in charity abides in God, and God in him.*

We can know and believe *the charity that God has **in us***. Even
though it is difficult to find words to describe charity (God's
love), we can experience it because John states that God has

---

125   See Appendix for use of the word "perfect" or "perfection" in the Jubilee Bible.
126   Greek *homologeo* – meaning to "demonstrate or authenticate the exact same
values, character, and word" (see footnote 120).

his charity (his love and mercy) **in us**. We will have both an inward awareness of his charity for us and a great sense of joy and fulfillment as we extend his charity to others.

The apostle Paul pronounced a benediction on the church at Corinth: *The grace of the Lord Jesus Christ and the charity of God and the communion of the Holy Spirit be with you all* (2 Corinthians 13:14). Clearly there is a very close and intertwined relationship between the grace of the Lord Jesus Christ, the charity of God, and the communion of the Holy Spirit as we trust and depend on them by faith as believers. This is how God's charity with us may come to perfection (same word in Greek as "maturity") until we reach the point where we permanently abide in charity and therefore abide in God. John goes so far as to say that *he that abides in charity abides in God, and God in him.*

> 4:17 *In this the charity with us is made perfect, that*
> *we may have confidence in the day of judgment,*
> *that as he is, so are we in this world.*

Jesus said, *Blessed are the merciful, for they shall obtain mercy* (Matthew 5:7). He told us we may ask God to *set us free from our debts, as we set free our debtors* (Matthew 6:12), and he went on to explain: *For if ye set men free from their trespasses, your heavenly Father will also set you free; but if ye do not set men free from their trespasses, neither will your Father set you free from your trespasses* (Matthew 6:14-15). Showing mercy is charity, setting our debtors free is charity, and freeing men from their trespasses is charity. Those who flow in the charity of God will have *confidence in the day of judgement*.

Remember that when Jesus appeared to his disciples on the day of his resurrection, he told them that *unto those whose sins ye release, they shall be released; and unto those whose sins ye retain, they shall be retained* (John 20:23). If we must decide to *release* or to *retain* someone's sins regarding whatever sphere of responsibility we are accountable for, we had best have the mind of Christ regarding all matters (Philippians 2:5).

> 4:18 *In charity there is no fear; but charity that is perfect casts out fear; because fear has torment; from which he that fears is not complete in charity.*

Make no mistake, *charity* (the *agape* love of God) *that is perfect casts out fear.* The human emotion that most people call love will not cast out fear. When we demonstrate charity by forgiving others (even our enemies) from the heart, when we pray for those who persecute us, when we set free our debtors, and when we liberate people from their trespasses, our hearts will be pure and clean and bold and joyful, and there will be no room left for fear.

Many people make most of their decisions based on fear of man and therefore live in torment. God wants us to make decisions led by the Spirit, based on *charity that is perfect,* so we can live in harmony with him.

> 4:19 *We love him, because he first loved us.*

Redemption, which is charity, began with God. If we love him, it is because we respond to *his* love and not the other way around.

> 4:20 *If anyone says, I love God and hates his brother, he is a liar; for he that does not love his brother whom he has seen, how can he love God whom he has not seen?*

Old Testament law puts it this way: *Thou shalt not hate thy brother in thine heart; thou shalt rebuke thy neighbour in sincerity, that thou not bear sin for him* (Leviticus 19:17). Note that "neighbor" and "brother" are virtually equivalent in this verse.

> 4:21 *And we have this commandment from him, That he who loves God loves his brother also.*

Look at how Jesus sums this up:

> *Ye have heard that it was said, Thou shalt love thy*
> *neighbour, and hate thine enemy. But I say unto*
> *you, Love your enemies, bless those that curse you,*
> *do good to those that hate you, and pray for those*
> *who speak evil about you, and persecute you* [the
> Greek word translated as "love" here is *agapao*];
> *that ye may be sons of your Father who is in the*
> *heavens, for he makes his sun to rise on the evil*
> *and on the good and sends rain on the just and on*
> *the unjust. For if ye love those who love you, what*
> *reward shall ye have? Do not even the publicans the*
> *same? And if ye embrace your brethren only, what*
> *do ye more than others? Do not even the publicans*
> *so? Be ye therefore perfect, even as your Father who*
> *is in the heavens is perfect.* (Matthew 5:43-48)

Jesus commands us to be *perfect* and holds up our heavenly
Father as the standard. But how can we possibly be perfect,
given our human condition?

If Jesus and the Father dwell in us, and we in them, then
our heart – including our motivation and goals – will change
dramatically. In our natural state, our hearts are *deceitful above
all things and desperately wicke*d (Jeremiah 17:9). Jesus' heart,
however, is perfect and is indissolubly linked to the Father's
heart. God desires to put Jesus' heart in us so that we will also
have a perfect heart to follow our heavenly Father. *And I will
give you a new heart, and a new spirit will I put within you; and
I will take away the stony heart out of your flesh, and I will give
you a heart of flesh. And I will put my Spirit within you and
cause you to walk in my commandments, and ye shall keep my
rights, and do them* (Ezekiel 36:26-27).

God will take away our stony heart and give us a heart of flesh because *Jesus Christ is come in flesh.*

There are many examples in Scripture of those who, according to God, had a perfect heart (1 Chronicles 12:38; 1 Chronicles 29:9), and there are 153 references in the Jubilee Bible to the word "perfect," "perfected," or "perfection."[127] Consider the following verses:

> *Noah was a just man and perfect in his generations, and Noah walked with God.* (Genesis 6:9b)

> *Surely none of the men that came up out of Egypt, from twenty years old and upward, shall see the land which I swore unto Abraham, unto Isaac, and unto Jacob; because they were not perfect in following me, except Caleb, the son of Jephunneh the Kenezite, and*

> *Joshua, the son of Nun, for they were perfect in following the LORD.* (Numbers 32:11-12)

> *For the eyes of the LORD run to and fro throughout the whole earth, to show himself strong in the behalf of those whose heart is perfect toward him.* (2 Chronicles 16:9a)

> *And above all these things put on charity, which is the bond of perfection.* (Colossians 3:14)

1 John 5

5:1 *Whosoever believes that Jesus is the Christ is*

---

127 In both Hebrew and Greek, the root word translated as "perfect" or "perfection" can also be translated as "mature" or "maturity." A seed that is planted must come to maturity or perfection in order to bear fruit. The seed might have some blemishes or deformities, but if it sprouts and grows and bears fruit in kind, then according to the way God uses this word, it has attained maturity or perfection, because God looks at the fruit, not the seed. And he uses the same criterion to determine if our heart is perfect before him. See Appendix.

> *born of God; and anyone that loves him that begat*
> *also loves him that is born of him.*

All true believers are *born of God*. They believe Jesus is the Christ, the promised Messiah: prophet, priest, and king (Deuteronomy 18:15; 1 Samuel 2:10; Isaiah 61:1; Luke 4:18; Psalm 110:4; Hebrews 5:5-6). Jesus Christ is the sovereign Lord and King of heaven and earth; he is the creator and owner of everyone and everything (Colossians 1:12-23). He is the new High Priest of the order of Melchisedec and only mediator of the new covenant (1 Timothy 2:5; Hebrews 6:20; 9:15). John also wrote at a later date that *the testimony of Jesus is the spirit of prophecy* (Revelation 19:10). To believe in him is to place our faith and trust in him as our Lord and Savior and Redeemer.

If we are *born of God* we will, of course, love our heavenly Father. And if we love *him that begat* Jesus, we will also love our brothers and sisters in Christ, who are likewise born of God.

> 5:2 *In this we know that we love the sons*[128] *of God,*
> *when we love God and keep his commandments.*

We can be certain that we love the sons and daughters of God *when we love God and keep his commandments.* To love God and keep his commandments is a matter that must begin from the heart. In practice, we will receive day-and-night guidance from the Holy Spirit. This guidance will begin more in our heart than in our mind; we will start to feel the presence of God and sense his feelings in our heart and then his thoughts in our mind. In fact, while God is dealing with our heart, it is possible – and even likely – that our mind will receive intense bombardment from the enemy.

When we begin to sense how God feels about wickedness and iniquity, this will have a radical effect on our behavior. When God develops our spiritual sense of smell and the stench

---

128   This word does not refer to gender; it includes both male and female.

of our own human abominations hit our nostrils, our discernment will be sharpened. Not only will we fervently seek his aid in abandoning any practices that are against the desires of his heart, we will soon actively delight in doing his will, and we will find that the more we obey him, the greater will be our joy and his. We will be able to tell when he is happy, and before long we will live to give him joy and will repent of anything that we might have been doing (or have failed to do) that has caused him grief. At this point, we will be so aligned with him that it will be natural for us to love others just as he does. We will also naturally hate what he hates.

> 5:3 *For this is the charity of God, that we keep his commandments, and his commandments are not grievous.*

> 5:4 *For whatsoever is born of God overcomes the world; and this is the victory that overcomes the world, even our faith.*

If we remain in communion with God and keep his commandments, not only will this be a great joy to us and to him but also it will lead to *victory that overcomes the world.* This is brought about by faith, by us depending on him, believing him, and doing what he commands. Soon he will have us carrying out very complex maneuvers that may not make sense to our natural mind. This is why we need the mind of Christ (Philippians 2:5).

> 5:5 *Who is he that overcomes the world, but he that believes that Jesus is the Son of God?*

Who is capable of overcoming the world? Only the person who believes that Jesus is the Son of God, because only such a person will completely depend upon Jesus for wisdom and strength. Jesus summed up his last instructions to his disciples with these words: *These things I have spoken unto you that in me ye might have peace. In the world ye shall have tribulation; but be of good cheer; I have overcome the world* (John 16:33). Now he wants all of his followers to overcome the world as well. This will inevitably involve trials and tribulation, since in order to overcome the world, we must take the same path he took: the way of the cross. The trials and tribulation are only on the outside, however. Inside, in Jesus, we have his peace.

> 5:6 *This is Jesus, the Christ, who came by water and blood; not by water only, but by water and blood. And the Spirit is he that bears witness, because the Spirit is the truth.*

There is an emphasis here on *water and blood*, two things that were obviously very important to devout Jewish people who loved the law. Under the law, water and blood were used for purification. Water is a symbol of the word of God that flows and cleanses (Ephesians 5:26), while blood (from a sacrifice) has to do with remission of sins, ransom, and redemption. Jesus came as the living Word of God who was sent by the Father *to give his life in ransom for many* (Mark 10:45), and *we have redemption through his blood* (Ephesians 1:7). Remember that the *life of the flesh is in the blood* (Leviticus 17:11).

> 5:7 *For there are three that bear witness in heaven, the Father, the Word, and the Holy Spirit; and these three are one.*

God the Father bears witness in heaven to his Son, Jesus the Christ. Jesus is the Word of God (John 1:1; Revelation 19:11-16), also known as the Word of Life (1 John 1:1). Following his resurrection, he is now seated at the right hand of the Father in heaven, with all power in heaven and in earth (Mark 16:19; Matthew 28:18). The Holy Spirit bears witness in heaven and in earth and is the bond between us and the Father and the

Son. The Father, the Word, and the Holy Spirit all witness the same thing: they are one.

> 5:8 *And there are three that bear witness on earth,*
> *the Spirit and the water and the blood; and these*
> *three agree in one.*

The Holy Spirit is the last of the *three that bear witness in heaven* but the first of the *three that bear witness on earth*. The second of these three, the testimony of the water, symbolic of the Word, bears witness that Jesus is the Lord of heaven, the Son of God. And the testimony of the blood bears witness that he is also the Son of Man and fully human, formed of flesh and blood. Therefore the fact that Jesus the Christ came by water and blood – not by water only, but by water and blood – bears witness that he is God and truly *is come in flesh*.

After Jesus died on the cross and *gave the Spirit*, a Roman soldier pierced his side with a spear, and John was a witness when blood and water flowed out (John 19:30, 34-35). Note that here the order is reversed, and instead of *water and blood*, it is *blood and water* that flowed from the wound in Jesus' riven side, beneath his heart. This is the source of God's river of living water that continues to flow from Jesus' heart and will flow in and through us if we have Jesus in our heart. It begins with blood because Jesus, coming in flesh, ransomed us by giving his life for us, and the life of the flesh is in the blood. *Now justified in his blood, we shall be saved from wrath by him* (Romans 5:9). *We have redemption through his blood, even the remission of sins* (Colossians 1:14; Ephesians 1:7). *For if, when we were enemies, we were reconciled with God by the death of his Son, much more, now reconciled, we shall be saved by his life* (Romans 5:10). After the blood pours out, living water flows from Jesus' side, from his heart, and it is this water that will form mighty rivers that bring cleansing, healing, and salvation (John 7:38; Ezekiel 47:1-12).[129]

Adam's bride was formed by God from material he took from Adam's side, below his heart, after which Adam declared, *This is now bone of my bones and flesh of my flesh* (Genesis 2:21-23). In other words, Eve was made of the same stuff as Adam.[130] *And so it is written, The first man Adam was made a living soul; the last Adam was made a life-giving Spirit* (1 Corinthians 15:45). Adam shared his life with Eve, and Jesus will share his eternal life with his bride (also known as the body of Christ). *The first man is of the earth, earthy; the second man is the Lord of heaven. As is the earthy, such are those also that are earthy; and as is the heavenly, such also are those that are heavenly* (1 Corinthians 15:47-48).

> 5:9 *If we receive the witness of men, the witness of God is greater: for this is the witness of God which he has testified of his Son.*

As we have seen, God bears witness on earth about his son by the Spirit, the water, and the blood.

> 5:10 *He that believes in the Son of God has the witness of God in himself; he that does not believe God has made God a liar; because he does not believe the witness that God has testified of his Son.*

If we believe in the Son of God, we will have the witness of God inside of us: the witness of the Spirit, of the water, and of the blood.

> 5:11 *And this is the witness, that God has given eternal life to us, and this life is in his Son.*

---

129 See *The River of God*, Russell Stendal, Aneko Press, Abbotsford, WI.

130 Adam's bride was corruptible like Adam. Jesus will have a bride who is incorruptible like him and shares his heart. *And as we have borne the image of the earthy, we shall also bear the image of the heavenly* (1 Corinthians 15:49). This change, however, will require resurrection.

Eternal life does not mean that the life that we inherited from Adam will continue forever. The word "eternal" primarily has to do with the quality of that life. Eternal life is God's life and is of a totally different quality from our own natural life. God is charity: that is, his specific form of love is an essential part of his life. We will never, ever be fulfilled or satisfied until we respond to that love. *Blessed are those who hunger and thirst for righteousness,* says Jesus, *for they shall be satisfied* (Matthew 5:6). Righteousness is primarily a state of being, and we must become what God wants us to be in order to be able to fully please him with what we do. We can taste eternal life even now, on earth, if Jesus and the Father dwell in us and we in them.

> 5:12 *He that has the Son has life; and he that does not have the Son of God does not have life.*

> 5:13 *These things I have written unto you that believe in the name of the Son of God, that ye may know that ye have eternal life and that ye may believe in the name of the Son of God.*

The name of the Son of God is linked to the nature of God, and eternal life is in God's nature. If we have the Son, we also have his life, and *we shall be saved by his life.* We cannot have eternal life apart from him.

> 5:14 *And this is the confidence that we have in God, that, if we ask any thing according to his will, he hears us:*

On what basis can we have this confidence?

> *If our heart does not condemn us, then we have confidence in God* (1 John 3:21). *For we do not have a high priest who cannot sympathize with our weaknesses, but was in all points tempted like as we are, yet without sin. Let us, therefore, come boldly unto*

*the throne of his grace, that we may obtain mercy
and find grace to help in time of need (Hebrews
4:15-16). According to the eternal purpose which he
[God] purposed in Christ Jesus our Lord, In whom
we have security and access with confidence by the
faith of him (Ephesians 3:11-12).*

*5:15 And if we know that he hears us in whatever we
ask, we also know that we have the petitions that we
asked of him.*

How can we know for sure that he hears us? Because *if we ask
any thing according to his will, he hears us.*

John's next verse is of tremendous interest:

*5:16 If any man see his brother sin a sin which is not
unto death, he shall ask God, and he shall give him
life that is, unto those that do not sin unto death.
There is sin unto death, for which I do not say that
you should pray.*

How do we know if someone has gone too far and sinned away
his or her day of grace? John had presumably been thinking
about those like Judas, but Peter too might have been in the
back of his mind. Judas's betrayal of Jesus was an appalling
sin, and in their shock, the disciples scattered. John was the
first to recover, and after going with Jesus into the house of the
high priest and persuading a maid to allow Peter to enter and
warm himself, John was able to observe the trial while Peter
remained in the outer courtyard, standing beside the fire and
denying the Lord. I think it very likely that even during the
trial and subsequent events, John was desperately praying and
interceding for Peter in order that his sin of denial should not
be considered a sin unto death.

Further indication that this indeed may have been the case

is that after his resurrection, Jesus organized events so that as he walked along the beach with Peter, John was following them and was close enough to overhear their conversation. John was thus able to learn the answer to his intercessory prayers as the two of them talked, for he could hear Jesus giving Peter the opportunity to reaffirm his love three times (once for each denial) and prophesying about the manner in which Peter's death would clarify God.

> 5:17 *All unrighteousness is sin, but there is a sin not unto death.*

There was nothing wrong with Peter's basic desire, goal, and motivation to follow Jesus no matter what. Satan, however, had sifted Peter as wheat, and the disciple had fallen into an unforeseen trap when, while Jesus was inside the building, surrounded by armed men and being sentenced to death, the maid confronted Peter about having been with Jesus earlier. Fortunately Peter's sin (*hamartia*) was not *unto death*.

What was the wrong target at which Peter, while under extreme and unexpected pressure, took three shots?

It was the target of saving his own life by denying Jesus.

Judas Iscariot's betrayal, on the other hand, was a vastly different scenario. He arrived at the last supper with thirty pieces of silver in his possession after having, in effect, sold Jesus to those who wished him dead. (Judas had a dubious history where money was concerned, being known to have helped himself to money from the group's funds.) At the supper, the other disciples were having incomparable communion with Jesus around the table, but when Jesus fed Judas a sop of bread dipped in wine, Satan entered into him. In Peter's case, Satan had been on the outside, and although he had set up a successful ambush, he had not managed to breach the disciple's heart. In the case of Judas, however, Satan finally got inside of him, and what was deep communion and blessing for the other eleven became the exact opposite for him, due to the unclean status of his heart.

Satan then maneuvered Judas into a final act of treachery whereby he would betray Jesus with a kiss. Judas subsequently felt intense remorse and attempted to return the thirty pieces of silver, but by then, it was too late. Driven to desperation, he hanged himself sometime between Jesus' death and the resurrection. Satan undoubtedly helped make sure that Judas was no longer alive when Jesus returned in resurrection to appear to the disciples. In this way, the Enemy strategy was to preclude even the remotest possibility that Judas could be restored. Judas is a classic case of a sin unto death.

> 5:18 *We know that whoever is born of God does not sin; but he that is begotten of God keeps himself, and the wicked one does not touch him.*

It is very clear Judas was not *born of God*. His love of money, which is *the root of all evil* (1 Timothy 6:10), put him in in such a bad position that the *wicked one* was able to touch him and then possess him. Despite knowing this would happen (being well aware that Judas was *the son of perdition*),[131] Jesus chose him to be one of the twelve so that the Scripture could be fulfilled (John 17:12).

Even so, Jesus was *troubled in spirit* when he testified to his disciples at the last supper that *one of you shall betray me* (John 13:21). Scripture is clear about the nature of God. God is charity, and he is *not willing that any should perish*; rather, he desires for *all to come to repentance* (2 Peter 3:9). Simon Peter was completely convinced of this.[132]

---

131 Judas, *the son of perdition*, is an example of the final antichrist when Satan will at last be completely unmasked prior to the *day of the Lord*, also known as the *day of Christ. Let no one deceive you by any means: for that day shall not come except there come a falling away first and that man of sin be revealed, the son of perdition* (2 Thessalonians 2:3).

132 See *What Religion Has to Hide (The Witness of Simon Peter)*, Russell Stendal, Aneko Press, Abbotsford, WI.

5:19 *And we know that we are of God, and the whole world lies in wickedness.*

If we are of God, we are in the light (John 1:7). If we are of God, then *the darkness is past, and the true light now shines* (1 John 2:8b). *He that loves his brother abides in the light, and there is no occasion of stumbling in him* (1 John 2:10) even though *the whole world* (not just part of it) *lies in wickedness* (1 John 5:19).

5:20 *But we know that the Son of God is come and has given us understanding, that we may know him that is true, and we are in him that is true, even in his Son Jesus Christ. This is the true God and eternal life.*

The Son of God is come. Again the verb tense is present continuous. Jesus came and died for us, but he continues to come and live in people like us so we can be part of the body of Christ. If Jesus lives in our hearts, he *has given us understanding*, and he does this so *that we may know him that is true* (the Father). *And we are in him that is true* if we are *in his Son Jesus Christ.* The true God and eternal life are changelessly linked together.

5:21 *Little children, keep yourselves from idols. Amen.*

Idols are anything that would distract us from *the true God and eternal life.*

Let us pray

Heavenly Father, may we receive understanding to know you. May your charity be completed in us. May we be perfect in one. May the world believe that you sent your Son, Jesus Christ. Amen.

Chapter 22

The Chosen Lady

2 John

1:1 *The elder unto the chosen lady and her sons,...*

There are differences of opinion among theologians as to the exact identity of the *chosen lady* mentioned here. I think that in the immediate natural realm, John wrote this epistle to Mary, the mother of Jesus. As you remember, when Jesus was about to die he looked down from the cross and apparently only John from among his disciples was there with some women, including Jesus' mother, Mary. *When Jesus therefore saw his mother and the disciple standing by, whom he loved, he said unto his mother, Woman, behold thy son! Then he said to the disciple, Behold thy mother! And from that hour that disciple took her unto his own home* (John 19:26-27).[133]

John, therefore, would have replaced Jesus as the eldest son in the natural household. It is also likely that John would have been older than Jesus' four half-brothers, and thus he refers to

---

133 I find it very interesting that Jesus waited until the last possible moment before delegating this important responsibility to the one who is known as "the disciple whom Jesus loved" and who, after a moment of panic at Gethsemane, faithfully accompanied him to the very end.

himself as *the elder*. The word translated here as "lady" is *kuria* in Greek, the female form of *kurios*, meaning "lord" or "master." When the disciples called Jesus "the Lord" in the gospels, the word used is *kurios*.

Mary, along with Jesus' brethren, also represents something very important in the spiritual realm, which is why this letter is made public as the sixty-third book of the Bible. There is a scene described in Matthew 12:46-50, Mark 3:31-35, and Luke 8:20-21 in which Jesus says, *My mother and my brethren are those who hear the word of God and do it.*

John was, therefore, in a unique position to write a universal epistle to Jesus' *mother and* (his) *brethren.* John was part of Jesus' family, who in turn were part of John's household. This is true in both a natural sense (with Jesus' natural family) and a broad spiritual sense (i.e., *those who hear the word of God and do it*).

> 1:1 ... *whom I love in the truth, and not I only, but also all those that have known the truth,*

> 1:2 *for the truth's sake, which abides in us and shall be with us for ever.*

For the sake of the truth (as embodied by Jesus), John and *all those that have known the truth* (all those who have known God) love Jesus' mother and also love his brethren (*those who hear the word of God and do it*).

> 1:3 *Grace be with you, mercy and peace, from God the Father and from the Lord Jesus Christ, the Son of the Father, in truth and charity.*

John lived in intimate communion with God the Father and with the Lord Jesus Christ, the Son of the Father, and therefore he could send (even command) grace, mercy, and peace from the throne of God to *the chosen lady and her sons, in truth and charity.*

> 1:4 *I have rejoiced greatly, for I have found of thy
> sons that they walk in the truth, as we have received
> the commandment from the Father.*

The sons[134] of Mary were named James (the lesser), Joses, Juda (Jude), and Simon. Jesus also had some sisters, one of whom was named Salome[135] (Mark 6:3; 15:40). John was able to give a wonderful report concerning Jesus' brethren.

> 1:5 *And now I beseech thee, lady, (not as though
> I wrote a new commandment unto thee, but that
> which we had from the beginning) that we love one
> another.*

> 1:6 *And this is charity, that we walk after his com-
> mandment. And this is the commandment, That ye
> walk in him, as ye have heard from the beginning.*

Even with all the respect that John demonstrates for *the chosen lady*, he still feels the weight of the responsibility that Jesus placed on him. Therefore he earnestly brings up this commandment from Jesus' position and perspective, writing as if he were Jesus and prefacing his remarks with "*not as though I write a new commandment unto thee, but that which we had from the beginning.*" John's position in Jesus' natural family is indeed that of a natural replacement for Jesus, since this is the position assigned to him by the Lord. Then John proceeds with the message: *that we love one another.* This, of course, is Jesus' commandment to all of us in his spiritual family.

> 1:7 *For many deceivers are entered into the world,
> who do not confess Jesus Christ coming in flesh. This
> same is a deceiver and antichrist.*

John felt it his responsibility to personally write *the chosen*

---

134 This word does not distinguish gender, these "sons" can be male or female.
135 My best understanding of the Greek indicates that Salome was a sister to the brothers (half-sister to Jesus).

lady and her sons and warn them of imminent enemy deception involving *many deceivers* who *do not confess Jesus Christ
coming in flesh*. Once again, the phrase is configured in such a
way as to denote continuous action (Jesus continues *coming in
flesh* as he lives in the hearts of his people by the Holy Spirit[136]),
and once again the Greek word *homologeo* (translated here as
confess[137]) is used, to show forth *that Jesus is the Son of God,*

> 1:8 *Look to yourselves, that we not lose those things
> which we have wrought, but that we receive a ful-
> filled reward.*

John sees fit even to admonish the chosen lady and her sons,
warning them: *Look to **yourselves**, that **we** not lose those things
which **we** have wrought.* The construction of this phrase is very
telling. John obviously includes himself as part of this family
and expresses deep concern that **we** *receive a fulfilled reward.*
He would not be writing this in such strong and certain terms
if he did not perceive the possibility of very real and imminent
danger that could affect their corporate and individual reward.

> 1:9 *Whosoever rebels and does not abide in the
> doctrine of the Christ, does not have God. He that
> abides in the doctrine of the Christ, the same has the
> Father and the Son.*

What is *the doctrine of the Christ*?

The doctrine of the Christ is set forth in the word (and
example) of those people Jesus Christ selects as apostles ("sent
ones"), such as John, who explains it as Jesus Christ and the

---

136 Before he died, Jesus told John and the other disciples: *If ye love me, keep
my commandments; and I will ask the Father, and he shall give you another
Comforter, that he may abide with you for ever, even the Spirit of truth, whom
the world cannot receive because it does not see him, or know him; but ye know
him, for he dwells with you and shall be in you. I will not leave you orphans; I
will come to you* (John 14:15-18, emphasis added). Jesus continues to come to
us by the Holy Spirit, and the spirit of antichrist continues to deny this.

137 Greek *homologeo* – meaning to "demonstrate or authenticate the exact same
values, character, and word" (see footnote 120).

Father being in us and we in them. The doctrine of the Christ operates in charity and truth. It brings Jesus' followers together and does not split them apart into factions. Under the doctrine of the Christ, we love one another even as Jesus loved (and loves) us. Christ's doctrine is the central theme of the New Testament. The apostle Paul summed it up like this: *Christ in you, the hope of glory* (Colossians 1:26-27). This is what the spirit of antichrist denies and can never confess. The spirit of antichrist can never give anyone a practical demonstration of the doctrine of the Christ because charity, the love of God, can never be part of any demonstration offered by such a spirit. Always and unfailingly, the spirit of antichrist will produce bad fruit.

> 1:10 *If anyone comes unto you and does not bring this doctrine, do not receive him into your house neither say unto him, Welcome:*

> 1:11 *For he that says unto him, Welcome, is partaker of his evil deeds.*

John is concerned that *the chosen lady and her sons*, in their joy of loving, might make a mistake and let a wolf in sheep's clothing enter their home. This is a warning for all of us.

> 1:12 *Having many things to write unto you, I would not write with paper and ink, but I trust to come unto you and speak face to face, that our joy may be full.*

John planned to come and speak with them face to face in the not too distant future. Even so, by the Spirit, he considered the message to be of such prime importance that he wrote this letter and sent it to them without delay. The letter remains just as pertinent to us today.

> 1:13 *The sons of thy chosen sister greet thee. Amen.*

Who are *the sons of thy chosen sister*?

Scripture mentions that Jesus' mother had a sister, who was also at the foot of the cross (John 19:25). John may have been referring to this sister's sons. Spiritually, the bride of Christ is made up of many congregations that form one universal body of Christ. In prophetic typology, groups are referred to many times as female (generally addressed as "women") and individual believers as male (usually called "sons").[138] The bottom line is that God's plan is to bring many sons to glory (Hebrews 2:10), joined together in the body of Christ as a *bride who has made herself ready* and is *without spot or wrinkle or any such thing*, and it is for this bride that Jesus will soon return (Ephesians 5:27; Revelation 19:7).

Let us pray

Heavenly Father, may we confess that Jesus is come in flesh. May we demonstrate your Word and truth and charity. May we have quick discernment to recognize and reject the many deceivers who are antichrist and are compatible, not with you, but only with the world. Amen.

---

138 Remember that Hebrew and Greek (and Spanish) consider all nouns to be either male or female. English does not have this issue. When Scripture mentions sons of God, the phrase does not refer to gender, as in Christ there is neither male nor female (Galatians 3:28).

Chapter 23

The Letter to Gaius

3 John

1:1 *The elder unto the wellbeloved Gaius,*[139] *whom I love in the truth.*

Interestingly, John does not present himself as "an apostle" or "the disciple Jesus loved" or any other high and important-sounding title. He is simply *the elder*, one who has reached maturity in Christ and therefore has authority.

1:2 *Beloved, I wish that thou be prospered in all things and be sound, even as thy soul prospers.*

John desired that Gaius *be prospered in all things and be sound* but added this qualifier: *even as thy soul prospers.* This echoes Jesus' well-known question, *For what shall it profit a man, if he shall gain the whole world and lose his own soul?* (Mark 8:36).

1:3 *For I rejoiced greatly when the brethren came and testified of the truth that is in thee, even as thou dost walk in the truth.*

---

139 The name "Gaius" is of Latin origin and means "to rejoice." This person was most likely someone John had led to Christ.

*1:4 I have no greater joy than this, to hear that my
sons walk in the truth.*

For John, there was no greater joy than to hear that those to
whom he had witnessed and ministered were walking in the
truth. The same should be true for any of us.

*1:5 Beloved, thou doest faithfully whatever thou
doest regarding the brethren and with the strangers,*

*1:6 who have borne witness of thy charity before the
congregation,*[140] *whom if thou wilt help them as is
convenient according to God, thou shalt do well;*

*1:7 because for his name's sake, they went forth, tak-
ing nothing of the Gentiles.*

The charity or love of Gaius for the brethren, and also for strangers, took tangible form as hospitality and even financial aid.

*1:8 We, therefore, ought to receive such, that we
might be fellow workers to the truth.*

This was a time when many Jewish Christians were being scattered all over the world as Jerusalem and Judea were about to be
destroyed (or possibly had already been placed under siege or
demolished). The "strangers" referred to could have been some
of those who had been forced to flee. If we receive those whom
the Lord would have us aid, either because they are displaced
persons persecuted for their faith or because they are traveling
in ministry, then we become *fellow workers to the truth.*

1:9 I wrote unto the congregation, but Diotrephes,[141]
*who loves to have the preeminence among them, did
not receive us.*[142]

---

140 Greek *ekklesia* – meaning "called-out ones."
141 "Diotrephes" means "nourished by Zeus" (or Jupiter, the supreme deity of the
pagan Greeks).
142 I wonder: was the letter (and ministry) that was rejected by Diotrephes the text
we know as 1 John?

Here is a strong whiff of what Jesus would later refer to as the Nicolaitans (Revelation 2:6, 15), meaning "those who conquer the people," a term denoting the emergence of a clergy class that – instead of being shepherds willing to give their lives for the sheep – would attempt to make the sheep subject to them rather than helping to join the people directly to the Lord as was the obvious ministry of true apostles like John.

> 1:10 *Therefore, if I come, I will cause his deeds to be understood, speaking against us with malicious words, and not content with this, he does not receive the brethren and forbids those that desire to receive them and casts them out of the congregation.*[143]

John began to confront this problem by writing to the congregation, but Diotrephes, who appears to have been the main one causing the problem, did not receive his ministry by apparently blocking the letter. Only after John was rebuffed did he write this letter to Gaius, an outstanding member of the congregation, letting him know where he stood regarding the problem and adding that he was considering making a personal visit to confront Diotrephes and *cause his deeds to be understood.*

> 1:11 *Beloved, follow not that which is evil, but that which is good. He that does good is of God, but he that does evil has not seen God.*

In this case, John does not encourage the notion (or even suggest it to Gaius) that they all should just love Diotrephes in spite of his evil behavior. John sums it up like this: *He that does good is of God, but he that does evil has not seen God.*

Gaius is exhorted and encouraged not to follow the evil example of Diotrephes, and John recommends the good example of Demetrius.

---

143 Greek *ekklesia* – meaning "called-out ones."

> 1:12 *Everyone gives testimony of Demetrius,*[144] *even the truth itself; and we also bear witness, and ye have known that our witness is true.*

John is very concerned that Gaius will be sucked into the wrong side of this controversy. Therefore he lists the witnesses: (1) *Everyone gives testimony of Demetrius* – that is, everyone who is in communion with John and has knowledge of this situation; (2) even *the truth itself* – this is the witness of God; (3) and he also bears witness – and reminds Gaius – that he and the others (*ye*) have known that *our witness is true* (John says "our witness" because Jesus and the Father dwell in him and he dwells in them).

> 1:13 *I had many things to write, but I will not with ink and pen write unto thee,*

> 1:14 *For I trust I shall shortly see thee, and we shall speak face to face. Peace be to thee. Our friends salute thee. Greet the friends by name.*

Let us pray

Heavenly Father, may we be prospered even as our soul prospers. May we have keen discernment to receive those whom you have sent and to reject those who are false. Amen.

---

144 "Demetrius" is also a name of pagan origin, meaning "belonging to Demeter." According to *Webster's Unabridged Dictionary*, Demeter was a goddess corresponding in some respects to the Latin Ceres, the goddess of agriculture and fruitfulness and a protectress of marriage.

Appendix

Use of the word "Perfect" or "Perfection" in the Jubilee Bible[145]

(1) Genesis 2:3

*And God blessed the seventh day and sanctified it because in it he had rested from all his work which God created in **perfection**.*

(2) Genesis 6:9

*These are the generations of Noah. Noah was a just man and **perfect** in his generations, and Noah walked with God.*

(3) Genesis 17:1

*And when Abram was ninety-nine years old, the LORD appeared to Abram and said unto him, I am the Almighty God; walk before me and be thou **perfect**.*

(4) Exodus 29:1

*And this is what thou shalt do unto them to sanctify them that they shall be my priests: Take one young bullock and two **perfect** rams …*

---

145 Emphasis added

(5) Leviticus 22:21

*Likewise when anyone offers a sacrifice of peace unto the LORD to present his vow or a freewill offering in bovine cattle or sheep, it must be **perfect** to be accepted; there shall be no blemish therein.*

(6) Numbers 19:2

*This is the ordinance of the law which the LORD has commanded, saying, Speak unto the sons of Israel that they bring thee a red heifer, **perfect**, in which there is no blemish, and upon which there has never been placed a yoke;*

(7) Numbers 32:11

*Surely none of the men that came up out of Egypt, from twenty years old and upward, shall see the land which I swore unto Abraham, unto Isaac, and unto Jacob; because they were not **perfect** in following me,*

(8) Numbers 32:12

*... except Caleb, the son of Jephunneh the Kenezite, and Joshua, the son of Nun, for they were **perfect** in following the LORD.*

(9) Deuteronomy 1:36

*... except Caleb the son of Jephunneh; he shall see it, and to him will I give the land that he has trodden upon, and to his sons, because he has **perfectly** followed the LORD.*

(10) Deuteronomy 18:13

*Thou shalt be **perfect** with the LORD thy God.*

(11, 12) Deuteronomy 25:15

*But thou shalt have a **perfect** and just weight, a **perfect** and just measure shalt thou have, that thy days may be lengthened in the land which the LORD thy God gives thee.*

(13) Deuteronomy 32:4

*The strong One, whose work is **perfect**: for all his ways are right; a God of truth and without iniquity, just and upright is he.*

(14) Deuteronomy 33:10

*They shall teach Jacob thy judgments and Israel thy law; they shall put incense before thy nostrils and a **perfect** sacrifice upon thine altar.*

(15) Joshua 24:14

*Now therefore fear the LORD and serve him in **perfection** and in truth and put away from among you the gods which your fathers served on the other side of the river and in Egypt, and serve ye the LORD.*

(16) 2 Samuel 22:24

*And I was **perfect** before him and have kept myself from my iniquity.*

(17) 2 Samuel 22:26

*With the merciful thou art good, and with the **perfect** thou art upright.*

(18) 2 Samuel 22:31

*As for God, his way is **perfect**; the word of the LORD is purified; he is a shield to all those that trust in him.*

(19) 1 Kings 6:7

*And the house, when it was built, was put together of **perfect** stones made ready before they were brought there; so that there was no hammer nor axe nor any tool of iron heard in the house, while it was being built.*

(20) 1 Kings 7:23

*Likewise, he made a molten sea, ten cubits from the one brim to the other; it was **perfectly** round, and its height was five cubits, and a line of thirty cubits did compass it round about.*

(21) 1 Kings 8:61

*Let your heart, therefore, be **perfect** with the LORD our God, walking in his statutes and keeping his commandments, as at this day.*

(22) 1 Kings 11:4

For it came to pass when Solomon was old, that his wives turned away his heart after other gods, and *his heart was not **perfect** with the LORD his God, as was the heart of David, his father.*

(23) 1 Kings 15:3

*And he walked in all the sins of his father, which he had done before him; and his heart was not **perfect** with the LORD his God, as the heart of David his father.*

(24) 1 Kings 15:14

*But the high places were not removed; nevertheless, Asa's heart was **perfect** with the LORD all his days.*

(25) 1 Kings 22:34

*But a certain man, shooting his bow in **perfection**, smote the king of Israel between the joints of his coat of mail; therefore, he said unto the driver of his chariot, Turn thy hand and carry me out of the host, for I am wounded.*

(26) 2 Kings 20:3

*I beseech thee, O LORD, remember how I have walked before thee in truth and with a **perfect** heart and have done that which is good in thy sight. And Hezekiah wept with great weeping.*

(27) 1 Chronicles 12:38

*All these men of war, that could keep rank, came with a **perfect** heart to Hebron, to make David king over all Israel; and likewise, all the rest also of Israel were of one heart to make David king.*

(28) 1 Chronicles 28:9

*And thou, Solomon, my son, know thou the God of thy father and serve him with a **perfect** heart and with a willing soul, for the LORD searches all hearts and understands all the imaginations of the thoughts. If thou seek him, he will be found of thee; but if thou forsake him, he will cast thee off for ever.*

(29) 1 Chronicles 29:9

*Then the people rejoiced to have offered willingly because with **perfect** heart they offered willingly to the LORD. Likewise, David the king rejoiced with great joy ...*

(30) 1 Chronicles 29:19

*Likewise, give unto Solomon, my son, a **perfect** heart, to keep thy commandments, thy testimonies, and thy statutes, and to do all these things, and to build the palace, for which I have made provision.*

(31) 2 Chronicles 4:21

*... and the flowers and the lamps and the tongs, he made of gold, of **perfect** gold;*

(32) 2 Chronicles 8:16

*16 Now all the work of Solomon was prepared from the day of the foundation of the house of the LORD and until it was finished. So the house of the LORD was **perfected**.*

(33) 2 Chronicles 15:17

*But with all this the high places were not taken away out of Israel; nevertheless, the heart of Asa was **perfect** all his days.*

(34) 2 Chronicles 16:9

*For the eyes of the LORD run to and fro throughout the whole earth, to show himself strong in the behalf of those whose heart is **perfect** toward him. Herein thou hast done foolishly, for from now on thou shalt have wars.*

(35) 2 Chronicles 18:33

*But a certain man drew a bow in all his **perfection** and smote the king of Israel between the joints of his coat of mail; therefore, he said to his chariot man, Turn thy hand, and carry me out of the camp, for I am wounded.*

(36) 2 Chronicles 19:9

*And he charged them, saying, Ye shall proceed thus in the fear of the LORD, in truth and with a **perfect** heart.*

(37) 2 Chronicles 25:2

*And he did that which was right in the sight of the LORD, but not with a **perfect** heart.*

(38, 39) Ezra 7:12

Artaxerxes, king of kings, unto Ezra, the priest,

perfect scribe of the law of the God of heaven, **per-fect** peace, and to Cheenet.

(40) Job 1:1

*There was a man in the land of Uz, whose name was Job; and that man was **perfect** and upright, and one that feared God and departed from evil.*

(41) Job 1:8

*And the LORD said unto Satan, Hast thou considered my slave Job, that there is none like him in the earth, a **perfect** and an upright man, one that fears God and has departed from evil?*

(42, 43) Job 2:3

*And the LORD said unto Satan, Hast thou considered my slave Job, that there is none like him in the earth, a **perfect** and an upright man, one that fears God and has departed from evil and that he still retains his **perfection**, although thou didst incite me against him to destroy him without cause.*

(44) Job 8:20

*Behold, God will not cast away a **perfect** man; neither will he help the evil doers.*

(45) Job 9:20

*If I justify myself, my own mouth shall condemn me: if I say, I am **perfect**, he shall prove me perverse.*

(46) Job 9:22

*One thing remains, that I say, He consumes the **perfect** and the wicked.*

(47) Job 11:7

*Canst thou by searching find out God? Canst thou come unto the **perfection** of the Almighty?*

(48) Job 12:4

*He who invokes God and he answers him is mocked by his friend; the just and **perfect** man is laughed to scorn.*

(49) Job 22:3

*Is it any pleasure to the Almighty that thou art justified? Or is it gain to him that thou makest thy ways **perfect**?*

(50) Job 28:3

*He set a border unto the darkness, and unto every **perfect** work that he made, he placed a stone of darkness and shadow of death.*

(51) Job 36:4

*For truly my words are not lies; for I share **perfect** knowledge with thee.*

(52) Job 37:16

Dost thou know the balancings of the clouds,

the wondrous works of the one who is **perfect** in knowledge?

(53) Psalm 18:23

I was **perfect** before him, and I kept myself from my iniquity.

(54, 55) Psalm 18:25

With the merciful thou wilt show thyself merciful; with a **perfect** man thou wilt show thyself **perfect**;

(56) Psalm 18:30

As for God, his way is **perfect**: the word of the LORD is precise: a shield to all those that wait in him.

(57) Psalm 18:32

It is God that girds me with strength and makes my way **perfect**.

(58) Psalm 19:7

The law of the LORD is **perfect**, converting the soul; the testimony of the LORD is sure, making wise the simple.

(59) Psalm 19:13

Keep back thy slave also from pride and arrogance; let them not have dominion over me; then I shall be **perfect**, and I shall be innocent of the great rebellion.

(60) Psalm 37:18

*The LORD knows the days of the **perfect**, and their inheritance shall be for ever.*

(61) Psalm 37:37

*Mark the **perfect**, and behold the upright, for the end of each one of them is peace.*

(62) Psalm 50:2

*Out of Zion, the **perfection** of beauty, God has shined forth.*

(63) Psalm 64:4

*That they may shoot in secret at the **perfect**; suddenly do they shoot at him and fear not.*

(64) Psalm 64:6

*They search out iniquities; they **perfect** and put into effect that which they have invented in the inward thought of each one of them and that which they have devised in their heart.*

(65, 66) Psalm 101:2

*When thou shalt come unto me, I will walk in the way of **perfection** and understand. I will walk in the midst of my house in the **perfection** of my heart.*

(67) Psalm 101:6

My eyes shall be upon the faithful of the land, that

they may dwell with me; he that walks in the way of **perfection**, *he shall serve me.*

(68) Psalm 119:1

Blessed are those who walk in the **perfect** *way, who walk in the law of the LORD.*

(69) Psalm 119:80

Let my heart be **perfect** *in thy statutes that I not be ashamed.*

(70) Psalm 119:96

I have seen an end of all **perfection**, *but thy commandment is exceeding broad.*

(71) Psalm 138:8

The LORD will **perfect** *that which concerns me; thy mercy, O LORD, endures for ever; forsake not the works of thine own hands.*

(72) Psalm 139:22

I hate them with **perfect** *hatred; I count them mine enemies.*

(73) Proverbs 2:7

He keeps the person of the upright; he is a buckler to those that walk **perfectly**,

(74) Proverbs 2:21

*For the upright shall dwell in the land, and the **perfect** shall remain in it.*

(75) Proverbs 4:18

*But the path of the just is as the light of the morning star, that shines more and more until the day is **perfect**.*

(76) Proverbs 10:29

*The way of the LORD is strength to the **perfect**, but it is terror to the workers of iniquity.*

(77) Proverbs 11:3

*The **perfection** of the upright shall guide them in the way, but the perverseness of transgressors shall destroy them.*

(78) Proverbs 11:5

*The righteousness of the **perfect** shall straighten his way, but the wicked shall fall by his own wickedness.*

(79) Proverbs 11:20

*They that are of a perverse heart are an abomination to the LORD, but such as are **perfect** in their way are his delight.*

(80) Proverbs 13:6

*Righteousness keeps the one of the **perfect** way: but wickedness overthrows the sinner.*

(81) Proverbs 28:6

*Better is the poor that walks in his **perfection** than he that is perverse in his ways, though he is rich.*

(82) Proverbs 28:10

*Whosoever causes the upright to go astray in an evil way, he shall fall himself into his own pit, but the **perfect** shall inherit every good thing.*

(83) Proverbs 29:10

*The bloodthirsty hate the **perfect**, but the just seek his soul.*

(84) Song of Solomon 5:2

*I sleep, but my heart watches for the voice of my beloved that knocks at the door, Open to me, my sister, my love, my dove, my **perfect** one: for my head is filled with dew, and my locks with the drops of the night.*

(85) Song of Solomon 6:9

*My dove is but one, my **perfect** one; she is the only one of her mother, she is the choice one of her that brought her into the light. The virgins saw her and called her blessed; yea, the queens and the concubines and they praised her.*

(86) Isaiah 18:5

*For before the harvest, when the fruit is **perfect**, and after the flower is past and the fruit is mature, then*

*he shall both cut off the sprigs with pruning hooks
and take away and cut down the branches.*

(87) Isaiah 26:3

*Thou wilt keep him in **perfect** peace, whose mind is
stayed on thee: because he trusts in thee.*

(88) Isaiah 38:3

*And said, Remember now, O LORD, I beseech thee,
how I have walked before thee in truth and with a
perfect heart and have done that which is good in
thy sight. And Hezekiah wept sore.*

(89) Isaiah 42:19

*Who is blind, but my slave? or deaf, as my messen-
ger that I sent? Who is blind as he that is **perfect**,
and blind as the slave of the LORD,*

(90) Isaiah 47:9

*But these two things shall come to thee in a moment
in one day; the loss of thy fathers and widowhood:
they shall come upon thee in their **perfection** for the
multitude of thy sorceries and for the great abundance of thine enchantments.*

(91) Lamentations 2:15

*All that passed by clapped their hands over thee and
whistled and wagged their heads over the daughter
of Jerusalem, saying, Is this the city that men called
The **perfection** of beauty, The joy of the whole earth?*

(92) Ezekiel 16:14

*And thy renown went forth among the Gentiles for thy beauty; for it was **perfect** because of my beauty which I placed upon thee, said the Lord GOD.*

(93) Ezekiel 23:12

*She fell in love with the Assyrians her neighbours, captains and rulers clothed to **perfection**, horsemen riding upon horses, all of them desirable young men.*

(94) Ezekiel 27:3

*And say unto Tyre, O thou that dwelleth at the ports of the sea, who art a merchant of the people for many isles, Thus hath the Lord GOD said; O Tyre, thou hast said, I am of **perfect** beauty.*

(95) Ezekiel 28:12

*Son of man, raise up lamentations upon the king of Tyre and say unto him, Thus hath the Lord GOD said: Thou dost seal up the sum of **perfection**, full of wisdom, and completed in beauty.*

(96) Ezekiel 28:15

*Thou wast **perfect** in all thy ways from the day that thou wast created, until iniquity was found in thee.*

(97, 98) Matthew 5:48

*Be ye therefore **perfect**, even as your Father who is in the heavens is **perfect**.*

(99) Matthew 14:36

*... and besought him that they might only touch the hem of his garment, and as many as touched were made **perfectly** whole.*

(100) Matthew 19:21

*Jesus said unto him, If thou desire to be **perfect**, go and sell what thou hast and give it to the poor, and thou shalt have treasure in heaven; and come and follow me.*

(101) Matthew 21:16

*... and said unto him, Hearest thou what these say? And Jesus said unto them, Yes; have ye never read, Out of the mouth of children and sucklings thou hast **perfected** praise?*

(102) Mark 10:21

*Then Jesus beholding him loved him and said unto him, One thing thou lackest: go, sell all that thou hast and give to the poor, and thou shalt have treasure in heaven; and come, take up the cross [Greek stauros – stake], and follow me taking up thy stake (if thy desire is to be **perfect**).*

(103) Luke 6:40

*The disciple is not above his master, but any one that is as the master shall be **perfect**.*

(104) Luke 8:14

And that which fell among thorns are those who when they have heard go forth and are choked with cares and riches and pleasures of this life and bring no fruit to **perfection.**

(105) Luke 13:32

And he said unto them, Go ye and tell that fox, Behold, I cast out demons, and I do cures today and tomorrow, and the third day I shall be **perfected.**

(106) John 17:23

I in them, and thou in me, that they may be **perfect** *in one and that the world may know that thou hast sent me and hast loved them as thou hast loved me.*

(107) Acts 3:16

And in the faith of his name, unto this man whom ye see and know, has confirmed his name; and the faith which is by him has given this man this **perfect** *soundness in the presence of you all.*

(108) Acts 18:26

And he began to speak boldly in the synagogue, but when Aquila and Priscilla had heard him, they took him unto them and expounded unto him the way of God more **perfectly.**

(109) Acts 26:5

… who knew me from the beginning, if they would

*testify, that after the most **perfect** sect of our religion I lived a Pharisee.*

(110) Romans 2:27

*And that which is by nature foreskin, but keeps the law **perfectly**, shall judge thee who with the letter and with the circumcision art rebellious to the law.*

(111) Romans 12:2

*And be not conformed to this age, but be ye transformed by the renewing of your soul that ye may experience what is that good and well pleasing and **perfect** will of God.*

(112) 1 Corinthians 1:10

*Now I beseech you, brethren, by the name of our Lord Jesus Christ, that ye all speak the same thing and that there be no divisions among you, but that ye be **perfect**, joined together in the same understanding and in the same perception.*

(113) 1 Corinthians 2:6

*For we speak **perfect** wisdom of God, and not the wisdom of this age nor of the princes of this age, that come to nought,*

(114) 1 Corinthians 13:10

*But when that which is **perfect** is come, then that which is in part shall be done away.*

(115) 1 Corinthians 14:20

*Brothers, be not children in understanding, howbeit in malice be ye children; but in understanding be **perfect**.*

(116) 2 Corinthians 7:1

*Having therefore these promises, dearly beloved, let us cleanse ourselves from all filthiness of the flesh and spirit, **perfecting** holiness in the fear of God.*

(117) 2 Corinthians 12:9

*And he said unto me, My grace is sufficient for thee; for my strength is made **perfect** in weakness. Most gladly, therefore, I will rather glory in my weaknesses that the power of Christ may dwell in me.*

(118) 2 Corinthians 13:9

*By which we are glad that we are weak and ye are strong, and even so we pray for your **perfection**.*

(119) 2 Corinthians 13:11

*For the rest, brethren, that ye may have joy, be **perfected**, have consolation, be of one mind, having peace; and the God of peace and charity shall be with you.*

(120) Galatians 3:3

*Are ye so foolish? having begun by the Spirit, are ye now made **perfect** by the flesh?*

(121) Ephesians 4:12

*... for the **perfecting** of the saints in the work of the ministry, unto the edifying of the body of the Christ ...*

(122) Ephesians 4:13

*... until we all come forth in the unity of the faith and of the knowledge of the Son of God unto a **perfect** man, unto the measure of the coming of age of the Christ:*

(123) Philippians 1:6

*... being confident of this very thing, that he who has begun a good work in you will **perfect** it until the day of Jesus Christ.*

(124) Philippians 3:12

*Not as though I had already attained it, either were already **perfect**, but I follow after, if I may lay hold of that for which I have also been laid hold of by the Christ, Jesus.*

(125) Philippians 3:15

*Let us, therefore, as many as are **perfect**, be thus minded; and if in anything ye are otherwise minded, God shall reveal even this unto you.*

(126) Colossians 1:28

*... whom we preach, warning every man and teaching in all wisdom that we may present every man **perfect** in Christ Jesus,*

(127) Colossians 3:14

*And above all these things put on charity, which is the bond of **perfection**.*

(128) Colossians 4:12

*Epaphras, who is one of you, a slave of Christ, salutes you, always labouring fervently for you in prayers, that ye may stand firm, **perfect** and fulfilled in all the will of God.*

(129) 2 Timothy 3:17

*... that the man of God may be **perfect**, thoroughly furnished unto all good works.*

(130) Hebrews 2:10

*For it was expedient that he, for whom are all things and by whom are all things, preparing to bring forth many sons in his glory, should **perfect** the author of their saving health through sufferings.*

(131) Hebrews 5:9

*... and being made **perfect**, he became the author of eternal saving health unto all those that hearken unto him,*

(132) Hebrews 5:14

*But strong food belongs to those that are **perfect**, even those who by reason of use have their senses exercised to discern both good and evil.*

(133) Hebrews 6:1

Therefore, leaving now the word of the beginning of the establishment of the Christ, let us go on unto **perfection***, not laying again the foundation of repentance from works of death, and of faith in God,*

(134) Hebrews 7:11

If therefore **perfection** *were by the Levitical priesthood (for under it the people received the law), what further need was there that another priest should rise after the order of Melchisedec and not be called after the order of Aaron?*

(135) Hebrews 7:19

… for the law made nothing **perfect***, but the bringing in of a better hope did, by which we draw near unto God.*

(136) Hebrews 7:28

For the law makes men high priests who have weakness; but the word of the oath, which was after the law, has made **perfect** *a Son forever.*

(137) Hebrews 9:9

Which was a figure of that time present, in which were offered both gifts and sacrifices, that could not make him that did the service **perfect***, as pertaining to the conscience,*

(138) Hebrews 9:11

*But Christ being now come, high priest of the good things to come, by a greater and more **perfect** tabernacle, not made with hands, that is to say, not of this creation,*

(139) Hebrews 10:1

*For the law having a shadow of good things to come, and not the very image of the things, can never make **perfect** those who come by the same sacrifices which they offer year by year continually.*

(140) Hebrews 10:14

*For by one offering he has **perfected** for ever those that are sanctified.*

(141) Hebrews 11:40

*God having provided some better thing for us, that they without us should not be made **perfect**.*

(142) Hebrews 12:23

*... to the congregation of the called out ones of the firstborn, who are registered in the heavens and to God the Judge of all and to the spirits of just men made **perfect** ...*

(143) Hebrews 13:21

*... make you **perfect** in every good work to do his will, working in you that which is wellpleasing in his*

sight, through Jesus Christ, to whom be glory for the ages of the ages. Amen.

(144) James 1:4

*... and the patience finishes the work, that ye may be **perfect** and entire, not lacking in anything.*

(145) James 1:17

*Every good gift and every **perfect** gift is from above and comes down from the Father of lights, with whom is no variableness neither shadow of turning.*

(146) James 1:25

*But whosoever has looked attentively into the **perfect** law of liberty and has persevered in it, not being a forgetful hearer, but a doer of the work, the same shall be blessed in their deed.*

(147) James 3:2

*For we all offend in many things. If any man offends not in word, the same is a **perfect** man, and able also to govern the whole body with restraint.*

(148) 1 Peter 1:13

*Therefore, having the loins of your understanding girded with temperance, wait **perfectly** in the grace that is presented unto you when Jesus, the Christ, is manifested unto you,*

(149) 1 Peter 5:10

*But the God of all grace, who has called us unto his eternal glory by Jesus, the Christ, after ye have suffered a little while, he himself **perfects**, confirms, strengthens, and establishes you.*

(150) 1 John 2:5

*But whosoever keeps his word, in him verily is the charity of God **perfected**: hereby know we that we are in him.*

(151) 1 John 4:17

*In this the charity with us is made **perfect**, that we may have confidence in the day of judgment, that as he is, so are we in this world.*

(152) 1 John 4:18

*In charity there is no fear; but charity that is **perfect** casts out fear; because fear has torment; from which he that fears is not complete in charity.*

(153) Revelation 3:2

*Be watchful, and strengthen the things which remain, that are ready to die; for I have not found thy works **perfect** before God.*

Meet the Author

Russell Stendal, a former hostage of Colombian rebels, is a lifelong missionary to that same group in the jungles of Colombia. He is an influential friend to military and government leaders in Colombia, Cuba, Mexico, Venezuela, and the United States. Russell's ministry shares the gospel via twelve radio stations, hundreds of thousands of Bibles, books, and movies distributed through airplane parachute drops, and numerous speaking engagements for groups of leaders, prisoners, and individuals. Russell goes wherever the Lord leads, whether it's to speak with a president or to go deep into the jungle to help an individual in trouble. He has witnessed thousands commit their lives to Christ.

Connect with the Author

Website: www.cpcsociety.ca

Newsletter Signup: www.anekopress.com/stendal-newsletter

Russell and his coworkers have built dozens of radio stations in Latin America that concentrate a clear message on remote and dangerous areas where persecution of Christians is rampant. More than 120,000 Galcom solar-powered radios have been deployed to those being discipled. Most of the programming is in Spanish, but they also transmit in almost a dozen native languages where a great move of  God is presently taking place. Russell preaches through the Bible, a chapter or so per message. More than 1,000 messages have been recorded and aired repeatedly. The chapters of this book are samples of these messages preached on the radio in the Colombian war zone about ten years ago. The key website is www.fuerzadepaz.com. Pray for Russell and his team as they expand Spanish-language radio coverage into places like Cuba, Venezuela, Mexico, and Central America.

Plans are in the works for new stations broadcasting in English that will provide coverage into Africa (where there are over 300 million English speakers) and possibly even into Asia and the Middle East. The first stage, as the programming is refined, will be Internet radio. After that, we want to begin shortwave radio transmission and distribution of Galcom radios in Africa and elsewhere as God opens the doors. The new radios have digital audio Bibles on board, and the goal is to move in the direction of digital shortwave transmissions within the next few years.

Connect with Russell's Ministry

Website

www.cpcsociety.ca

Receive newsletter updates

http://goo.gl/amBsCD

Buy books

http://amzn.to/1nPLcNL

jubilee
B I B L E

In the Jubilee Bible, the usage and context tends to define each key word so you don't need to depend on theological dictionaries or reference materials. Careful attention has been made to properly translate the first usage of each key word and through to the last occurrence. Then, as the word makes its way across the Old Testament and you make the correct match with the corresponding Greek word in the New Testament, an amazing pattern emerges. The Jubilee Bible is the only translation we know of that has each unique Hebrew word matched and mated with a unique English word so that the usage (number of occurrences and number of verses where the word occurs) sets forth a meaningful number pattern and a complete definition of what God means by each word.